THE LOST
BATTLEFIELDS
OF BRITAIN

THE LOST BATTLEFIELDS OF BRITAIN

MARTIN WALL

AMBERLEY

For Andrew

First published 2022

Amberley Publishing
The Hill, Stroud
Gloucestershire, GL5 4EP

www.amberley-books.com

Copyright © Martin Wall, 2022

The right of Martin Wall to be identified as
the Author of this work has been asserted in
accordance with the Copyright, Designs and
Patents Act 1988.

ISBN 978 1 4456 9708 6 (hardback)
ISBN 978 1 4456 9709 3 (ebook)

British Library Cataloguing in Publication Data.
A catalogue record for this book is available
from the British Library.

1 2 3 4 5 6 7 8 9 10

Typesetting by SJmagic DESIGN SERVICES, India.
Printed in the UK.

I came not to bring peace but a sword...

Matthew, 10:34

CONTENTS

INTRODUCTION

The title of this book is deliberately somewhat misleading. A brief glance at the contents will reveal that the majority of the battles are perfectly well known, marked on Ordnance Survey maps with the appropriate cross-swords symbol and date. Enough enthusiasts of military history and local antiquarianism still exist to ensure that the memory of these conflicts of olden times will not be utterly effaced. But I would contend that something has changed in our cultural consciousness, perhaps not unconnected to the long period of peace we have enjoyed in Great Britain since the last battle on British soil, the Battle of Culloden in 1746, which has sundered us from the grim realities of war on our own territory. We understand that blood was shed and lives were lost in such and such a place, but we don't actually 'know' what that experience meant, how the world was changed by it.

This change in the way we think and feel about war is something I have lived through, for I can remember a different Britain – one very much in the shadow of the bloodiest conflicts ever waged by the human race. In that time war did not seem so ethereal or mysterious, as I feel it does now. Mercifully, these conflicts were fought for the most part overseas, but I can still remember seeing bomb damage as a boy, and steel helmets, both British and German, were in use as flowerpots in my grandparents' outhouse. Seemingly ordinary men of a certain age turned out to have been distinguished heroes, or ruthless killers trained in the Commandos. My grandfather had served on the Western and Italian fronts in the First World War. As I helped him polish boots as a small boy, he would tell me of his encounters with German *Ulans*, cavalrymen armed with the lance. It seemed to my young mind that since there had already been two world wars, a third was more or less inevitable. As if to confirm my hunch, the Vietnam conflict began to escalate right on cue.

These martial predilections were actively encouraged by my early reading material – 'comics' as they were known, though the content was really more in the province of tragedy, lionising the heroes of Britain and its former empire, as in *The Victor* and *The Valiant*. Invariably, the exploits of these men (this was a 'boy thing') concluded with the award of some prestigious British military honour, more often than not the Victoria Cross 'For Valour', that most rare honour. It was very satisfying for a pedantic mind such as my own that the stories were not mere inventions but based on real 'historical' events, though I doubted that the real enemies of the British Army were quite the hapless caricatures depicted therein. This was confirmed when my father, who was obsessed with war – and in particular 'the war' as he called the 1939–45 conflict – began a subscription to Purnell's *History of the Second World War* in 1966. Every week, the magazine would be on the kitchen table, and although I could not yet read properly, it was lavishly illustrated. It was noteworthy that the jolliest and best photographs, in vivid colour depicting smiling soldiers (at least at first) – were German, usually derived from the Nazi propaganda magazine *Signal*. Although my understanding was limited, I felt an immediate and natural bond with these times, and looked forward each week to the next instalment of the 'story' much as a boy would await delivery of a 'comic'. But then, one week, the weekly episode was missing. This was unprecedented, because my father was meticulous about collecting the volumes, and even ordered the binders to keep them safe. Where was it? As it turned out, my father had concealed it from me, because this was the issue called 'Inside the Camps'. The cover displayed a mangled pile of violated, starved, degraded human beings – all now mercifully dead, lying in a heap in a filthy death camp. The moment I discovered it I burst into tears. This was not war – this was murder! Let no one say that they cannot tell the difference when a five-year-old boy knew it intrinsically.

So, for that cohort of people who usually examine a book of this sort, the aficionados of military history, wargaming or local antiquarianism – do not abandon hope. This is very much a project aimed at you – and the author would be proud beyond measure if it became a set text for students at Sandhurst and West Point. And yet, for a very long time, these matters have been far from my mind, and I fear that by the very act of my broaching them the war machine may creak and turn more readily. The more one learns of war, either experientially or by research, the more one realises what an ultimate catastrophe it really is. Entire university departments are devoted to 'War Studies', in an age when any major conflict would immediately result in the complete extinction of all human and most animal life on Earth. What would the Prussian military theorist Carl von Clausewitz (1780–1831) have made of that? War is, in the words of a popular ballad, good for 'absolutely nothing'. It is, in anthropological terms, mere ritualised murder, and no matter how glamorised it may be in a time of emergency, it represents a massive failure, a basic flaw in the human spirit. How can it, when all is said and done, have come to this? What demons are there in us which drive us to whet our swords and gird our daggers against those who, until all too recently, were our friends and neighbours? This is the key question, and it has been asked since the beginning of human civilisation. In the *Bhagavad Gita*, an ancient Indian text, the hero Arjuna leads out an army to confront rebels, many of them his erstwhile friends and relatives. Can it really be that he must ride forth in his chariot to maim or kill these once beloved comrades? The prospect is simply too much to endure:

> I do not wish to kill ... though they kill me ... I do not wish for victory nor sovereignty, nor pleasures, nor even life.

With that, the poor man retires in tears, puts aside his bow and arrows, and resolves to yield rather than to kill his fellow men, for he has realised, all too late, that the 'enemies' are exteriorised aspects of his own 'self'. Arjuna is most fortunate that his charioteer, who comforts him during this crisis, turns out to be none other than an avatar of the god Krishna. In one of the most shocking exchanges in literary history, Krishna completely challenges Arjuna's inflexible ideas about life and death – and war and peace:

> Never did I not exist, nor you, nor these princes; nor will any one of us ever hereafter cease to be ... There is no existence for that which is unreal; there is no non-existence for that which is real ... He who thinks one to be the killer and he who thinks one to be the killed, both know nothing. He kills not, is not killed. He is not born, nor does he ever die ...

And then, in spite of all the horror, the heartache, the wretched suffering, the famine and the grief which must inevitably ensue, Krishna exhorts Arjuna not to retire to a monastery or to capitulate in abject surrender, but rather says instead:

> Therefore, fare ye forth, and fight on![1]

Something rather along these lines was reiterated to me by my father, whose rather obsessive interest in military history came to dominate my early years.

---

1. *Bhagavad Gita*, 11:18

My mother had worked in all the local cinemas before I was born, so there was a convenient arrangement that my father could go and watch for free. When my mother was working, he would have me in tow, and so I would be allowed in with him. This was not something that happened often, but when it did the film would always be either a Western (usually with Clint Eastwood), an historical drama (usually with Peter O'Toole), or a war movie. One of the first of these treats was *Zulu* (1964), the superb dramatization of the defence of a tiny mission station at Rorke's Drift, Natal, by men of the South Wales Borderers Regiment and other elements in 1879. Some of our ancestors had originated near Brecon, and I think I had already been to the Regimental Museum there not long before seeing the film. Now – and, it must be said, at quite a young age – I saw something of what this thing called war was really about. When we emerged from the cinema, my father was somewhat disconcerted when I began praising the spirit and martial *elan* of the 4,000 Zulu attackers rather than the force of just over 100 who had defended the place. But his point was, I think, to inculcate the idea that – and this can happen with lightning swiftness – a time comes when diplomacy and bargaining, conciliation and compromise, have failed. The enemy is here now, and there is nothing left to do but prepare for battle.

The battlefields in this book are arranged chronologically. The earliest are often 'lost', in the sense that we cannot know their precise location so long after the events, but they all (with the possible exception of Camlann) really happened. In such cases we must simply weigh up the options and take an inspired guess – but this was always a favourite game of mine as a boy. The first battle related herein was a source of endless speculation of this kind. As a boy I often searched for 'Caer Caradoc' in the Welsh borderlands, looking out from the Stretton Hills and vividly imagining two Roman legions advancing towards me, as depicted in the film *Spartacus* (1960). It will be objected, perhaps, that a great many of the conflicts are located in the English Midlands. There is almost certainly an element of personal bias and nostalgia in this, but it is also a reflection of the sad fact that the Midlands has been the main battlefield for countless wars – and it could not really be otherwise. Britain is a small island, and a few obvious facts dictate military planning in respect of it. The main objective of any British defence has always been to prevent an invading force setting foot onshore. Until the Roman occupation, when the Roman *Classis Britannica* patrolled the Channel, no unified national authority existed to construct and maintain a British fleet. This inability to oppose the Romans at sea, and the desultory efforts to dislodge them when they had carved out a beachhead, were what ensured eventual defeat for the British tribes.

To penetrate inland, an invader, at least until very recent times, had to attempt any substantial ingress from the sea. Hilaire Belloc, in his *Warfare in England*, proposed that five 'gates' exist which facilitate rapid penetration into the hinterland. These are the Solent and the estuaries of the Humber, the Thames, the Severn and the Dee. I must here make a somewhat grim admission: I no longer possess a copy of Belloc's classic. However, the following principles were inculcated so thoroughly in my youth that they may as well be in quotation marks, so well do I recall them. They are as follows.

No invader can truly be said to have control of the country unless they have gained possession of the five aforementioned strategic gateways, and any defender who has lost them – or the cities which lie on or near them, like London, Bristol, Hull, Southampton or Chester – has lost the country. In respect of London, this is the most important of all the cities, the national centre of government and of course the financial and economic centre too. For many centuries London boasted that it could laugh a siege to scorn behind its ancient walls, and possession of the city was usually the key to victory in any civil conflict. London had vast reserves of manpower and money, and was usually well supplied with foodstuffs and armaments. It was also a depot and a port, and until a few hundred years ago possessed the only major bridge over the Thames. To besiege it was usually too protracted and expensive an exercise to contemplate, though both Cnut and William of Normandy attempted it. But to ignore it was dangerous as well, because it could be used as a sally port from which offensive operations by the forces within could be advanced in any direction. Therefore, in the long history of warfare on the island, possession of this city has always been a priority – if not *the* priority – in any campaign.

In terms of topography, the mountainous regions of the island lie to the north and west, but even there the mountains are not exceptionally forbidding as military obstacles. The same is true of the major rivers. Although the Severn is wide in its lower reaches, it is not deep enough to prevent its being carried by assault or bridged with pontoons by a determined aggressor. The Thames, however, is a more serious challenge, and hostile military planners have had to contend with that problem, from the Romans to the Germans during the Second World War. Fortunately, the *Wermacht* never made an amphibious landing, and like Philip II of Spain and Napoleon Bonaparte before them were frustrated by English and then British supremacy at sea (and, in 1940, in the air).

I have deliberately selected the more obscure battles because there exist plenty of other accounts of major and decisive conflicts like Hastings, Marston Moor and Naseby. Some of the battles described herein were desperate and vicious affairs involving many tens of thousands of men; others were hardly more than local skirmishes involving a few hundred. These smaller conflicts will, therefore, take up less space than the major ones, but I would not wish that to imply that they were somehow less important.

Once it had begun, the fissiparous nature of war affected every community, no matter how remote. What united them all was the intense waste and sadness, the keening of women for lost fathers, husbands and sons who never returned from some blood-soaked field far away – and that those men gave up all their tomorrows for causes too precious and honourable to set aside. If this book reminds us of their sacrifice, and ensures it is not forgotten, then it will have served its purpose. May they all rest in eternal peace.

PART ONE

I

THE FIRST 'BATTLE OF BRITAIN'
(50–51)

Rather than being a glorification of war, the author hopes this book serves as a valediction for an activity which will have outlived its usefulness. In the afterword, I will explain why I think we may stand on the threshold of a new era of peace, in which even simulations of war may be thought socially deviant, and that the ultimate peace will truly come to pass, of which the prophet Micah spoke: 'And He shall judge among many people; and they shall beat their swords into ploughshares, and their spears into pruning-hooks; nation shall not lift up sword against nation, neither shall they learn war any more.'[2] At the Regiment Museum in Worcester a touching exhibit always drew my eye. It detailed how, at the end of the First World War, the local Yeomanry Cavalry found itself posted to Palestine. At the conclusion of hostilities, they took Micah's words literally, and had their cavalry sabres smelted down and fashioned into a ploughshare. They sowed wheat, which they harvested and milled into the flour that formed the communion host at a field service for the regiment,

---

2. Micah, 4:3

for perhaps there has never been a time when universal peace was more devoutly wished for across the world than in 1919.

This now seems like a utopian dream, but the alternative is a nightmare – the pointless annihilation of the human race and perhaps life itself. One of the reasons for the diminishing space that war takes up in the modern consciousness, and why battlefields are clearly marked on maps but are fading from our minds, is that there is a growing and definite distaste for it among the younger generations. In 2019 it was reported that the army was 40 per cent below strength,[3] and regulations forbidding tattoos and beards were being relaxed so that young men were not instantly disbarred from the RAF. Not only is there a detestation of discipline and order, but there is a question about physical efficiency, since so many applicants are clinically obese.[4] Similar conditions pertained during the Boer War, when sheer poverty meant that recruits were often stunted and unhealthy, resulting in the Haldane Reforms to professionalise the army. Similar modern reforms would be welcome, because peaceful cooperation is not yet the natural condition of human consciousness – and for our forebears quite a different mindset obtained, in which war was the most honoured and esteemed activity of all, the epitome of valour, comradeship, loyalty, self-sacrifice and glory.

For the British Celtic tribes, among others, there was only one way to achieve undying fame: to be a warrior-hero. One had to either die fighting the enemies of the tribe or return to victory feasts, where vast amounts of roasted meats would be washed down with rich wines and mead in honour of the glorious fallen. Before we begin the story of Caratacus, the first folk hero of this

---

3. 'UK army combat units 40% below strength as recruitment plummets', *The Guardian* (2019), https://www.theguardian.com/uk-news/2019/aug/09/uk-army-combat-units-40-below-strength-as-recruitment-plummets
4. 'Almost One In Ten British Troops Are "Clinically Obese"', *Forces* (2018), https://www.forces.net/news/almost-one-ten-british-troops-are-clinically-obese

island (his name means 'well-beloved one'), we should first try to imagine the psychopathic belligerence towards tribal enemies which was the very foundation of this society. Here was a culture entirely geared to constant warfare and feasting, male-dominated and aristocratic, with an entire class of men whose only purpose in life was to kill or be killed.

There was no higher calling among these Brythonic (hereafter 'British') Celts than to die in battle on behalf of the tribe. In their philosophy there was no absolute annihilation of the soul at death in any case. Like Arjuna's divine charioteer, they believed the spirit to be immortal, indestructible. This gave them a fearsome reputation for reckless bravery in battle like the Japanese *kamikaze* suicide pilots of the Second World War. When the Roman Emperor Claudius dispatched a huge invasion force to Britain in AD 43, his 40,000 troops faced these formidable adversaries, whose bards had sung them poems of the deeds of their great-grandfathers. These glorious ancestors had, they believed, sent the mighty Julius Caesar packing when he had dared to invade almost a century before. Claudius, they knew, was no Julius Caesar; he was reputed to be a drooling fool, a cripple, a stammering idiot – in short, unmanly in their eyes. When news reached the Celtic chieftains of this fresh Roman landing, far from being alarmed and panicked, they were eager to show that they had inherited the martial skill and courage of their ancestors, and that the well-beloved Caratacus and his brother Togodumnus of the Catuvellauni tribe – 'the battle experts' as they called themselves – would soon throw these new Roman interlopers into the sea. But, as we will see, Claudius was very far from being a fool, and the Romans had come to stay.

This insouciant attitude to the threat posed by Roman imperialist expansionism was a consequence of a certain hubris which had grown up among the kings of the Catuvellauni tribe. Britain was home to between twenty and forty main tribal groupings, each with its own ruler. In a time of supreme emergency such as the Roman invasion, however, these tribal rulers would cooperate, electing a *Brenin* or 'over-king' as a sort of commander-in-chief, a 'high king' of the Britons – at least until the emergency was over, when they immediately began fighting among themselves again. When Caesar had invaded in 55 BC and 54 BC, it had been Cassivellaunus, great-grandfather of Caratacus, who had fulfilled this role. Conventional histories portray Caesar's expeditions as, in effect, a conquest of south-eastern Britain that was rudely interrupted by rebellion among the Gauls across the Channel and political intrigues in Rome. It is true that Caesar's expeditions were partially successful, and the Britons were very pleased to see him leave, but the story the Britons told themselves about the affair was very different, and only grew in the retelling in the decades that followed.

In previous books, I have examined how the cryptohistory or 'national' mythology of the insular British Celts, conveyed to them in oral tales told by Druids and bards, became the spiritual underpinning for their resistance to various invaders for 1,500 years. The Druids, organised in three distinct orders, controlled all aspects of spiritual and political life. It was they who advised the tribal chieftains, and ultimately the *Brenin*, after first consulting the departed spirits of the ancestors using seers who entered trance states known as *Awenyddion*. One of the main attributes of the Druids was their knowledge of the history of the tribes, and of the island people as a whole, which they learned orally, by means of reciting mnemonic poems or triads. Caesar related that the Druids devoted up to twenty years to such studies. A great heroic king, once deceased, became elevated to the status of a god, not 'dead' as we would think of it but dwelling now in a parallel realm coterminous with this one, overlooking the affairs of the living and standing ready to advise the Druids through visions or signs in nature – even in the last resort, reincarnating once more to lead the Britons to victory. These sacrosanct traditions formed, many centuries later, the basis of the Arthurian myth cycle, but the very first such 'British' hero was Caswallawn ap Beli – or, in Latin, Cassivellaunus. So famous was he that his legend endured for over 1,000 years, when it was recorded by the historian Geoffrey of Monmouth in his *Historia Regum Britanniae*, written in around 1136.

One of the abiding features of these Brythonic or British warrior heroes was that they were never content to concern themselves merely with insular affairs. Instead, they are portrayed as taking the war to the Continent, usually Rome, by mounting seaborne expeditions with large armies. Arthur, for example, leads just such an expedition against the Romans. In the tales which encrusted around Caswallawn, he leads a huge host of 61,000 warriors of Britain to rescue Fflur ('Flower'), a renowned beauty who has been abducted by a chieftain from Gaul named Mwrchan or Morgan. A Roman army comes to intercept him, but Caswallawn easily brushes this aside, recaptures Fflur, and settles down to retire in Gascony. Other traditions clearly identify Caswallawn as the 'high king'. In the *mabinogi* of Manawyddan, one of the oldest Welsh tales, Pryderi, a mythical ruler of what is now Dyfed, visits Ryt Ychen (Oxford) to offer Caswallawn homage and tribute. Whatever the historical facts behind this legend – and we will almost certainly never know – Caswallawn's descendants came to be seen as the epitome of the British heroic tradition.

Within a few years of Caesar's departure, the Catuvellauni tribe reneged on their promises to send slaves and tributes of gold to the Romans, as had been agreed with 'Iwl Caisar' or 'Ukessar', as the Britons called Caesar. All punitive obligations were repudiated once Caesar was dead, and no retaliation followed. The Catuvellauni, emboldened by their own propaganda, now emerged as the dominant power in the south of the island, and under the able leadership of Cunobelinus ('the hound of Beli' or Apollo), eldest son of Cassivellaunus, their territory expanded from its core in what is modern Hertfordshire to encompass most of the south-east. The 'battle-experts' were living up to their fearsome reputation. Cunobelinus, the model for William Shakespeare's Cymbeline, took the legends and made them fact. Not only did he consider himself to be the 'High King of Britain', but the Romans concurred. Suetonius, a Roman historian, calls him just that. A modern text calls him 'the Iron Age equivalent of a Mafia godfather: dangerous, strong, politically powerful and in control of all economic and financial transactions for his region'.[5] But powerful as he was, Cunobelinus took great care not to offend the Romans in any way. It was a wise policy, but as so often before and since, the sagacious policy of the father was rapidly unravelled by his tempestuous and feuding sons – and especially by our hero, Caratacus.

Even now, when two millennia have elapsed, Caratacus is a 'national' hero in Wales, where the proud descendants of the Brythonic tribes still live and speak a language descended from theirs. Here, he is known as Caradoc or Caradawc, and the Welsh Marches still contain examples of hill forts named 'Caer Caradoc' in his honour. In the 1560s, the itinerant Welsh folklorist Humphrey Llwyd spoke with shepherds who told him of a famous hero they (mistakenly) called 'Caratactacus'. The Roman historian Tacitus, whose account of the campaign remains the only reliable historical source on the matter, called him 'Caractacus' – the Latin form of the name. Celtic linguistic experts assert either Caratacos or Caratacus as being the most accurate form, so I will use the latter form herein. Strangely, Tacitus was not translated into English until the 1570s, fully a decade after Llwyd recorded his tale. It is highly unlikely that these presumably illiterate border rustics could have come by the works of Tacitus in Latin, and so it seems that, garbled as they were, these traditions had been passed down orally from one generation to the next for over 1,500 years.

From the outset, Caratacus seems to have been determined to antagonise Rome, which he regarded with contempt. He was one of many brothers, and we know two of them by name: the aforementioned Togodumnus, perhaps the eldest, who fought and died alongside him against the Romans; and Adminius, who

5. Russell, J. B & Laycock, S., *UnRoman Britain: Exposing the Great Myth of Britannia* (Stroud, 2010)

had been set up by his father as the ruler of the Cantiaci tribe of Kantion or Kent, which controlled the vital cross-Channel trade with Gaul. During their father's more senescent years, the two eldest brothers had gradually expropriated territory and tribute from most of the southern British tribes, among them the Trinovantes, Atrebates, Regni and Dobunni of the lower Severn Valley. When their father finally died in AD 41, Togodumnus and Caratacus divided the spoils between them, excluding the furious Adminius, who fled overseas to plead for help from the Roman emperor. Another British king, Verica, had preceded him, and Caratacus immediately demanded his extradition, threatening to impose economic sanctions on Roman goods. The new co-ruler of the Catuvellauni was proud, headstrong, militant and arrogant (the tribal rulers may have been descended from a people called the Belgae, or 'boastful ones'). He minted coins depicting himself as the mythic Hercules on the obverse, and on the reverse an eagle aggressively swoops on a snake, which it grips in its fearsome talons. So, we can surmise that Caratacus was the model of the British warrior tradition – a man who feared no one, least of all the decadent Roman Empire with its mad and disabled emperors.

But these provocations came at precisely the time when the supposedly imbecilic Claudius desperately needed to prove his political virility. His insane predecessor, Caligula, had already planned an invasion of Britain but had aborted the mission, ordering his bewildered troops to collect seashells from the beach which he then paraded in a Roman triumph as 'tribute from the sea-god, Neptune'. Claudius was extremely astute and well read, and he had studied Caesar's account of his invasions of Britain in minute detail. Although Caligula's legions had been stood down at the last minute, the transports at Boulogne intended to convey them to 'Britannia' had been completed, and it was a relatively simple matter to revive the plan. The great statesman and historian Cassius Dio related that Claudius appointed his most accomplished general, Aulus Plautius, to command the expedition. No expense was spared, and the military complement was twice the size of

Caesar's force almost a century before. He selected 40,000 of the finest troops in the empire to spearhead the expedition – and this time the Romans meant to subdue the entire island. But it was one thing to provide expertise and military heft, and quite another to persuade superstitious soldiers to cross the sea. The fearful troops were demoralised to be dispatched 'beyond the inhabited world' to fight rumoured head-hunting 'barbarians' whose weapons included the curses of the dreaded Druids, who claimed the ability to control the weather and conjure storms at sea.

The massive preparations for the operation could not be completed covertly, and the four legions and their activities were closely observed by Gallic spies who kept their British cousins well informed about Roman preparations. A vast British army was called up, and watched the sea anxiously. But the weeks and months elapsed, and when the spies reported that the Roman legions were openly mutinous, many British commanders concluded that this expedition was doomed to end in farce like its predecessor a few years before. The tribesmen, many of them levies from vassal tribes of the Catuvellauni, grew increasingly restless and demanded to go home to tend to their farms. So, the British army was stood down rather too prematurely, and when Aulus Plautius and his four legions finally landed at Richborough in Kent, they were completely unopposed. Cassius Dio, our only source for what happened next, takes up the story:

> They landed on the island, and found none to oppose them. For the Britons, because of reports that had reached them, did not expect the Romans to come, and had not assembled an army. Even when they did muster, they would not attack the Romans openly, but lurked in the marshes and woods, hoping to wear down the invaders so that – as had happened in Julius Caesar's time – they would sail away without achieving anything. Plautius therefore had a great deal of difficulty finding them, but when he finally did so, he defeated first Caratacus and then Togodumnus, the sons of the late Cunobelinus ... the Britons were not independent, but ruled by

the kings of other tribes ... when these kings fled, Plautius received the submission of the Bodunni (Dobunni), a subject people of the Catuvellauni. Then, leaving a garrison behind, he marched on until he came to a river...[6]

The resentful Dobunni ('the victorious ones') were only too eager to leave their overlords to do the fighting. They had little reason to love Caratacus, and probably calculated that he would soon be overwhelmed by the numerous and well-trained Roman legions. But Caratacus was to defy the invaders for nine long years, and was destined to become a legend, not only among the Britons, but also the Romans themselves.

The two brothers, Togodumnus and Caratacus, took council as to their next move. The defection of the Dobunni was only to be expected, but their hold on their nearer neighbours was still strong, and the threat to their own tribal homeland north of the Thames was now so urgent that there could be no alternative but to fight a pitched battle. Roman historians had a habit of vastly inflating the numbers of their defeated enemies so as to make the victory of Roman arms seem all the more glorious. It was claimed that the British army which mustered to halt Plautius' army on the River Medway consisted of over 60,000 men – almost certainly an overestimate – but this battle did, nevertheless, offer the Britons their only hope of victory. Perhaps a more modest estimate of 40,000 would be more accurate, and with a river obstacle in front of them the defenders presumed that a Roman assault would either fail or prove so costly that the enemy would ultimately withdraw, as in Caesar's campaigns. Cassius Dio:

The barbarians believed that the Romans would be unable to cross the river without a bridge, so they camped on the far bank without taking precautions. But Plautius sent across a

---

6. Cassius Dio, *Roman History*, ed. & trans. J. Jackson (London, 1924)

detachment of Celts (actually, Batavian auxiliaries from what is now the Netherlands) ... who were trained to swim in their full armour ... these took the enemy by surprise, but instead of shooting at the men, they unleashed or wounded the chariot horses, so that even the charioteers could not escape in the confusion. Then Plautius sent across Flavius Vespasian (who later became the Roman emperor) and his brother Sabinus, his lieutenant ... who also took the enemy by surprise.

The Romans greatly feared the British charioteers, whose skill had so impressed Julius Caesar many years before. These superbly crafted and expensive vehicles were the 'secret weapon' of the tribesmen, but only an elite could afford them. The nobleman was not the passenger, as in Arjuna's day, but controlled the chariot as it was deployed at high speed, turning and manoeuvring with astonishing agility. Beside him, either one or two men, heavily armed, could leap out to attack the stunned enemy, even moving along the yoke at full speed to hurl deadly javelins into their ranks. It may even be true that some models included vicious, whirling, razor-sharp blades attached to the wheel hubs, designed to panic infantry and cavalry alike.

Thanks to the efforts of the Roman-allied 'Celts', as Dio called them, the threat of the chariot was now negated. In normal circumstances this would have been the denouement of the engagement, but on this occasion, and probably due in no small part to Caratacus' leadership, the Britons rallied the following morning. The Roman line was very nearly broken by the enraged tribesmen, but an officer named Gnaeus Hosidius Geta fought so bravely that the day was saved. He later received a Roman triumph for his bravery – the highest honour the emperor could bestow.

The Britons were broken but not disconsolate. The survivors fled north to the Thames – a much more formidable river barrier. Once again, the 'Celtic' Batavian auxiliaries were called upon to swim the river, but emerged to find themselves trapped in

Hackney Marshes. The British army, knowing the country well, extricated themselves, but Togodumnus was not so fortunate. He may well have sustained wounds at the Medway battle, and perhaps died of these during the frantic retreat. Finally, the Romans located a bridge, though it must have been somewhat west of what is now London. Although some sort of trading settlement existed there, the famous city called *Troia Nova* or Trinovantum – allegedly founded by the Trojan exile Brutus as 'New Troy' in around 1185 BC – had long since been abandoned, if indeed it was ever more than legendary. Caratacus, grieving for his brother, retired to Camulodunum (modern Colchester, in Essex). Here, he prepared to make a last stand, but to his surprise the Roman advance stalled. Plautius had done his job, but for propaganda purposes the emperor himself had to be summoned from Rome to observe the final showdown.

Claudius took a month to make the journey, bringing with him his own Praetorian Guard, cavalry reinforcements, and some 'secret weapons' of his own – war elephants (fully armoured and trained to attack infantry) – and camels, whose unusual scent panicked the British warhorses. Neither animal was familiar to the Britons, and Claudius remarked that the inhabitants were so horrified by them that he saw not one native on his journey from the coast to the Thames (Plautius would have anyway been very careful about security, in case of assassination attempts).

Roman siege artillery, and overwhelming numbers, ensured that the 'city' of Camulodunum was stormed swiftly and at no grievous loss. A delegation of eleven British sub-kings from a variety of tribes soon came to surrender to the emperor in person, but Caratacus does not seem to have been among them. Claudius had covered himself in glory sufficient for a huge Roman triumph upon his return to 'civilisation', and after just sixteen days in Britannia he returned home. Plautius was commanded to subjugate the rest of the country, and to establish a Roman colony at Camulodunum, where a mighty temple, dedicated to Claudius as a living deity, was to be established, using the finest materials and the most skilled craftsmen in the empire. 'Mission accomplished,' the emperor may have thought. But now one man was to show that a determined foe could take on the whole Roman imperial apparatus: Caratacus.

The surviving ruler of the Catuvellauni was too intelligent to be caught in the trap at Camulodunum. He escaped with his wife, daughters and younger brothers, along with such treasures as he could carry. A typical Celtic war band traditionally numbered 300 men, and this close personal bodyguard of elite warriors may have been his only remaining strike force. Along with their best horses and cattle, this tiny group seems to have made for the West Country. The Iceni of East Anglia, traditional enemies of his tribe, went over to the Romans, making a treaty with them. The south-east was already lost. The Midlands tribes also capitulated or made terms; one of the tribes whose king surrendered to Claudius on his brief visit were the Cornomagni, the 'great Cornovii' of the north-west Midlands. They were the traditional enemies of all other tribes in Britain, especially their southern neighbours the Dobunni. The latter had mixed feelings about submitting to Rome, but their co-rulers initially sued for peace with the Romans. This treachery would not go unavenged, and although it is impossible to know exactly what happened, archaeological evidence suggests that Caratacus moved swiftly to punish them.

Plautius too, looked westward. To secure the south coast and its harbours was a pressing priority for him; but one of the main economic motives behind the invasion was to secure the tin and lead of the south-western peninsula. Additionally, it was known that there were rich deposits of gold at Dolocauthi and large copper mines near Llandudno in present-day Wales. As the legions moved west, all resistance was ruthlessly crushed. The Durotriges of Dorset were forced to capitulate by Vespasian, and the famous archaeologist Mortimer Wheeler may have been correct to suggest that the Romans stormed their mighty hill fort of Maiden Castle near Dorchester. Although he was still too weak to chastise the northern Dobunni, Caratacus brought their southern component back into line. At Minchinhampton in Gloucestershire excavations have revealed a strong fortress built at this time from which the patriotic Britons still loyal to Caratacus could have visited savage reprisals on collaborators. Many men must have joined him by this point, for the site encloses over 600 acres. These new recruits would have comprised resentful refugees from the new Roman order; the Roman army was as brutal and cruel to the 'barbarians' of Britain as were the German invaders of Russia and the Ukraine during the Second World War – at least at first. Until Caratacus was eliminated, there could be little scope for introducing the more benevolent aspects of the *Pax Romana*. In AD 47, Plautius decided to fan out into the unconquered territories and dispose of the troublesome warlord once and for all.

The legions pushed north and west until a line had been established from *Isca Dumnoniorum* (Exeter) to *Lindum Colonia* (Lincoln). These operations were co-ordinated offensives by three legions plus their auxiliary elements – probably in excess of 30,000 troops all told. No individual British tribe could match these numbers, nor the discipline and efficiency of the professional Roman army. But Caratacus had one factor in his favour. The further the Romans advanced, the more stretched their lines of communications grew as they moved into a hinterland which was less well developed than the south-east, and broken up by tracts of impenetrable woodland and fenland. A military road, known today as the Fosse Way, was the slender thread linking the three prongs of the Roman trident.

By now, Caratacus had repeated the time-honoured British tactic of putting a river obstacle between himself and the enemy, this time the Severn (or Hafren as the Britons called it). The tribe to the east of the Severn in the west Midlands, the Cornovii, seems to have colluded with the Roman offensive. A huge military base was built at a junction with an ancient British trackway into Mid Wales, the Hen Fford or 'old road' just outside the village of Wall Heath in south Staffordshire. This was the hub for communications between *vexillationes*, or detached elements of the Roman Fourteenth Legion. The 'old road' pointed straight as an arrow to the great hill fort of the Ordovices tribe at Cefn Carnedd between Caersws and Trefeglwys, which many contend was the scene for the final, epic encounter in this chapter. In the nineteenth century, excavators at nearby Wrottesley, outside Wolverhampton, were said to have discovered British blades and spearheads of the period, and the site was dubbed 'the camp of Caratacus'. While it is unlikely that Caratacus would have dared to venture so far east at this point, it is known that he fought a very deadly guerrilla campaign which exasperated the Roman high command.

By now Plautius had served four long years in Britannia, and his weary troops were growing more and more disgruntled. Claudius decided to replace him as governor of the province, and to withdraw his veterans so that they could be replaced with fresh troops. During the complicated business of the changeover, which took place during the autumn, when military campaigning usually ceased until the following spring, Caratacus struck his blow. Tacitus describes it:

> ... the new governor, Publius Ostorius was greeted by chaos ... the enemy, not believing that a new commander would take the field against them with an army unfamiliar with the country, and in the winter season, burst through the frontier into the territory of our allies ... but Ostorius rushed forward his light troops at once, cutting down those who resisted and pursuing the broken fugitives. Then, he resolved to disarm all suspects and to subdue the entire area south-east of the Rivers Severn and Trent.[7]

This may provide a context for the finds at Wrottesley, for the Roman depredations which followed were aimed at pacifying the Deceangli of modern Clwyd. It was a tradition among the Britons

---

7. Tacitus, *Annals*, ed. J. Jackson (London, 1937)

that every free man had the right to bear arms. As soon as Roman troops arrived to search for weapons and malcontents, trouble flared; soon, even the hitherto cooperative Iceni tribe erupted into rebellion. Perhaps the Roman-allied tribes, such as the Cornovii, simply hid their weapons away until the Roman threat was gone. In any case, Roman reprisals were swift and brutal. Tacitus writes, 'The countryside was laid waste, and booty taken on every hand. Ostorius had almost reached the Irish Sea when rebellion among the Brigantes to his rear called him back.'

Ostorius had made an elementary mistake: he had taken the offensive before properly securing his rear. Furthermore, he had antagonised previously friendly tribes. The still active Druids intensified their anti-Roman propaganda, and Caratacus, whom many Britons had previously seen as a fanatic, became a 'national' hero and a potential liberator. Those brave souls who were able now made their way west to join his renegade army – for an army it was. Two of the most warlike tribes in Britain had rallied to the 'beloved one': the Ordovices of northern Wales and the Silures of southern Wales. It was this latter tribe who were to prove the most dangerous enemy the Romans had yet faced.

These hill tribesmen reminded Tacitus of the Iberians of Spain and Portugal, with their swarthy complexions and dark, curly hair. They were virtual aborigines, perhaps the last remnants of the folk who had taken to the hills and forests when the 'Bell-beaker' people from what is now the Netherlands displaced a more primordial stock, commencing around 2,500 BC. They were ferocious in battle, and were equally undaunted whether fighting a 'bandit war from woods and marshes', as Tacitus put it, or in pitched battles. Later they would refuse to yield against all odds, and under the leadership of Arviragus they would confront a full Roman legion and put it to flight, taking many Roman prisoners. The Silures were not numerous, and so couldn't afford to immediately massacre these captives, as was their time-honoured custom; instead, the prisoners were enslaved for five years before being sacrificed at a quinquennial festival. They worshipped the cunning and elusive wildcat as their totem animal, which perhaps indicates the nature of their method of war – swift, savage and furious assaults that seemed to come from nowhere.

These formidable tribesmen now threw in their lot with Caratacus, threatening to smash through the Roman frontier and destabilise the entire colonial venture. Ostorius was determined to redeem himself by crushing Siluria, and vowed that he would take no prisoners in doing so, declaring his resolve to exterminate the entire tribe. In AD 50, once his methodical preparations were completed, he deployed his entire field force, as well as a considerable fleet, in St George's Channel, or the *Mor Hafren* as the Britons called it. But the Silurians were determined they would not be obliterated from history without a fight, as Ostorius was to find to his cost.

The recalcitrant Silurians now in effect faced the onslaught of the entire Roman Empire – which was then at peace save for this one corner of Britannia. The Fourteenth Legion, called 'Gemina', concentrated in the western Midlands for an offensive down the valley of the River Wye, aiming to block Caratacus in from the north. The Roman fleet landed a large force of auxiliaries in modern-day Dyfed, as well as a vexillation of the Second Legion. These joined the Demetae tribe, ancient enemies of the Silures, with the aim of preventing Caratacus's retreat to the west. The main assault force, though, was the Twentieth Legion, called 'Valeria Victrix' or the 'Valiant and Victorious', whose emblem was the ferocious wild boar. This legion had constructed a massive fortress on the Severn outside Gloucester – for each legion was a heavy construction company as well as a military unit.

In the summer of AD 50, the Twentieth deployed along the valley of the River Usk. Tacitus tells us that the Silures resisted 'most obstinately'. But there was no sign of Caratacus. As the Romans penetrated into the Silurian valleys his warriors seemed to disappear into the landscape like wraiths. Tacitus, echoing Ostorius's frustration, simply says that Caratacus, 'superior in his knowledge of that treacherous terrain, cunningly shifted the war into the territory of the Ordovices'. The fighters of this northern component were just as redoubtable and fearsome as their Silurian neighbours. Their name means 'the hammer-wielders'. For hundreds if not thousands of years, Wales had been mined for various ores, and so stone hammers were ubiquitous. These ancient mountain folk were adept at throwing such weapons and skilled in the use of the bow and arrows. Any small child could be trained to proficiency with a sling, which in the right hands could penetrate full Roman plate with just a small stone.

Ostorius was furious; all his careful preparations had failed to deliver up his quarry. Slowly but surely, the governor's mental and physical health began to deteriorate as the elusive tribesmen mocked the seemingly impotent empire – and the whole empire was watching. News of the campaign in Cambria was on the lips of everyone in Rome, and the defiant British king was discussed not with contempt but a grudging respect. To his own oppressed and dispirited countrymen, meanwhile, he had become a superhero, a 'warrior of destiny' – he who was fated to deliver his people from slavery. The climax of this long drama drew near.

The most tantalising aspect of this final battle from nearly two thousand years ago is that Tacitus gives us all the small details but, crucially, neglects to mention its precise location. This has meant that a multitude of sites all over Wales and the Marches have been postulated over the intervening centuries, and the name of the hero, like Arthur's, naturally became associated with various local landmarks. The hunt for the battlefield began, for me, in childhood. Now, in my dotage, it seems to me that four 'contenders' are worthy of consideration, which I will explicate here ranked in order of likelihood, from the least likely to most likely. These are the 'British Camp' on the Herefordshire Beacon in the Malvern Hills; Caer Caradoc hill fort near Church Stretton in Shropshire; Cefn Carnedd hill fort between Caersws and Trefeglwys in Powys; and, finally, Stowe Hill near the tiny village of Chapel Lawn in south-west Shropshire. At various stages of my life I have been convinced of the merits of each of them in turn, but the obduracy of old age makes me think that I shall not now be persuaded otherwise.

First, the 'British Camp'. My mother grew up in extremely straitened circumstances during the Great Depression of the 1930s. Several of her siblings died of tuberculosis, and she, the youngest and frailest in health, and her sister who was a year or so older, were sent away to what was known as the 'Open Air Hospital' in the Malvern Hills to ensure they did not contract the illness. This decision saved their lives, for which reason my mother always retained a deep love for the area, and the English countryside in general. She loved nothing more than days out to Malvern, and would set off up the Worcestershire Beacon past St Ann's Well at a furious pace, while my father, holding me aloft on his shoulders, brought up the rear. At the summit there was then a café, and sheltering here one rainy, squally day in spring we met a glamorous American lady. She was extremely interesting as well as very kind to me (she bought me a bottle of exotic 'pop', possibly Vimto). She pointed at the massive hill fort on the adjacent Herefordshire Beacon, and told me how the great composer Edward Elgar used to walk these hills and how a great battle had taken place there. All the tribes from every corner of Britain, she said, had congregated there to defy the haughty Roman legions, led by the great hero 'Caractacus' (as she called him).

Then, when the rain cleared, the lady left us to follow in Elgar's footsteps. She had been a shaft of glamorous sunlight on a grey day. When we stood outside to survey the wide panorama my father said not to mind too much what the nice lady had said. He pointed away to the blue hills to the north, in Shropshire. That was where the great battle had been fought, he declaimed, at the place called Caer Caradoc. Elgar, he thought, was a great composer but a bohemian dreamer who had fallen for his own fantasies. The American lady was probably the same type. We needed no 'foreigners' to tell us our own history! He promised we would go to the real battlefield on our next day out.

As was so often the case, I think my father was right – or mostly right. The British Camp is much too far east, it seems to me, nowhere near the territory of the Ordovices, which Tacitus states was where the battle was fought. Nor can the Severn be called 'a stream', and it is anyway some miles away from Malvern. Church Stretton seemed much more promising, and as we walked along Carding Mill Valley towards the Long Mynd I gazed up at the forbidding mountainside, imagining it packed with howling Celtic warriors clad in plaid, heard the skirling of the carnyx trumpets and the beating of shields. These were my glorious ancestors, come to fight for the fate of Britain against the Roman foe – but I had to admit what worthy adversaries they must have been to climb such a mountain in full armour, pelted with missiles and obstructed by a stone wall. How had they prevailed? Atop Caer Caradoc, we sought out 'Caradoc's cave' where the great man was supposed to have hidden from the Romans after the battle. The site has more to recommend it than Malvern, perhaps, but still does not comport well with Tacitus's description.

Several sites in Wales have been postulated and are situated in the Ordovician heartland as stated by Tacitus. One is Cefn Carnedd hill fort near Caersws, which lies beneath a great spur of high land that rises as a wall just west of the Caersws basin. Caersws was a major Roman base and a hub for military roads during their conquest of Wales. The huge Ordovician fort dominated the confluence of the Rivers Severn and Carno. Although the first Roman base there cannot be precisely dated, it is quite possible that the legions marched along the Kerry Ridgeway to mount an assault on the heartland of the Ordovices. But Tacitus also states that the main action of the battle was an attack up steep, almost vertical cliffs, atop which the defenders had erected a crude wall of stones and a palisade. There are no vertical cliffs at Cefn Carnedd that I could find, and so although I do not lightly dismiss the possibility of the battle having been fought there, I am of the opinion that the author Charles Kightly was correct to surmise that the 'first Battle of Britain', as I call it here, was in fact fought outside Chapel Lawn near Knighton.[8] Kightly was the first to draw my attention to the fact that folklore sources, though they may seem academically unsound, can sometimes retain a valuable link to the past, an unbroken chain of information transmitted from mouth to ear, even over a period of 1,500 years. In fact, in rural areas in a pre-literate society these 'stories' and traditions could only be passed down in this way.

This was no ordinary battle but the 'main event' of the war for control of the island. Now in his fifties, Caratacus could no longer run or hide. The Ordovices and Silures needed a decision, a victory which, even if it did not dislodge the enemy from the entire island, would at least preserve their own liberty. The Druids, too, must have been pressing for a battle, as the legions stood poised to strike into Wales, and their headquarters on Ynys Mon or Anglesey. Perhaps the Archdruid had a vision of a great victory where the Britons, inspired by the gods and goddesses of old, would finally prevail. And so, in the summer of AD 51, Caratacus assembled the military strike force of the Ordovices and Silures, his own Catuvellauni veterans and 'all others who hated Roman rule' at the hill fort overlooking the River Teme that is still called 'Caer Caradoc' and lies just outside Chapel Lawn on the River Redlake. (Could that name, 'Red Lake', be a clue in itself, perhaps?) Humphrey Llwyd spoke to shepherds there who said that the hill fort had been the site of a great battle where 'Caratactacus (*sic*) had been at last conquered, and taken by his enemies'. After many visits to this place, I am quite convinced that this was indeed the battlefield.

In the late spring of AD 51, Roman scouts would have begun to report increased hostile activity near Bravonium, now Leintwardine in Herefordshire. This was exactly at the mid-point between the Twentieth Legion at Kingsholm and the Fourteenth Legion, then at Viriconium Cornoviorum (now Wroxeter) in Shropshire. It was also the mid-way point between the Silures

8. Kightly, C., *Folk Heroes of Britain* (Thames & Hudson, London, 1982)

and the Ordovices, and soon the 'bidding-stick' or 'war-arrow' was sent out to summon their clans to Stowe Hill. Like Harold Godwinson at Hastings and the Duke of Wellington at Waterloo, Caratacus had studied the lay of the land well beforehand. The hill fort in which he ensconced his immediate family members lies atop a steep massif of high ground overlooking the River Teme, which must be the 'stream with an unsure ford' mentioned by Tacitus. The tiny settlement of Stowe itself is nestled in the crucible of the battlefield, just beneath 'steep, almost vertical cliffs', now called Holloway Rocks. These rocks were now assembled into a defensive wall atop the cliffs – the 'ill-built heap of stones' Tacitus mentions – with a timber palisade behind that. Chariots and cavalry stood ready to contest any crossing of the ford on the north-west bank of the Teme where a small bridge now stands. These formidable defences were necessary because Caratacus was outnumbered by a significant margin – his entire force perhaps consisted of fewer than 15,000 warriors. The rule of thumb in military strategy is that an attacking force aiming to storm a defensive position ought to be superior by a factor of three to one. Ostorius did not have such a luxury, but he made very sure to position his two legions, plus auxiliaries and scouts, so as to maximise his superior manpower. When the legions had drawn up on the south bank of the Teme, about 15,000 to 18,000 men gave him a slight advantage in numbers.

Tacitus, whose father-in-law Julius Agricola fought in the campaign (he must have witnessed many a 'pepper-pot' diorama over lunch), gives us a vivid description of what happened next:

> The site of the battle was so chosen that approaches, escape routes and everything else were unfavourable to us and most advantageous to his (Caratacus') own men. On one side rose steep hills, and wherever there was an easy ascent the enemy had piled up boulders into a kind of rampart. In front of the position flowed a river with an untested ford, and all the defences were bristling with armed men …

As soon as the Romans had formed into ranks a tremendous noise erupted from the British defenders, designed to show that the invaders faced no mere British chieftain with a raiding party but the assembled host of all Free Britain, led by the high king himself. Tacitus continues:

> The British chieftains, meanwhile, went around encouraging their tribesmen, uplifting their spirits by making light of fear, inflaming them with hope and otherwise inciting them to battle. Caratacus himself, almost flying from one position to another, proclaimed that this day and this battle would mark the beginning either of the recovery of freedom or of perpetual slavery. He also called on the names of the ancestors, they who had driven out the dictator Julius Caesar; it was valour alone that had kept them from the axes of the Roman executioners and the demands of Roman tax-gatherers, and the bodies of their wives and children undefiled. The warriors responded with great shouts of approval, and every man swore by his tribal oath that neither wounds nor enemy weapons would make him give way ...

It was a rousing speech that put fire in the bellies of the assembled British host. The uproar atop the cliff tops struck fear into the hearts of the legions, and according to Tacitus even their general was dismayed:

> ... (He) was already apprehensive about the intervening river, the reinforcing ramparts, the overhanging cliffs, and the crowds of savage defenders who thronged everywhere. But his soldiers demanded battle, crying out that no strong position was proof against courage, while their officers, using the same arguments, spurred them on to greater zeal. Then Ostorius, having carefully examined the enemy lines to see which points were impenetrable and which might be vulnerable, led his eager troops forward.

The first Battle of Britain had begun. The initial and most pressing task for Ostorius's men was to cross the river under a hail of missiles, with British cavalry and chariots swarming on the far bank, at exactly the point where the little bridge is nowadays. The Teme is not deep, and in summer the flow is not strong, so this obstacle, Tacitus states, was negotiated without difficulty. But as their comrades followed them the Romans soon realised that they were being funnelled into a killing zone, where any hesitation or reverse would end in catastrophe. As they climbed the hill under a hail of arrows, stones and spears, the Romans began to take heavy casualties:

> But when they got up to the ramparts, and the fight was being decided by an exchange of missiles, the Romans had decidedly the worst of it, and many of them fell. So, after they had locked their shields together into a defensive 'testudo' (or 'tortoise' formation) ... they undermined and pulled down the crude and ill-built heap of stones: this turned the combat into a hand-to-hand struggle on equal terms, and the barbarians began to retire to the hilltops. Even there they were pursued by both light and auxiliary troops, and caught between these and the heavy legionary infantry, the former skirmishing with their spears, and the latter advancing shoulder-to-shoulder. The British ranks, lacking the protection of breastplates and helmets, were thrown into chaos: if they resisted the auxiliaries, they were laid low by the javelins and stabbing swords of the legionaries, but if they turned to face the legionaries they fell to the lances and slashing swords of the auxiliaries. It was a famous victory, and Caratacus's wife and daughters were captured, his brothers being allowed to surrender.

Caratacus must have known that the battle was lost. He fled with a handful of comrades on their swift horses over the Black Hill. The British casualties were very heavy, perhaps over 8,000 slaughtered, with more than 1,000 Roman dead. But Caratacus was still at liberty, and while he lived the war went on. His only hope now was to stir up resistance in the north, among the Brigantes. It was known that Venutius, the consort of the Brigantian Queen Cartimandua (meaning 'sleek pony'), was sympathetic to the cause of freedom. So, Caratacus headed towards what is now Manchester. Here, near the Roman fort of Rigodunum on the bleak moors of Castleshaw, he was cruelly betrayed. He would have been assured of a safe passage to meet with Venutius, but Cartimandua was too cunning and intelligent to risk a war with Rome. Caratacus was arrested, to be handed over to the Romans in chains.

Reunited with his family members, Caratacus was speedily conveyed to Kent and thence overseas to the Continent. From there the family were taken under heavy guard to Rome to be paraded through the streets, mocked and spat upon, before the final act: ritual strangulation before the Roman emperor and senate. But now, at the darkest moment of all, Caratacus won his last victory.

Caratacus was by no means held in contempt by the Roman population. Tacitus is explicit that his fame had spread far and wide throughout the whole empire:

His fame had spread from the islands of Britain into the neighbouring provinces, and he was well known in Italy itself; everyone was desperate to see the man who had scorned our might for so many years. Even in Rome the name of Caratacus was not without honour, and the emperor, seeking to enhance his own splendour, only made him seem more glorious in defeat. For the people were summoned as if for some magnificent spectacle, while the Praetorian Guard stood to arms on the parade-ground before their camp. There, while Caratacus's lesser retainers were herded past, the neck-rings and other trophies he had won from other British tribes were displayed: next his brothers, his wife and his daughters were put on show, and finally the king himself appeared. Fear made the rest of the prisoners degrade themselves by appeals for pity, but Caratacus sought mercy neither by words or downcast looks ...

Then, in an incredible moment, the captive king strode forth to look the assembled senators – and the emperor himself – full in the face:

Coming to the emperor's dais, he spoke in this manner: 'If my high birth and good fortune had been matched by moderation in the hour of success, I would have come to this city as a friend rather than a prisoner: nor would you have rejected a peaceful alliance with a man of such noble ancestry, the ruler of many nations. But as things turned out, I am humbled, while you are glorified. Once I had horses and many warriors, fine weapons and splendid treasures; is it any wonder I was unwilling to lose them? Just because you want to conquer the world, does it follow that everyone else wants to be a slave? If I had been dragged here before you after surrendering without a blow, neither my misfortune nor your triumph would be worthy of fame: if you execute me, both of us will be forgotten soon enough. Spare my life then, to be an everlasting memorial to your mercy.' The emperor answered by granting pardon to Caratacus, his wife, daughters and brothers.

As the relieved Britons were led away to their palace on the Palatine Hill in Rome, where the great man indeed lived out the remainder of his days, he looked about him at the monumental buildings of the Forum, the triumphal arches and the great temples and said, 'Why, when you have all this, do you envy us our miserable huts?'

Even under house arrest in Rome the beloved leader could not resist causing more trouble for the Romans. When a new and supposedly seditious religious sect known as Christians began to be persecuted for their beliefs, Caratacus sheltered Linus, the second Bishop of Rome, under his roof. His daughter Gladys, meanwhile, had been forced to adopt the Roman name of Claudia and married a Roman senator named Rufus Pudens. This man was also sheltering one of the despised Christians – St Paul himself. It is said that after Caratacus's death, his daughters were allowed to return to Britain where they joined the small Christian community at Glastonbury, allegedly founded by Joseph of Arimathea. For those who wish to traduce these tales as wishful thinking, that is their business and their loss. The theologian

Tertullian of Carthage mentions that there were parts of Britannia over which the Romans had no authority, but which 'had been conquered by Christ'. Reginald Pole (1500–1558), in turn a cardinal and Archbishop of Canterbury, and who was within a whisker of being elected as the second English pope, put up a scholarly defence of the tradition that the first Christian church had been built in Britain. He had nothing to gain, and much to lose, by defending these stories.

But of one thing we can be sure: so long as British blood flows in the veins of the folk of these islands, the story of Caratacus, his determination in the face of impossible odds, and above all his unyielding pride in the face of death, will never fade from our minds or relinquish its grip on our hearts.

2

'THE TREACHEROUS LIONESS': BOUDICCA AND THE GREAT BRITISH REVOLT (60–61)

When the sixth-century British historian Gildas wrote his *De Excidio et Conquestu Britanniae* ('On the Ruin and Conquest of Britain'), he referred to his first-century countrywoman Boudicca (to the Romans 'Boadicea') as 'that Treacherous Lioness' – a somewhat disparaging term, we may think, for our first 'national' heroine. Gildas was not an historian in the modern sense of the term, though his book went on to become a cornerstone of our national story. He was, rather, a moral commentator, a theologian, and a sort of 'prophet of doom'.

When Gildas lived, the Romans had been gone for a century. Before that, they had controlled most of Britain for four hundred years. With their departure came the rapid collapse of civic infrastructure and the financial and economic system. There were immediate large-scale incursions by 'barbarian' Picts, Irishmen, Angles, Saxons, Jutes, Franks, Frisians, and other Germanic pirates. Gildas therefore regarded the Roman occupation with a wistful nostalgia, and saw the invasions by the foreigners as a punishment from God for the Britons' apostasy and sinfulness. For him, any enemy of the old Roman order represented barbarism and chaos. Therefore, Boudicca, a bitter enemy of the empire, was a dangerous and disturbing reminder of the days before the Roman order and the Christian faith; 'treacherous', as he puts it. But she is also a 'lioness', implying qualities of courage, nobility and power. That Gildas recorded her actions, from over five hundred years before his day, is evidence that Boudicca, warrior queen of the Iceni and the living embodiment of the goddess Andrasta ('the Victorious One'), was part of the folk psyche of the Romano-Britons long after the imperial collapse. For this was a woman who was destined to leave her mark on history in blood and fire – the avenging fury who unleashed the most desperate conflict ever to have engulfed this island.

The Roman historian Cassius Dio gives us a description of Boudicca. Though written long after the events he was describing, it may well have been based on records available to him but no longer extant:

> She was very tall, the glance of her eye most fierce; her voice harsh. A great mass of the reddest hair fell down to her hips. Around her neck was a large golden necklace (torque) and she always wore a tunic of many colours over which she fastened a thick cloak with a brooch. Her appearance was terrifying ... then she clutched a spear to strike fear into all who beheld her. Then she let loose a hare from within the folds of her robes ... which running in a direction considered propitious for victory ... the whole host gave a mighty cheer. Boudicca then raised her hands to heaven and said; 'Praise to you Andrasta, I call on you as one woman speaking to another ... to beg you for victory and the preservation of liberty ... Mistress, be you forever our leader!'

Nothing in the above description rings false; all details accord with what we know of British costume and cult practices of the time. Many thousands of prisoners were taken after the revolt, and some of these must have been interrogated. Could the above description be derived from a genuine eyewitness? What is depicted is an invocation of the goddess Andrasta through which Boudicca would have ceased to be human. From now on, she was the personification of a goddess of destruction and vengeance, her sacred mission to erase the Roman colony in Britain. How had a seemingly inoffensive woman come to embody such furious passions?

Of all the tribes which inhabited pre-Roman Britain, only one is still remembered in the popular imagination: the Iceni, the tribe Boudicca came to rule. Their territory consisted of the whole of modern East Anglia plus parts of Cambridgeshire, some of the richest agricultural land in the island. At first, they had chosen to be compliant with the Roman invaders, because the legions were a powerful counterweight to their traditional adversaries, the Catuvellauni to their south. Furthermore, the Romans offered the tribe generous loans for what we would today call 'economic development'.

In AD 50, however, all this was put in jeopardy by Ostorius, the governor of Britain, whose decision to disarm all suspected malcontents south of the Trent and east of the Severn meant that the Iceni were not exempt from roughly executed searches for weapons, persecution of the Druids and seizure of cattle and horses – with rapine and pillage into the bargain as well. The Iceni rebelled, but the insurgency was swiftly crushed when the legions surrounded their 'crude rustic earthwork'. Ostorius led the Roman army in person as the fort – probably Stonea Camp in Cambridgeshire – was stormed, and although the Britons 'performed many famous prodigies of valour' their defeat was a foregone conclusion. But the usual crucifixions, enslavement and desolation of the land did not follow. Instead, Ostorius insisted on a more compliant puppet ruler being installed as his price for tolerating some form of notional independence for the Iceni. The choice seems to have been Prasutagus, Boudicca's husband, and the couple became king and queen of the now resentful and oppressed tribe.

Prasutagus was all too aware that the precarious independence of his people depended very largely on his own longevity. He had two young daughters but no sons, and so he conceived a plan which he thought might appease the Roman emperor following his eventual decease. Tacitus tells us:

> King Prasutagus of the Iceni, long renowned for his wealth, had died leaving the emperor (Nero) as joint heir with his own two daughters; he believed that such an act of submission would secure both his kingdom and his family fortune from harm. Just the opposite happened, for both his realm and his household were plundered as if they were spoils of war, the former by Roman centurions and the latter by the procurator's slaves ...

But then, the ultimate desecration:

> First of all, his wife Boudicca was flogged, and his daughters cruelly raped in front of her. Then the Iceni nobility were all stripped of their ancestral lands – as though the Romans had been gifted the entire country – while the king's relatives were reduced to serfdom. Faced with these outrages, and fearing worse to come once Roman dominion had been established, the Iceni reached for their weapons. They also incited rebellion among their neighbours, the Trinovantes and others who, still unbroken by subjection, had secretly plotted together to regain their freedom.

The decision to rebel was a desperate gamble, as the Iceni knew to their cost, but the violated queen had one thing very much in her favour: virtually the entire Roman field force in Britain was committed to a campaign in Wales, well over 200 miles to the west.

While the moment was opportune, the uprising was more significant because it was led by a woman. Roman attitudes to women were cynical and patronising, as well as cruel; female babies were regularly exposed at birth. But among the British tribes, a long tradition of comparative gender egalitarianism obtained so that females could rule in their own right – we have encountered Queen Cartimandua of the Brigantes in the previous chapter, for example. The desecration of Queen Boudicca and her daughters, then, was the vilest form of blasphemy. Such contempt meant that revenge was expedited amid an atmosphere of the most intense savagery. To add material insult to spiritual injury, Roman procurator Catus Decianus was demanding immediate repayment of the forced loans which had been disbursed by the previous emperor, Claudius, thus bankrupting the entire tribal aristocracy at a stroke.

The insurgency spread like wildfire. Every able-bodied man, and very probably many women too, flocked to join this war of national liberation. Now Boudicca rode in a chariot with her daughters beside her as a force of nature, Andrasta – her very tribal name, Boudicca, means 'Victoria', and we know the British revere their queens above any king. In his account of the rising, Charles Kightly is explicit that despite our prosaic modern interpretations of the political and economic motives behind it, the religious context had primacy in the ancient mind: 'But we should not ignore the strong possibility that Boudicca – whether as sacred queen, priestess, or inspired representative – was first and foremost the heiress of the ancient, bloody and orgiastic goddess of life and death, and that the savagery of the rebels was a direct outcome of the Roman insult to that goddess's power.' The Romans estimated the final British host to have numbered between 100,000 and 250,000. If so, it would seem that, rather like in the much later Peasants' Revolt of 1381, the entire mass of the population armed themselves and then concentrated on eliminating the main power centre. Even then this was London. But first, Boudicca had more immediate matters to address.

In AD 58, Gaius Suetonius Paulinus had taken over the governorship of the restless colony of Britannia. Although he was well into his sixties, his reputation was that of an experienced and tough-talking commander with a strong sense of mission. He had conquered the Moors of North Africa by striking over the Atlas Mountains, and this exploit recommended him for a similar task in Britain. It was clear to the new emperor, Nero, that no peace was to be had on the island until the Druidic religion was finally extirpated. The Archdruid resided on Ynys Mon, or Anglesey, shielded by the high mountains of Snowdonia and moated by the Menai Strait. Suetonius took two legions and marched them through the mountains to smash the Druids' headquarters. As they landed on the holy island, the Roman troops were unnerved to see Druids and black-gowned women invoking the gods against them, as Tacitus related:

> Drawn up on the seashore was a dense mass of armed warriors. Among them, bearing flaming torches, ran women with funereal robes and dishevelled hair like Furies, and all around stood the Druids, raising their hands to heaven and calling down dreadful curses. This weird spectacle temporarily stopped the Romans in their tracks ... but then they advanced their standards, cut down all who stood against them, and pushed the enemy back into their own fires. Afterwards they destroyed the groves sacred to the cruel superstitions of the Druids, whose religion dictated that altars must smoke with the blood of prisoners and the will of the gods be discovered by examining the entrails of men. At this moment news reached Suetonius of a sudden and unexpected uprising in the Roman province ...

The final invocations of the Druids had, it seems, worked after all; the Romans would now pay a horrific price for their blasphemy. An orgy of violence was unleashed against them.

The Iceni had now been joined by their long-standing enemies, the Trinovantes, and their combined forces moved quickly to overrun the hated Roman colony of Camulodunum (modern Colchester). The citizens of the town were seized with dread as eerie cries echoed around the senate house and the incoming tide foamed with blood – perhaps forms of 'psychological warfare'. Although the centrepiece of the *Colonia* was the great temple of Claudius, one of the most impressive buildings in the empire outside Rome itself, with a magnificent equestrian statue of the emperor within its precincts – the majority of the buildings were of timber construction. The defenders consisted of retired Roman soldiers, veterans long past their prime who had been settled on plots of land for what they expected to be a comfortable retirement. There may have been only a few hundred of these men, and a desperate appeal was sent to Londinium for extra troops. Catus Decianus sent a measly force of less than 200 men as reinforcements 'and these without proper equipment'. Even this scanty force idled away precious time, not even bothering to build a rampart and ditch for protection. The colossal temple of Claudius would, they thought, provide an adequate refuge in an emergency, so the women, children and the elderly were not evacuated. But then the storm finally broke:

> While they (the Romans) were still acting as heedlessly as if they were living in the midst of peace, they were engulfed by a horde of barbarians. Everything was overwhelmed and burnt in the first enemy assault: only the temple, where the soldiers had rallied, held out for two days before being stormed and taken. Petillius Cerialis, commander of the Ninth Legion, was marching to the rescue when he was intercepted by the victorious Britons who routed him and cut his infantry to pieces: Cerialis and his cavalry managed to escape to their fortress, and took refuge within its defences.

In the ruins of Camulodunum the tribesmen were running amok, smashing everything that spoke of Roman culture. A bandsman's gear was stamped upon before the owner's house was torched. The tomb of a Roman cavalry officer, Longinus, was defaced with special venom because it depicted the brave Roman crushing a cowering British warrior beneath his horse's hooves. Longinus's face was painstakingly destroyed and the stone broken into two pieces. A similar fate befell the tomb of a haughty Centurion called Facilis. The statue of the Emperor Claudius was decapitated and the head thrown into the River Alde. The temple itself was so massive that it could not be completely erased, but all inside were massacred. The death toll cannot be known with any precision, but there were no survivors. Even the professional Ninth Legion had been routed and 2,000 soldiers slaughtered. In the countryside isolated Roman farms and villas were swiftly overrun and burnt, their inhabitants cruelly murdered, and the contents looted. While Cerialis cowered in Longthorpe Fort in Cambridgeshire, and with the other three legions hundreds of miles away in Wales and Exeter, British morale was sky high.

The signs for victory seemed propitious, but to ensure that the deity continued to bestow her favours, a blood sacrifice was required. Perhaps 15,000 people had died in Colchester, but many living prisoners were taken, as well as those prisoners taken when the Ninth Legion had been ambushed. It was not Boudicca's intention that these hapless captives should survive, however. Cassius Dio spares us none of the gory details:

> Those who were taken (alive) by the rebels were subjected to every conceivable kind of outrage, but the worst and the most bestial atrocity was this. They hung up the noblest and most high-born women naked, and then they cut off their breasts and sewed them to their mouths, so that the victims seemed to be eating them: afterwards they impaled the women on sharp stakes, which they thrust lengthwise through the whole body. Accompanied by sacrifices, feasts and sexual orgies, these things were done in all their holy places, but especially in the sacred grove of Andrasta. This was their name for 'Victoria', and they worshipped her with particular reverence.

These blood-crazed rituals must have been very satisfying for the folk after all the immiseration the Romans had inflicted, but they wasted precious time. Napoleon is said to have uttered the dictum, 'Space we can get back – time never.' While the Britons dallied around Colchester, Suetonius was riding hell-for-leather towards the undefended city of London.

Although it was not a *colonia* like Camulodunum, Londinium was already the largest town in Britain, with perhaps between 30,000 and 40,000 inhabitants, 'famous for its merchants and merchandise'. Two forms of 'merchandise' were especially dangerous: wine and olive oil. The Celts were infamous drunkards and made straight for the wharves and warehouses where imported wine was stored. Olive oil was used for lamps, and was therefore highly combustible. All that was required to ignite this dangerous mix was an angry mob, now numbering over 100,000 or more. Suetonius, with just a small bodyguard, entered the panic-stricken city only hours before Boudicca.

London as yet had no city walls and no artillery emplacements; there had not even been enough time to erect a rampart. The wealthy citizens and Roman officials had already fled in terror. Suddenly, Suetonius realised that he had been lured into a trap, and that the rebel strategy was to concentrate the Roman army in one place where it could be wiped out. A general's first duty is to his troops, and reluctantly the old warrior made the decision to sacrifice London to save his legions. Boudicca's outriders probably watched as Suetonius left London with a few hundred cavalry and such evacuees as could keep pace with him. There can be no knowing how many old or vulnerable residents he left behind, but their doom was now assured.

Boudicca's enraged mob engulfed Aldgate. In the Walbrook, a (now underground) tributary of the Thames, huge wine jars have been discovered looted and smashed. Then, the whole town was looted and put to the torch, and the inhabitants were dragged into the area around modern Liverpool Street to be ritually slain by decapitation. Hundreds of severed human skulls have been discovered beneath what is now the City of London or the 'Square Mile'. This was, in fact, the heart of Roman London, and when the deep foundations necessary for tall office buildings are dug in this area a thick layer of soot and ash is always found; it is all that remains of the first city.

The tribesmen would not have stayed long in the inferno, 'for the barbarians, rejoicing in plunder but shunning hard work, steered clear of fortresses and garrisons and headed for places where the spoil was richest and the defence lightest'. This is the key to understanding the whole campaign. Boudicca's force, though huge, was an undisciplined, untrained, ill-equipped, drunken and heavily encumbered mob, incensed by religious fervour and a thirst for blood, true – but still a mob. Suetonius and his legions were something quite different; drilled with an iron discipline, highly trained, superbly equipped, with an experienced general who had been in many tight spots over a career of forty years. Not only this, but they now had no way out but to conquer or die, for there would be no escape or mercy if they were defeated. But time was not on their side, for if Boudicca moved rapidly up the Watling Street – the main Roman military highway to the north-west – they would have no time to choose a defensive position. Fortunately for them, another Roman *colonia*, Verulamium (St Albans), lay in the path of Boudicca's host, who tarried there long enough to buy Suetonius a vital few days. Needless to say, Verulamium was pillaged and burned and all remaining inhabitants butchered – but the climax of this carnage could no longer be delayed. Not until the Battle of Towton in 1461 was there to be a bloodier slaughter in Britain than the impending engagement – but maddeningly, the exact location remains a mystery.

The Roman position was now desperate, trapped deep in a hostile hinterland, cut off from the coastal ports which were their only means of evacuation, and with a baying mob perhaps numbering 200,000 hard on their heels. Tacitus says, 'Never before or since has Britain ever been in a more uneasy and dangerous state ... We had to fight for life before we could think of victory.' Roman fortunes had fallen so low, in fact, that the Second Legion, besieged in Exeter, refused a direct order from Suetonius to link up with his remaining two legions in the Midlands. (Poenius Postumus, commander of the Second Legion, later took his life by falling on his own sword.) If the British colony was to be saved, everything now depended on the courage and military skill of Suetonius. Tacitus takes up the story:

> At this time Suetonius, having with him the Fourteenth Legion, together with detachments of the Twentieth and auxiliaries from the nearest forts ... prepared to abandon delay and join battle. He chose a position in a narrow defile, protected to the rear by woods ... he was sure there were no enemy forces except to his front, where the open plain was without cover, so there was no fear of a surprise attack.

So, we are in the same position with regards to this battle as we were in the case of Caratacus and his last stand – we have a description of the battlefield but not where it was. Over the years many places have been suggested, from King's Cross in London to Exeter, Chester, or even a suburb of Birmingham. But logically, we should look for the site somewhere to the north of St Albans, perhaps around Towcester on the Watling Street – along which Boudicca's tribesmen, together with their wives and families and vast quantities of loot – were now marching. They must have felt invincible, euphoric with victories bestowed by the living goddess. Little did they know they were being drawn into a deadly trap – and their doom.

It is astonishing that a paltry force of 12,000 Roman legionaries could have annihilated a gigantic host of well over 100,000, a feat of arms which must surely rank among the greatest military exploits of all time. How did they do it? Tacitus, quoting Suetonius giving an inspirational speech to his troops before the battle, gives us all the clues we need:

> Thus he drew up the legionaries in close order, with the light-armed auxiliary infantry on either side of them and the cavalry massed in readiness on the flanks. The British forces, however, ran riot all over the field on horseback or foot. They had never

appeared in greater numbers, and they were so full of confidence that they had even brought along their wives to witness the victory, stationing them on wagons arranged round the extreme edge of the battlefield.

This bravado was a typical demonstration of Celtic machismo, and the presence of the women may be accounted for when we think of the violation of Boudicca and her daughters. It must have seemed only fitting to the Britons that their women should witness the final destruction of the Roman beasts who had committed the crime. Moreover, they were led by a woman, and it is conceivable that some took up arms and fought alongside their menfolk.

Seeing so many women among the enemy ranks, either as spectators or combatants, Suetonius addressed his men:

> Don't worry about these yelling savages and their empty threats. Look at them, they have more women than warriors in their ranks! They are untrained and badly armed, and they'll break straight away when they see Roman courage and the weapons that have routed them before. Even when many legions are in the field, it is always just a handful of brave soldiers who decide the issue – so just think of the glory coming to you when a few men win fame against an entire army! Now, just remember, stick close together: throw your javelins – then push into them, knock them down with your shields and finish them off with your swords. Don't worry about booty or plunder. When the battle is won, then you can have the lot!

These were brave words indeed, spoken by a seasoned general, and they have about them a grim determination to get the job done. But across the battlefield, another leader was addressing her warriors, and they have echoed through almost 2,000 years. It was an emotive and heartfelt appeal for vengeance and liberty from a woman whose day of destiny was nigh.

The incarnation of Andrasta, goddess of victory, now appeared (according to Tacitus) as Boudicca, with her violated daughters, rode in her chariot to address her troops. Her speech, even if invented by Tacitus, would linger in British memory:

> We Britons are used to women war-leaders, but I don't come to you as one of noble descent, trying to protect my own realm and treasure … rather I come as an ordinary woman, striving to revenge my lost liberty, my lash-tortured body, and the violated honour of my daughters. Roman lust and greed know no bounds, they even violate virgins and old women – they leave no-one undefiled! But now the gods are granting us our just revenge: the one legion they sent against us we cut to pieces, and the rest hide in forts or look for means of escape. The enemy won't even stand up to the shouts and battle-cries of so many thousands of men as we have, let alone endure our blows and assaults! Consider our numbers, and the reasons why we are fighting: then you will either conquer or die in this battle. That's what I, a woman, am resolved to do – you men live as Roman slaves if you like!

Their blood now very much up, the unarmoured Britons immediately charged the Roman line in a howling mass. As soon as they were within 40 feet of the Roman line, 8,000 *pila* (javelins with detachable heads) were discharged into the dense British front ranks. Even if the Britons at the front held shields, a *pilum* would lodge there and weigh it down, forcing its owner to discard his only protection. Thousands of tribesmen fell after this first volley, which was immediately followed by a second hail of javelins that brought down the next rank. Tacitus:

> At first the legionaries stood their ground, using the narrow defile as a fortress: then as soon as the enemy came close enough for them to be sure of their aim, they all hurled their javelins together and burst forward in a wedge formation. The auxiliaries charged in the same way and the cavalry, thrusting with their lances, rode

down all who opposed them. The rest of the Britons turned and ran – but found their escape difficult, for they were trapped in the ring of wagons round the field. The Romans did not fail to slaughter even the British women, and even the bodies of the baggage animals, bristling with spears, added to the heaps of dead. It was a glorious victory, worthy of the triumphs of ancient times ... they say that nearly 80,000 Britons were slain, while the Romans lost only about 400 dead and very few more wounded.

So, ultimately the Britons were victims of their own overconfidence; the very wagons which had been circled into a sort of grandstand to observe an expected famous victory were now the obstacles which prevented them from fleeing to fight another day. What is more, this great host of chariots and wagons may provide us with a clue as to the precise location of the battlefield, as we will see.

For the Britons the battle had been a catastrophe of terminal proportions. Boudicca herself escaped the slaughter, but there could be no surrender. She was responsible for perhaps as many as 70,000 Roman deaths, so there would be no reprieve for her as there had been for Caratacus. It is indeed quite possible that Caratacus, in his palace in Rome, even heard news of the epic defeat of his fellow Britons. Cassius Dio states that Boudicca took poison and was then buried secretly with 'great honour' (and presumably fabulous treasures). A tradition exists which says that her daughters took poison too, and that sometimes, on damp and misty nights in the Fenlands, her spirit rides in a phantom chariot with her daughters.

For the few Iceni and Trinovantes who had survived, revenge was swift. Forced to replace his losses, Suetonius soon embarked on a campaign of destruction so severe that even the imperial authorities were shocked. Even in the middle of a harsh winter Suetonius continued his campaign to exterminate the Iceni (it may not have been clear to him that Boudicca was already dead). A force of 2,000 legionaries, 6,000 auxiliary infantry and 1,000 cavalrymen were sent over from Germany to help finish the campaign. But the Iceni were incapable of further resistance. Tacitus simply states, 'The enemy's worst affliction was famine, for they had neglected to sow their fields and had brought everyone available into the army intending to seize our supplies.' The Roman revenge extended well beyond East Anglia, for other tribes had given Boudicca assistance or proven contumacious. Eventually, Roman procurator Julius Classicianus – successor of the hated Catus Decianus, whose avarice had sparked off the revolt – grew concerned that if the punitive campaign lasted into a second winter the whole British race may become extinct. Writing to the emperor, he appealed for Suetonius to be replaced. Dead British subjects would pay no taxes – and taxes were what Classicianus desperately needed to rebuild London. (His lavish tombstone was incorporated into the city wall of the later Anglo-Saxon city, and so still survives.)

Suetonius, the man who had won one of the greatest military triumphs of all time, was relieved of his command on trumped-up charges of malfeasance. The Iceni were left in such a weak position that Venta Icenorum, the Roman town built to contain their wretched remnant, failed to thrive. No tribe could endure such a ruthless revenge. The extraordinary rebellion, though, was a salutary lesson to the Romans. A new generation of public officials sought to ensure no such insurgency would be repeated, and they did this not by using fire, famine and crucifixion but by seeking to win 'hearts and minds':

> To ensure that men who, because they are uncivilized and lived in isolated dwellings, were easily roused to warfare, should grow used to peace and leisure (Agricola) would encourage them personally, providing public grants to build temples, forums and town-houses. The obedient were praised, the sluggish censured, and so a competition for honour replaced coercion. Indeed, he took in hand the provision of a liberal education for the sons of nobles ... the next stage was that Roman dress became fashionable, and the toga was worn ... little by little there was a relapse into demoralizing

luxuries like colonnades, hot baths and sumptuous dinners. The Britons thought they had become civilised, but really, these luxuries were a mark of their servitude.

So complete was the success of the 'Romanization' programme that five hundred years later a British historian, Gildas, remembered Boudicca not as a national heroine but as a treacherous rebel against the imperial order.

But where was the battlefield? The pioneering archaeologist Dr Graham Webster (1913–2001) became convinced that he had pinpointed the exact location of the battlefield in a small valley between the villages of Hartshill and Mancetter near Nuneaton in Warwickshire. The site is directly on the Watling Street along which Boudicca's vast host must have advanced. The ancient Roman name for the place, Manduessedum, means 'the place of chariots' – a fitting name for a place in which thousands of chariots and wagons would have probably been left abandoned after the appalling massacre. The little River Anker bisects the battlefield, which is exactly as described by Tacitus – with a 'narrow defile' on sloping ground, a flat open plain to the front and dense woodland to the rear to prevent the legions being outflanked. A small Roman fortlet protected the Roman left flank, and a double ditch that had been dug in front would have required much more labour than the small fort could have supplied. Roman coin hoards have been found nearby dating to Boudica's time; they were probably concealed by unfortunate Roman soldiers who did not survive to retrieve them.

The key to understanding Dr Webster's identification is the strategic importance of the place. It lies just north-east of the most crucial Roman road junction in Britain, High Cross near Hinckley in Leicestershire, where the Watling Street and Fosse Way meet. It was along the latter route that Suetonius expected help to arrive, in the shape of the Second Legion, which had been commanded to meet him in the Midlands. By the time news came of the insubordination of the temporary commander of the Second, it was too late for Suetonius to change his mind.

There is now a project to raise funding for further excavations, and to turn the site into a centre for ramblers and cyclists – an area of peace and repose amid what may once have been the scene of carnage never to be repeated in the history of these islands. The vast heaps of human and animal corpses would have been burned on huge pyres. About 10 miles away, a large Roman base was established with a *gyrus* for training captured British horses. There was no mercy for the British tribesmen, or for their oxen, but the fine horses of the Iceni were too valuable to slaughter.

And so ended the whole terrible affair, a convulsion without equal in British history. For nearly 400 years the lowland Britons became compliant and obedient, proud to be a part of the Roman imperial scheme, but they never forgot their living goddess, and her spirit inspired the British imperialism of the eighteenth century. William Cowper (1731–1800) wrote lines in his *Ode on Boadicea* which attempt to render her noble struggle for liberty an outworking of an inchoate British national destiny. His words are inscribed on her magnificent monument on the Thames Embankment in London – the very city she had once so ruthlessly destroyed.

> Then the progeny that springs
> From the forests of our land
> Arm'd with thunder, clad with wings
> Shall a wider world command
> Regions Caesar never knew
> Thy posterity shall sway
> Where his eagles never flew
> None invincible as they.

3

'THE LAST OF THE FREE': MONS GRAUPIUS, SCOTLAND (83–84)

By AD 77, Vespasian, who had fought with such gallantry during the initial Roman invasion of AD 43, had risen to become the Roman emperor. He was determined that all remaining resistance in the island should be crushed, and indeed looked beyond Britain to Ireland, whose liberty remained a potential threat to Roman hegemony. In the far north of Britain, tribes still defied Roman rule and clung on to their traditional way of life – the Picts and Caledonian tribes of modern-day Scotland were a serious thorn in the imperial flesh. There were other, minor limitations too. Every so often, the wild and rebellious tribes of what is now Wales, or the confederacy of the Brigantes in the Pennine range of Lancashire and Yorkshire, would rise in insurgencies which could not be tolerated if the provinces of Britain were to become fully fledged members of the imperial system. Therefore, Vespasian appointed Gnaeus Julius Agricola (AD 40–93) as his new governor in Britain, with a commission to finally pacify the last free remnants of the British race.

Agricola was to retain this office for a period of seven years, a very long stint indeed, and his achievements are very well recorded. His son-in-law was Tacitus, the Roman historian whose account of the Roman conquest of Britain has already furnished us with so much detail. It is very probable that much of this history was related to him by his father-in-law, leading many subsequent commentators to suspect that it contains a strong element of bias, and even falsehood. Indeed, it has been claimed that the battle under consideration in this chapter may have been entirely invented – and that the Caledonian resistance fighter Calgacus, 'the swordsman', was a figment of the historian's imagination. I do not subscribe to this view, as will become clear.

Agricola's commission was nothing less than to subjugate the entire island of Great Britain. After crushing guerrilla insurgents in the mountains of north Wales he advanced through what is now the north of England, and then up the coastline of eastern Scotland. His land forces were shadowed by a strong fleet which hugged the eastern coast. The main task of the fleet was to ensure the army was abundantly supplied, but amphibious landings and raids in strength were made from the sea by Roman marines. Another mission for the Roman admirals was to finally establish whether Britain was, in fact, an island, and once Agricola had settled accounts with the Caledonian tribes, the fleet rounded Cape Wrath in Sutherland and elements of it circumnavigated the entire island for the first time in conventional history.

The campaigns in Caledonia were protracted and costly, because the Caledonian and Pictish tribes were too canny to face the large and experienced Roman army in open battle. Instead, they resorted to their time-honoured practice of guerrilla warfare, inflicting many casualties on Agricola's men in hit-and-run attacks before withdrawing into the dense forests, marshes and mountains to fight another day. They were fearsome warriors, the ancestors of the wild highland clans who mustered at Culloden Moor in 1746. They were physically bigger and stronger than the Romans, with Tacitus writing that they were large-limbed, with red hair and painted designs on their naked upper bodies. They wielded long slashing swords designed to cleave a man in two at a blow – the ancestor of the later claymore or great sword – and this weapon was greatly feared by the Romans.

Agricola decided to force the issue, and just after the harvest was home he sent out raiding parties to immolate and destroy all local granaries and seed-corn. He knew this would draw the ire of the entire highland zone, and that they would have no choice but to stand and fight in one final, desperate struggle for control of the island. After forty long years, the 'last of the free', as Tacitus calls them, now had no option but to turn at bay by the seashore among the mountains and fight to the death for their liberty. According to Tacitus, a final Celtic hero emerged to lead the clans against the legions – 'Calgacus', which means 'the swordsman', probably after the huge blade he carried with him. As we will see, the Romans had mastered tactics to neutralise the deadly effect of this weapon – just as the Duke of Cumberland (1721–1765) would train his men to withstand its deadly power many centuries later.

Many historians have doubted that the speech of an obscure Celtic chieftain in a remote mountain redoubt could have somehow been recounted to the Roman enemy, thence to be rendered into Latin by Tacitus. The speech is most likely his own invention – a device he used to criticise the imperial system he privately despised. Any actual personal criticism of the emperor in writing would have been suicide. The temptation, though, is to go further, and suggest that the entire affair – Calgacus, the battle, and the famous speech – were figments of the chronicler's imagination. While seemingly contrived, however, the speech may have been composed out of statements taken from prisoners and hostages following the campaign, who may have overheard the actual oration. Agricola was given a Roman triumph, and the emperor must have been convinced that a battle had taken place to bestow such an august honour. Tacitus makes it sound as if his father-in-law defeated an army of 35,000 barbarians without breaking into a sweat – not even bothering to commit his main legionary force, and only committing his auxiliaries and the cavalry. But in the previous two chapters we have seen precisely this phenomenon: large British forces completely outclassed by a disciplined, experienced, professional Roman army. There is no reason why the same ineluctable force should not have triumphed yet again.

Archaeological finds of precisely this date corroborate a large Roman military concentration in the neighbourhood of Readykes camp, a Roman marching camp 3 miles outside Stonehaven in Aberdeenshire. This was large enough to accommodate three full legions, so 18,000 men. It seems very likely that this was Agricola's final base camp before the confrontation, and that either the nearby mountain of Bennachie, or Kempstone Hill, which was also close, could be potential sites for the battlefield. Whatever actually happened, the rousing speech of this last free Briton at the edge of the world has a bitter ring of truth about it:

When I see this confederation, and the desperate situation which has brought us together, I know that today, and this hour will be the beginning of freedom for us. We know nothing of slavery, and there is nowhere else to go; there is no more land beyond us, and the Romans have conquered the sea, so we must fight, whether we be brave or cowards. When other battles were fought, we could rest content that we were safe from slavery here in the uttermost confines of the earth, but now our last sanctuary of freedom is breached. We are between the waves and rocks, and the even more terrible Romans from whose oppression there is no escape by obedience or submission. Having stolen the whole earth they now plunder even the sea! They steal from the rich and the poor alike, nothing satisfies their lust for dominion. To robbery plunder and slaughter they give the lying name of peace – they make a desolation and call it peace!

But as we have seen before, brave speeches do not win battles on their own.

The tribesmen had the advantages of superior numbers and the higher ground, which they occupied in a horseshoe-shaped formation in vast tiers rising from the level plain beneath; there were 35,000 of them. Their chariots cavorted in front of the Roman line seeking to provoke them by discharging spears and other missiles, but Agricola had taken care to hold his main legionary force well to the rear of the main action in case of a concerted attack by the wild clansmen. When he was convinced that no such attack was coming, he gave the order for two cohorts of elite Tungrian auxiliaries and four cohorts of Batavian auxiliaries to assault the Caledonian front ranks on the lower slopes. The front ranks gave way and retreated up the hill, and Calgacus gave the order to attack the flanks of the auxiliary force, which comprised about 3,000 men.

At this crucial point, when the melee was at its most intense, Agricola ordered his cavalry to sweep in and attack the charging tribesmen on their flanks in turn, where their lances made short work of the enemy infantry. Some 10,000 tribesmen were rapidly overwhelmed, and these were dispatched with ruthless celerity by the auxiliaries who had managed to retain their formation. The great swords of the Britons required the wielder to raise his arm in a slashing motion, so that his body was exposed to the short vicious stabbing swords of the Roman wedge formations, in which each man rotated to take his place at the front for five vicious minutes of concerted stabbing. All this was achieved without the necessity of committing the heavy shock troops – the legions themselves – but now these began to move forward. Panicked, Calgacus and his remaining force fled for the woods, leaving 10,000 dead on the battlefield to the Romans' 390 killed, according to Tacitus. The surviving clansmen disappeared like wraiths into the Highland mists (most experts think that the battle was fought sometime in the autumn of AD 83).

Once again, the British tribes had tasted bitter defeat at the hands of the Romans. However, their bravery and sacrifice were not to be in vain. Agricola's conquests in Scotland could not be maintained for long, and the ancestors of Calgacus and his comrades would one day prove the nemesis of the haughty Roman conquerors.

After forty years, the British resistance had finally been broken. But Mons Graupius marked the peak of the Roman military conquest of Britain. Tacitus saw Agricola as a Roman exemplar, and his ultimate ambition of subduing the wildernesses of the far north, the western promontories and even Ireland as a sort of sacred mission. This was the reason for his insinuations against the Emperor Domitian, using Calgacus as his mouthpiece in his speech. Emperor Vespasian – Domitian's father, who had appointed Agricola – was deeply personally interested in the British project. He had, after all, won his spurs there fighting on campaign as a young officer, alongside Agricola. He supported Agricola's governorship, which was an unusually long one. Domitian, though, was of a different stamp, and his concerns were more concentrated on establishing a frontier along the Danube. The lack of any further clear military objective in Britain led to increasing demoralisation among the Roman troops still on active service there.

To prevent the troops becoming mutinous, or simply going to seed, there was a tried-and-tested way of giving a large body of men something useful to do – large-scale construction work. A decision was taken to abandon the Roman military installations and fortresses in Caledonia, and to withdraw to the south, where two military frontiers were established bisecting the island from coast to coast. The massive fortress at Inchtuthil on the River Tay was completely deconstructed and all the materials either removed or rendered useless. The whole process was completed with the usual Roman military efficiency, but the truth could not be hidden from the Caledonian warriors still spying on them from the mountains: this was a retreat, not a conquest. Rome was relinquishing territory, not extending it. It would take many long years, but with the establishment of the Antonine Wall, and more significantly Hadrian's Wall, the great game of strategy had entered a new phase. The tide had turned.

Domitian was something of a 'glory hunter', and he saw little glory to be won amid the mountains and bogs of some misty wilderness with few of the luxurious conveniences to which the Flavian dynasty had grown accustomed. After forty years of excitement with the likes of Caratacus, Boudicca and Calgacus there were no more 'big names' among the Britons, and the Roman emperors came to see it as a remote outpost which required rather too much military investment for the profits it yielded. Emperor Trajan (reigned AD 98–117) was incautious enough to remove parts of the military complement in Britain, including some of the elite units, to supplement his forces along the Danube and much further east. Instead of four legions, Britain was now to be garrisoned by three – and these somewhat smaller than before, and consisting of more and more auxiliary units, and even a small number of native-born ones.

This insouciance about Britain may well have resulted in a military disaster rumoured to have occurred in about AD 108. The Ninth Legion *Hispana* seems to have left its base in York to march against a rising in Caledonia. After that, we hear nothing more about the unit, and there are plausible reasons for suspecting that they were lured north by a feigned rising, only to be cut off to their rear by a sudden rising of the Brigantes of the Pennines. For an entire legion to be taken in ambush seems like a remarkable victory for an insurgency – but the Germanic chieftain Arminius destroyed three Roman legions using just such a stratagem. Irish legends tell of a tribe of foreigners who came and begged their king for safe passage to Spain at just this time. Could they have been the traumatised survivors of the Ninth trying to reach their Spanish homeland? At any rate, Emperor Hadrian (reigned AD 117–138), was alarmed enough to visit Britain in person, where he concluded that 'the Britons could not be kept under Roman control'.

It seems plausible that an uprising was coordinated between the Brigantes of northern England and the Caledonians of Scotland, and that a legion had been wiped out so completely that it ceased to exist in the Roman military lists. To prevent any such cross-tribal cooperation in the future, the tribes were to be separated by a gigantic military obstacle to control any subsequent uprising; in other words, the world-famous Hadrian's Wall was intended to be effective in both the north and south. In support of this theory, it can be no accident that the Roman province in the north, *Britannia Inferior*, remained a militarised zone until the end of Roman rule. The sheer scale of the wall is astonishing, and at its peak it required a complement of 30,000 (mainly auxiliary) soldiers to keep its defences fully manned.

*

We have now reached the conclusion of the first part of this military history. Let us sum up, then, the Roman military achievement in Britain. A partition had been introduced to segregate the discontented tribes still at liberty in the north, those with the most reason to reject Roman rule. Nevertheless, as late as AD 154–155, the Brigantes rose again. It took Septimius Severus, a Roman emperor from North Africa, to finally take the matter in hand. By this time, it was possible to concentrate a very large number of troops from all over the empire in Britain. Severus assembled an army of as many as 60,000 men to accomplish the mission, many of them Libyans and other Africans, completely unused to the harsh conditions of northern Britain. Severus imagined that here, at last, in this wilderness on the far frontiers, a glorious triumph awaited him; it was a fatal mistake, both for him and the tens of thousands of Roman soldiers who perished during his three-year campaign. This would be Rome's very own Vietnam.

In AD 211, the frail Severus was carried on a litter to his imperial palace at York, where he died a broken man. Many tens of thousands of his troops died too, and with them went any dream of a final Roman conquest of Britain. The cultivated, civilised, increasingly wealthy elites would remain members of the empire for two centuries more, but all around them enemies were gathering. The Roman project was doomed, and the *Pax Romana* was finished. Here, in the wild moors and craggy valleys of Northumberland, Roman power had reached its final limit.

PART TWO

4

MONS BADONICUS/MOUNT BADON
(490–516)

However compromised, the Roman peace endured in lowland Britain for about 400 years. The inhabitants of the four main Roman provinces of Britain spoke in Latin, used currency with the emperor's head on it, worshipped the Roman pantheon in public and private, and embraced Christianity to some extent when that became the state religion. They were, at least superficially, Roman. This book does not concern itself with peace, however, so the leap forward in time from Septimius Severus to the close of the fifth century may be accounted for by the fact that no major military engagements took place during the intervening period. There is one exception, though.

As some have pointed out, 'Brexit' is actually nothing new – in AD 286 a Roman admiral from what is now the Low Countries declared himself as the emperor of that area, plus parts of Gaul and all of Britain. His main asset was his control of the *Classis Britannica*, the British fleet, whose main bases were in south-east Britain, and whose purpose was to interdict and destroy Germanic pirate vessels infesting the English Channel and the North Sea. This usurper emperor, Carausius, managed to keep the legitimate imperial fleet at bay for seven years before being assassinated by his deputy, Allectus. In AD 296, this new 'emperor' faced an invasion by Julius Asclepiodotus, a legitimate imperial officer, who landed in the Solent under the cover of a dense fog. Allectus quickly gathered an army composed of the Frankish mercenaries who garrisoned London and all the auxiliary troops from Hadrian's Wall – a motley army led by a cowardly assassin. Outside Silchester, this ramshackle force was easily beaten. Allectus, seeing all was lost, desperately tore off his imperial insignia and tried to pass as a junior officer. This tawdry affair need not concern us, except to remark, perhaps with a degree of satisfaction, that Allectus was put to death.

Following this episode Britain re-joined the wider empire, remaining a troublesome member for more than a century, but the relationship had now changed. Before we commence our journey into the so-called Dark Ages, then, a brief account of the disintegration of the imperial scheme in Britain will prove germane to what follows.

The key date to consider if we are to understand the collapse of Roman imperial control in Britain is AD 367. In that year a *conspiratio barbarum* – 'barbarian conspiracy' – was enacted. It saw co-ordinated attacks on the Roman imperial provinces from the north, west and east: by the Picts and Caledonians in Scotland; by the Irish slave traders in the west; by the Germanic peoples on the south and east coasts; and by Loire-based Saxons on the south-western peninsula. Following the earlier withdrawal of practically the entire garrison of Hadrian's Wall by Allectus, an incursion from the north had led to the whole northern region being ransacked by the Caledonian tribes, who even plundered the empty legion fortresses of York and Chester. A kind of peace had gradually been restored, and the wall's complement brought back up to strength – but the nature of the garrison had changed.

Increasingly, many of the auxiliary troops in Britain were what was called 'island bred'; that is, they were native Britons rather than foreign draftees. These troops resented the prospect of being redeployed to other parts of the empire, and as auxiliaries they had the right to take wives and raise families among the local populace – a right not accorded to professional legionaries before their retirement at the age of forty-four. It became a common practice for the forts along the wall to recruit from the children of these liaisons, and this meant that the entire border zone became a sort of hereditary military fiefdom, very much 'doing its own thing'. Another practice had grown up, too, whereby the tribes just to the north of the wall were more or less bribed to keep the peace and accept the presence of Roman military scouts, many of whom were of rather dubious loyalty. According to the historian John Morris (1913–1977), it was these scouts who were responsible for the greatest catastrophe to befall the island since Boudicca's day.[9]

Perhaps because they were suborned by bribes, or perhaps due to resentment at their treatment by the imperial regime, the scouts agreed to open the main gates to the 'barbarians' from the north on an agreed signal, and the clansmen immediately broke through in strength, where they harried the north. Meanwhile, whether as a result of some complex pact or simply out of opportunism, the Irish, Angles, Franks, Saxons, Jutes, Frisians and other freebooters raided in strength far inland, killing two of the main Roman commanders sent to interdict them. The Roman army, which was now a rather thin force south of the wall, soon lost control. Many of its soldiers deserted, having not been paid for some time, and joined in the looting – some even went over to the 'barbarians'.

This situation lasted for about eighteen months, until in 369 Count Theodosius was dispatched by the Emperor Valentinian I (reigned 364–375) to restore order. Four elite auxiliary detachments were embarked at Boulogne. Upon landing, Theodosius quickly chased off any bandits he found roaming in the south and marched on London, which was surrounded by

---

9. Morris, J., *The Age of Arthur* (London, 1973)

brigands. He entered the city, liberated it, and then cleverly offered an amnesty to all Roman troops who had deserted, promising that no recriminations would follow. This proved sufficient to stabilise the situation, and in short order the insurrection collapsed, the wall was recovered, and the pirate slavers were driven out. This was a remarkable military achievement considering the limited forces at his disposal, but the provinces in Britain never truly recovered – and new and deadly enemies from across the 'German Ocean' were now emboldened, telling stories in their damp polders and frozen fjords of the rich pickings to be had in the Roman island for warriors unafraid of hard fighting.

The economic fallout from this episode seriously undermined the prosperity of the urban elite, and particularly the large estates of the rural villa economy. Many of the slaves whose labour made the estates viable took the opportunity to liberate themselves during the disturbances, and they were not easily replaced. Pottery manufacturing – a key economic indicator – slumped immediately following the 'conspiracy', according to historians Russell and Laycock.[10] Villas were either 'downsized' to serve as family homes rather than bases for large-scale agriculture and manufacturing or simply abandoned altogether. As the tax take from the provinces of Britain declined correspondingly, the security the empire could provide was severely compromised – especially after large tribal groupings crossed the frozen Rhine and roamed around the heartland of the empire. Another theory espoused by Russell and Laycock, albeit controversial, is that a paramilitary force was encouraged in Britain to make up for the shortage of professional Roman military units. If true, this early vigilante movement could well have been the distant ancestor of the later King Arthur and his knights of the Round Table. The Roman historian Zosimus stated explicitly:

---

10. Russell, J. B & Laycock, S., *UnRoman Britain: Exposing the Great Myth of Britannia* (Stroud, 2010)

The barbarians from beyond the Rhine attacked without hindrance and prompted those living in Britain and some of the Celtic peoples to leave Roman control and live their own lives, free of Roman laws. The Britons took up weapons, and facing every danger themselves, liberated their cities from the barbarian threat.[11]

There were other methods of assuring safety. Hired militias were available to those who could afford them, called *bucellarii*, and as 'tyrants' or regional warlords gradually emerged they often resorted to encouraging Germanic warriors to relocate wholesale to Britain to provide military protection. These units, known as *Laeti* and *Foederati*, were settled in areas vulnerable to coastal raids like Yorkshire, the Thames Valley, Kent and Essex. As the Roman pool of manpower declined, a great many 'Roman' military units in Britain were in fact Germanic, including a king, Fraomar, whose whole tribe was shipped to Yorkshire. Although it was not very satisfactory, this arrangement enabled the imperial infrastructure to carry on in a diminished form. But then, in 380, the entire apparatus was unravelled by a Spaniard by the name of Magnus Maximus, who arrived to quell a rising in Caledonia. His appointment was the denouement for Roman Britain. Like his predecessor Carausius, Maximus was soon seduced into making a bid for the imperial purple himself – a decision which was to plunge Britain into the darkness for hundreds of years.

The Roman provinces in Britain were one part of what was known as the 'Prefecture of the Gauls', which included all of what is now Spain and France (Gaul) as well as most of Great Britain. Although he was from Spain, Maximus was to become 'more British than the Britons', and was destined to become a legendary figure. In many respects he was also a prototype for Arthur, as we will see. Maximus, or 'Macsen' as he became known to the Britons, took a British wife called Elen, and as soon as he was

---

11. Zosimus, *Historia Nova*

confident that he had the support of the Roman military units in the island he declared himself as the emperor of the 'prefecture'. Unlike his predecessor Carausius, however, he was not content to sit tight and wait for an invasion from Rome. Instead, and with momentous consequences, he mustered the entire military might of the island, much of it now native to Britain, and crossed the sea to Gaul – before marching on Rome itself.

Incredibly, this 'British' army captured the 'Eternal City', but the emperor of the separate Eastern Empire at Constantinople, Theodosius 'the Great' (reigned 379–395), marched against Maximus and defeated him at the Battle of Aquileia in 388. This was, of course, a catastrophe of the first order for Britain. The reassuring military presence which had protected them for 400 years was gone, never to return, and the imperial structure in the west was on the verge of total collapse. The British historian Gildas was explicit that this episode was the beginning of the end for the Roman Britain he remembered with a sort of phoney nostalgia – for the Britain he mourned was long gone by the time he was born (about 490). But there is a strange motif in British history whereby national disasters are recast as legendary exploits. Maximus, whose foolish ambition had left the country defenceless, was reinvented by the Romano-Britons as 'one of their own' – a mighty warrior who had captured the greatest city in the world with his gallant British soldiers. In Welsh legend he is still remembered to this day as 'Macsen Wledig' or 'Macsen the Commander'.

Despite all that had happened, the British remained recalcitrant about the imperial scheme, and another rebellion in 406 repeated the process when another usurper emperor, Constantine III, scoured the very last dregs of the Roman military in Britain, nearly all of them British by now, and attempted to invade Spain. They never returned, for Constantine's deputy, Gerontius, betrayed him. Then, on 24 August 410, Rome itself fell to Alaric, King of the Visigoths. The issue of who should lead the Western Empire was now academic; it was gone. The Roman story in Britain was finally over.

But history does not fall into neat chapters. The Roman legacy lived on, and ironically for the Britons, but entirely in keeping with their national character, they now began to remember the imperial order with a tender affection, whereas when they were actually part of it they were petulant and troublesome members. In the year 410, Emperor Honorius sent a message from his temporary capital of Ravenna, advising the Britons to see to their own defence – there was little else he could have done. The entire Western Empire was disintegrating, and barbarian tribes roamed with impunity. But for Britain the consequences were to be especially dangerous, for it became the target for some of the most aggressive pagan tribes from across the seas – Saxons, Angles and Jutes, many of whose warriors were already serving as militia in Britain under the patronage of Romano-British warlords who emerged to fill the political vacuum.

Abandoned to their fate by the Roman Empire, the thin veneer of 'civilisation' among the inhabitants of the island was swiftly worn through. In the *Pagani* or rural districts the imperial apparatus was somewhat distant. Once it had disintegrated, old customs, myths and previously suppressed religious practices now re-emerged, including many ancient (and at least pseudo-Druidic) local cults. The psychological motive for this was likely the new threat of the Germanic invaders in particular. They were hostile heathens, inveterate pagans, with a different language, religion, culture and history – in short, aliens.

The invaders, then, were a threat to the entire social order, and to the Celts 'order' was something in their blood. Their social stratification was as rigid as that of the Hindu castes, and it is postulated that a Proto-Indo-European (PIE) word, something similar to the ancient Sanskrit, *rta*, is the ancestor of the word 'order'. But this sounds similar to the word *arktos*, or in Latin *ursus*, which meant 'bear'. It seems that in very ancient times there was a cult of bears in northern Europe which had a taboo of directly mentioning the animal, perhaps lest its very dangerous presence manifest itself. The bear hibernates, seeming to die and then reawaken, usually in an irascible and aggressive mood. This is perhaps the ultimate race-memory for the cult of 'Arthur' – a sleeping hero who, reawakened from his cave, grows into an ineluctable force, restores order, and terrifies lesser enemies such as the Saxon 'wolves' (as Gildas called them) before retiring to his repose once more. As will become clear, it is my view that such a person did exist as a genuine military commander, and that he became the greatest legend of all time – Arthur, 'the Bear'.

In 2004, a film called *King Arthur* attempted to pin down the Arthurian legends to an historical personage, Lucius Artorius Castus, a second-century Roman officer whose cavalry unit may possibly have served on Hadrian's Wall and in that military zone. This process, of trying to pin down the legendary in the 'historical', is a philosophical legacy derived from a late fourth-century BC philosopher named Euhemeris. His thesis, which became very entrenched in the classical philosophical world, was that all legendary characters and archetypes could be ultimately traced to 'real' historical exemplars, those who had inspired the mythic lore. This idea was extremely enduring, and seemed to be borne out by the discoveries of Heinrich Schliemann (1822–1890), a German businessman turned archaeologist. As a boy, Schliemann became intuitively or empathically convinced that he was destined to discover the 'real' site which was the inspiration for the Homeric myths that obsessed his young imagination. After many years, and inspired by something somewhat more than conventional historical scholarship, he was eventually successful, and excavated the ruins of ancient Troy.

From a process of what the scholar and poet Robert Graves called 'analeptic thought', a huge leap forward in ancient historical knowledge had been achieved. This gave rise to the inevitable speculation: if the Homeric myths were true, and could be excavated as an archaeological 'fact', why couldn't the same thing be done with the Arthurian mythos and Camelot? In other books I have examined all these matters in some detail, but for the purposes of this work I confine myself to the most ancient texts with regard to historical events. Although they were adulterated and altered, their origins spurious, and their contents mostly mere 'shadows' of the events they purported to record, ancient Welsh, Irish and early Anglo-Norman texts such as William of Malmesbury and Geoffrey of Monmouth were based on more authentic sources than we can command today. My view is that the mythical 'Uther Pendragon', Arthur's father in the legendary lore, was a brother of the last usurper emperor of Britain, Constantine III, and that another of Constantine's brothers, Ambrosius Aurelianus, was the mentor and uncle of Arthur, the *Dux Bellorum* as he became known to history – 'the Leader of Battles'.

The most extraordinary fact of the immediate sub-Roman period in Britain is the emergence of an indigenous resistance movement in the island that, uniquely for a former region of the Western Empire, managed to repel the barbarians and impose treaty arrangements upon them which endured for half a century. Someone organised and paid for this, and the person who seems to have initiated the movement was Ambrosius Aurelianus, by no means a legendary character but a genuine Romano-British leader. Many have thought that it was he, and not Arthur, who was the victor over the Saxons at a site Gildas calls 'Mons Badonicus' or 'Mount Badon', a battle which he says was the final victory over the 'gallows' crew' and the 'Saxon wolves', and which, he proudly tells us, was fought in the very year of his own birth (about 490). Gildas does not mention the victor of this national deliverance by name but other texts do, such as the *Annales Cambriae*, a compendium of ancient Welsh texts most likely derived from contemporary originals. In these annals it is stated: 'Battle of Badon in which Arthur carried the cross of our Lord Jesus Christ on his shoulders (*sic*) for three days and nights and the Britons were victorious.' So, who was this 'Arthur', and where was this momentous battle? More importantly, who was it fought against? This is a 'riddle, wrapped in a conundrum, inside an enigma' as a great historian remarked about another matter; but we must attempt to unravel it.

The memory of the usurper emperor Magnus Maximus or 'Macsen', by now lionised, was utilised by many pretenders to various Celtic kingdoms to legitimate their claims and to ground them in the old imperial practice of allocating dangerous border fiefdoms to regional warlords. One of those supposed to have dignified his authority in this way was the legendary Vortigern, the 'tyrant' or overlord who, according to tradition, was responsible for inviting three shiploads of Jutish mercenaries into Britain. According to the *Anglo-Saxon Chronicle*, Hengist and Horsa, two brothers who led this small force, landed at Ebbsfleet in Kent in 449. Vortigern was the husband of Magnus Maximus's daughter Severa, who bore him three sons. Now, it was a custom among the Celts that a foreigner was immediately accepted as a *combrogi* or 'fellow-countryman' if he married a woman of the tribe, and this is precisely what Maximus had done when he took Elen, or 'Helen of the Hosts' as she was known, as his wife; he had become 'British by marriage' as Geoffrey Ashe remarked.[12] Ashe is almost certainly correct to locate Vortigern's power base as being in central Wales, at Gwertherynion, 'the fortress of Vortigern' in Radnorshire. Vortigern seems like a title ('overlord') rather than a personal name, and Welsh texts call him a *gwledig* or commander. Basically, these men amounted to petty Celtic warlords from the liminal, mountainous, dangerous zones at the western and northern margins of the old Roman Britain. As Celtic culture rapidly replaced the Roman ways, as even currency ceased to be minted and town life died away, these tough men and their personal retinues of warriors, sometimes no more than a few hundred strong, became the new powers in the land.

But these puny forces were insufficient to deal with any serious emergency, and according to tradition the Jutes were invited

---

12. Ashe, G., *The Quest for Arthur's Britain* (London, 1968)

into Britain to meet the threat of a fresh incursion by the Picts. Another group of Saxon mercenaries were settled in East Anglia, but there seems to have been a problem in delivering the food tributes or *annonae* which Vortigern had promised to deliver to his dangerous new allies. The Jutes, Angles and Saxons must have now numbered in the thousands, for in fury they immediately broke out of their reservations and ransacked the whole lowland zone from coast to coast, according to Gildas. Welsh traditions state that Vortigern arranged a peace conference where all the leading men from both sides would attend unarmed. The Saxon leader, Hengist, instructed his men to conceal daggers about them, and at an agreed signal all the British nobility were massacred at a stroke. Vortigern was held hostage until he renounced his legitimate wife and took Hengist's daughter, Rowena, in her place. Vortigern's three legitimate sons immediately repudiated him, and Vortimer, the eldest, gathered a British army with the intention of driving the Germanic peoples out of their settlements for good.

The *Anglo-Saxon Chronicle* is not a completely reliable source, but it is about all we have, and it states that a battle took place at Aylesford in 455. It seems that to counter the new threat from Vortimer, the Saxons concluded an alliance against him with their former Pictish enemies. Two years later, in 457, the Britons were defeated decisively at the Battle of Crayford, and all 'Welsh' were driven out of Kent, forced to take refuge behind the mighty Roman walls of London. Vortigern, disgraced and powerless, seems to have taken refuge in his fortress; tradition states that he was finally burned out of it and killed by his countrymen. At any rate, he disappears from the historical record, and it is in the aftermath of this appalling national calamity that the heroic figure of Arthur emerges.

There is no reason to dismiss the existence of a real as well as a legendary Arthur, and so I will proceed on the basis that the Battle of Mount Badon did take place, and that Arthur may have been the victor there. In the ninth century, a Welsh monk named Nennius collected all the legends, history, ballads and references in older chronicles relating to Arthur and 'made a heap of all I could find'. These ancient Welsh texts go into some detail about Arthur's military exploits:

> Then Arthur fought against them (the Saxons) in those days with the kings of the Britons, but he himself was the leader of battles (*dux bellorum*). The first battle was at the mouth of the River Glein. The second, third, fourth and fifth on another river called the Dubglas in the district of Linnius. The sixth battle was on the River Bassas. The seventh battle was in the Forest of Celidon, that is called Cat Coit Celidon. The eighth battle was in the fortress of Guinnion in which Arthur carried on his shoulders an image of St Mary the Virgin, and the pagans were put to flight and a great slaughter made amongst them through the virtue of Our Lord Jesus Christ and his holy maiden-mother, Mary. The ninth battle took place at the City of the Legion. The tenth battle was fought on the banks of a river called the Tribruit. The eleventh battle took place on the mountain called Agned. The twelfth battle was on Badon Hill, in which on that one day, by one assault of Arthur, nine hundred and sixty men were slain, and no-one slew them but Arthur ... and in all the battles he was victorious.[13]

This rather detailed and comprehensive documentary evidence has been dismissed by some Anglo-centric historians as a tapestry of Celtic wishful thinking, derived from bardic traditions which had every reason to portray Arthur as an immortal hero. But there is a great deal of useful information here as to what may have been happening in Britain in the misty decades at the close of the fifth century.

It seems that the war was one of religion. Vortigern was almost certainly heretical, perhaps even pseudo-Christian, and he could well have been a Pelagian – a peculiarly 'British' heresy.[14]

---

13. Nennius, *Historia Brittonum* (828)
14. See Wall, M., *The Magical History of Britain* (Stroud, 2019)

Ambrosius, by contrast, seems to have cleaved to the Roman Catholic faith, and the party he led were devoutly Roman, not only in religion but in their whole worldview. The eminent historian John Morris was absolutely convinced that both Ambrosius and Arthur were the spearhead of this movement, which equated all things Roman with social order and Christian civilisation – in short, it was nothing less than a national crusade. The list quoted by Nennius really is national in its scope. The battles are very widely dispersed, and so whoever fought them was using a small, compact cavalry force which fought off the invaders in an all-out war. But something else is clear too – this was an *offensive* war until the very last battle at Badon itself. Morris's basic contentions about this campaign are very difficult to refute, as well as being ingenious, and the following owes much to his theories about the period. To summarise, the Britons were, in strictly military terms, outmatched. The small warbands of petty Celtic chieftains simply could not prevail against an aggressive, militaristic and predatory Anglo-Saxon enemy, whose strength grew year by year as fresh immigrants arrived. By contrast, in the Celtic west the population was declining due to emigration, plague and economic and climatic adversity. But despite their numerical inferiority and lack of martial experience, there were some things the Britons could utilise to their advantage.

The excellent Roman road system in Britain, and the posting stations along it, with smithies and stabling for a network of messengers, was still in fairly good order. It was not, therefore, logistically difficult to convey a well-equipped and trained force of say, 300–500 men from one end of the country to another, where they could act as a rallying point for inferior, but more numerous, local British forces. In these border wars, the Anglo-Saxons, who fought as infantry, were at a disadvantage, because as soon as they deployed forward into British-held areas they left their own settlements exposed to counter-raids by British 'Commando'-style mounted units. Any pioneering Germanic settlers with a mind to clear woodland or erect homesteads in the frontier zones were also exceptionally vulnerable. But the Nennius document implies a larger project than this.

The project of national recovery initiated by Ambrosius appears to have been rooted in the legends that had encrusted around Magnus Maximus. Not only did Ambrosius have 'imperial' pretensions, but Gildas tells us that his ancestors 'had worn the purple' – that is, they had been emperors. But if Badon was really fought in 490, Ambrosius would by then have been either very old or, more likely, dead. By this time, after more than fifty years of warfare, the British national force was composed of a generation entirely inured to continual war, militarised as a culture, and led by a new generation of commanders. Welsh traditions state that Arthur was one of this new generation of eager officers, and that they had revived Roman military titles. One of these, *Dux Bellorum*, is referred to by Nennius as being a specific title bestowed on Arthur. Now, this sounds very similar to genuine Roman military commanders, who were given special commissions by the emperor to repel barbarian threats. It is unlikely Nennius would have been aware of this, and in fact it must have been somewhat of an embarrassment from his point of view that Arthur was not depicted as a 'king' as in the myths, but someone with a roving commission to galvanize resistance against the national enemy – the 'Saxon wolves'. In fact, Morris was convinced that all foreign interlopers were attacked and, in some cases, expelled by 'Arthur's men' – a mysterious warband which soon appeared in Brythonic ballads.

Gildas, a more reliable source, was writing in around 533. He describes the battle as 'the last great victory of the fatherland', but for reasons too complex to examine here, Arthur's name is not mentioned by him. Nevertheless, that there was a great British triumph over the Saxons is indisputable. Pottery evidence for Anglo-Saxon settlements suddenly disappears in the early sixth century in precisely those places where their forefathers had carved out small kingdoms, such as Sussex and Essex. Sir Frank Stenton, still regarded as being in the front rank of Anglo-Saxon historians, confirmed that there was a sudden influx of Saxon settlers in northern France and Normandy at just this time, and concluded that they no longer saw their holdings in Britain as defensible. It took fifty years for the Anglo-Saxon momentum to recover itself after what must have been a shocking defeat.

Of course, there are many eminent historians who simply refuse to take these matters seriously. J. N. L. Myers was scathing about the speculation regarding Arthur, which he considered to be a huge waste of academic time.[15] After all, we have precisely no evidence about a flesh-and-blood Arthur in archaeological terms. But absence of evidence does not mean evidence of absence, and one can interpret the battle list as a description of a sustained war derived from actual events. If we take care to put these battles together in the context of military strategy, all then becomes clear.

It should be explained that there are many contenders for the title of King Arthur's original heartland. The three most likely contenders are Dumnonia, which comprised Devon and Cornwall, which has the strongest folklore traditions; Wales, and in particular Gwent and Denbighshire/Flintshire; and finally, the area near to Birdoswald Roman fort on Hadrian's Wall, far off to the north. My own hunch is that Arthur had his main base in the south-west somewhere near Glastonbury, the place which has the most enduring traditions about him – and reputedly his final resting place 'in the Isle of Avalon'. I believe that this base became the nexus for the British national resistance, both military and spiritual. This was the last redoubt of the old Romano-British nobility, where the elite had long enjoyed a civilised and luxurious lifestyle under the Romans. But the barbarian threat was multifarious and came from all directions. If Arthur's strategy was to take the war to the invaders, whether Teutonic or Celtic, he had to travel far from his secure base to fight the heathens wherever they tried to exert an influence – if John Morris was

---

15. Myers, J. N. L., *The English Settlements* (Oxford, 1986)

correct. But the key to this strategy of raiding combined with an elastic defence was the all-important cavalry.

Two main regions of Britain were famed for breeding horses in ancient times. One was East Anglia, Boudicca's old heartland, but this had fallen to the barbarians long before. Without sturdy, well-trained mounts the British resistance was doomed to failure, and one relatively secure area which had all the necessary resources was the south-west. If the British cavalry were heavily armoured with mail in the manner of the last Roman mounted forces, specialist breeding stock would have been necessary and foreign contacts with sources maintained by sea. I do not think it can be an accident that, when the later Norman knights reimagined the Arthurian tradition over 500 years later, they were fascinated by these tales of men just like themselves – armoured horse soldiers, devoutly Christian and instilled with a strict cult of chivalry.

The eleven previous victories ascribed to Arthur are located all over the country. There were many battles on rivers, and one river, the 'Dubglas' or Douglas in 'Linnius' (Lincolnshire, in all probability), is the site of no less than four separate battles. This makes perfect strategic sense, because the Anglian settlements of Bernicia and Deira in the north-east were not as yet contiguous with Linnius or Lindsey in Lincolnshire and the Fens. If Britain was ever to be free of the Germanic threat, these territories had to be prevented from merging. Other engagements seem to have been fought against the Picts or Caledonians in the 'Forest of Celidon'. This must have been some attempt to restore Hadrian's Wall as a frontier, even if it were merely symbolic. Other battles were fought further south, probably against the Irish 'Scotti', who were already settling parts of Wales. According to Morris, there is indisputable evidence of the expulsion of the Irish precisely at this time. These spectacular successes must have completely transformed the morale of the beleaguered Britons, but conversely they must have horrified the Saxons – who were now faced with an existential threat from a dangerous and unpredictable enemy. The Anglo-Saxons were, therefore, faced with a desperate choice: eliminate Arthur once and for all, or abandon their British projects altogether. With typical Teutonic efficiency, they chose the former course. But how do you kill a legend?

We have now arrived at a period where much history is in fact legend. But there are two ways of dealing with this. One can either dismiss virtually all the traditions we know from non-academic sources as 'mere' folklore or conjecture, or one can try to use them as a basis for intuitive 'imagineering' of the past when the need arises. Making no apologies for that, let us now look at the probable strategic situation in southern Britain just before Badon. The Anglo-Saxon colonisation of Britain was now in serious jeopardy. Arthur 'the Soldier', as the Britons called him, with his retinue of elite mounted warriors (known as 'Arthur's Men' in later ballads), had seriously disrupted their advances all across the country. The most sustained campaign, though, had been in the north, and it was against the Angles that the main focus of British offensive operations had been concentrated. The West Saxons, South Saxons, East Saxons and Jutes of Kent knew that they were bound to be the next target for Arthur.

In such a situation, there are three basic options. Firstly, it is advisable to sue for peace; in this case, that was out of the question. The British were full of confidence after so many victories, and they were experiencing what Gildas admits was 'an unexpected recovery'. Arthur had been bred for this war and had prepared for it as his divine mission, and after the so-called 'slaughter of the long-knives', when Hengist's men had assassinated all their British counterparts at such a peace conference, no diplomatic contacts were kept up. Indeed, among the British at this time all contact with the 'Sais' or Saxons was taboo, and they were shunned. Centuries later, British pilgrims still refused to stay in rooms where Saxons had slept or eat from plates they had used when they stayed in lodging houses. St Augustine was astonished at the hostility of the Britons to the Anglo-Saxons when he visited British bishops over a century after these events. No compromise was to be had.

The next option, and the one which seems to have prevailed, was to decide the issue by mounting a pre-emptive strike against the main British military base, to force Arthur to commit himself to a major pitched battle in which he would be heavily outnumbered. Although this strategy was bold, it required co-ordination and co-operation between all the Germanic peoples of the south, and above all, a leader, someone with an authority among them comparable to Arthur's among the Britons. Covert planning and complex rapid deployments were necessary, and it would have been absolutely imperative for surprise that all of the junior commanders deferred to someone equivalent to a *Bretwalda* or over-king, but at this crucial time there was no one acting in this role that we know of. It was necessary to concentrate the entire available military forces of the southern English for the project.

Some hundreds of years later, the Vikings managed to deploy their 'Great Heathen Army' into just this territory, probably using the same routes – including the Ridgeway, an ancient trackway. Their army was probably between 3,000 and 5,000 strong, and so a similar-sized force was likely assembled for the Badon campaign by the Saxons. This was a truly extraordinary effort, and all this treasure and labour was not spent for nothing. Arthur was a deadly enemy who must be destroyed at any cost. One of the most feared and brutal Anglo-Saxon leaders, Aelle of Sussex, was probably chosen as the temporary *Bretwalda* and, risking everything on a final pitched battle, his allied army marched towards Arthur's fabled fortress in the south-west. This supreme effort by the Anglo-Saxons tells us much about how high the stakes were in Britain. But there was also another option the Saxons could have taken.

This other option, one favoured to this day among gangsters and hoodlums, was assassination. Of course, this stratagem is nothing new; indeed, at the time it was the first recourse in any conflict of interests. We have seen how Carausius was dispatched by his deputy in this way, and Vortimer, Arthur's predecessor as the British resistance leader, traditionally succumbed to poisoning by the Saxons. The massacre of 300 British leaders at a peace conference was still very fresh in Arthur's mind, and would have made him very wary. Later, King Edwin of Northumbria was almost killed by a poisoned dagger, and only survived with divine aid. Peada, eldest son of King Penda of Mercia, was poisoned during Easter celebrations by his own wife, and so this inexpensive and very effective means of waging war made sense. But Arthur would have been extremely well protected by a select body of oath-sworn bodyguards, men who may well have convened in some mead hall at a 'Round Table'.

As an aside, this need for absolute security against raiders and assassins perhaps offers insight as to why Arthur's 'historical' identity has always been so strangely obscure – especially when compared to his legendary presence. It may well be that the real 'Arthur' was deliberately anonymised. Among certain Roman auxiliary cavalry units on the northern frontier, the officers wore strange ceremonial helmets with a full-face visor, totally concealing the wearer's identity. Such a bronze helmet was discovered by a detectorist near Hadrian's Wall a few years ago. This unnerved the enemy, as well as protecting the wearer against reprisals from hitmen. If, as suggested, the unit Arthur commanded was a reconstruction of older Roman cavalry types, then Arthur's real identity may have been a closely guarded secret. Gildas, usually so opinionated, chose to completely ignore Arthur's role in the victory at Mount Badon. There are various theories as to why; it is speculated that Arthur was responsible for the death of a younger brother of Gildas, and that he therefore excised the section about Arthur from his book out of spite. Another theory is that Gildas actually did refer to Arthur in the book, using the device of a complicated acrostic code. But in light of the above, it could be that the person called 'Arthur' was almost deified after his death, and so it was unnecessary to record his heroic deeds; after all, every Briton would have been familiar with them.

In light of Arthur's protection, assassination was rejected. One spring day in the late fifth century, British scouts saw smoke rising from the beacons atop the hill forts. Aelle, at the head of an immense army, had crossed into British territory.

Arthur would have responded immediately with all the local forces he could muster. It is plausible that his core force, his 'companions' in Welsh tradition, was organised along the same lines as the later Roman cavalry unit called an *ala*, which traditionally numbered 500 men. This elite force was what the Saxons were intent on destroying, both men and mounts. Arthur would have had only two days to summon levies using a network of beacons atop local hill forts. If 2,000 such militia mustered to him, he would have been fortunate, so his army was small. But a lightning offensive by the Saxons must have been anticipated by him, and so there was time to concentrate his limited forces at a prepared rendezvous, a hill fort well supplied with water and fodder near to a road junction which Aelle needed to capture. Aelle's plan was to eliminate Arthur and to achieve one of the strategic priorities examined in the introduction – to break through to the Severn estuary and divide the Celts of south Wales from their cousins in Devon and Cornwall.

Within days, the Saxons arrived at Mount Badon and confronted Arthur's forces. Aelle's intention was to lure Arthur's forces out by laying siege to the hill fort, but this was a dangerous gamble; such a large force could not have carried much in the way of supplies, and could not sustain itself by foraging alone. The final conflict could not be long delayed. In this tense atmosphere, the two armies waited.

The question must now be asked: where exactly *was* Mount Badon? The short answer is that no one has the foggiest idea, but there is no shortage of candidates, and a new theory is advanced every year or so. The term *Mons*, which Gildas used about the battlefield, had by his time come to be used almost exclusively in relation to refurbished hill forts. It is often a shock to modern people to discover that the most basic construction techniques, even the skill of laying bricks with mortar, rapidly disappeared following the Roman withdrawal. Not only was the technical ability lacking, but also the logistical, financial and strategic planning, plus sufficient organised labour. The *civitates* or 'county' towns did have defences, but these could no longer be repaired and maintained, let alone properly manned. Instead, the Britons turned to older but still effective solutions – they reoccupied the ancient hill forts of their ancestors, abandoned since early Roman times.

There are a great many such hill forts in our target area, and other sites such as Bath, which have been traditionally associated with the battle. Geoffrey of Monmouth was convinced that Bath and Badon were synonymous, but the entire area around Bath was known in Brythonic/Welsh as 'Caer Badon', and so it would be better to concentrate our search on the most likely hill forts nearby. One of these, South Cadbury, has very ancient folklore traditions about Arthur. It was part of a defensive chain of such forts all across Somerset, each with a beacon for signalling enemy movements. When the antiquary John Leland (1503–1552) visited the place in 1542, the locals were in no doubt about their momentous local heritage: 'At South Cadbyri standith Camallate, sumtyme a famose toun or castelle. The people can tell nothing thar but that they have heard say Arture much resorted to Camallate.'

The area around the hill fort is saturated with Arthurian references too – 'King Arthur's Well', 'King Arthur's Palace' – and folktales say that Arthur and his knights lie sleeping in a vast hollow chamber beneath the hill. In the late 1960s, archaeological excavations there seemed to confirm something very unusual had been going on at precisely the time we are considering. A massive palisade and revetments were constructed enclosing the old fort, including tall watchtowers and a great gateway, heavily defended. The ditches and banks were restored, and inside stood a huge feasting hall, alongside lesser buildings such as kitchens and stables. The foundations of a unique cruciform chapel of a design seen nowhere else in the British Isles were also discovered. So, this was no ordinary hill fort, and it was commissioned by someone with wealth and authority far beyond what any petty British chieftain could have commanded. I contend that Arthur was that someone. Two experts involved in the excavations, Leslie Alcock and Geoffrey Ashe, agree:

> The lord of Cadbury was a person so like Arthur as makes no matter; a person living on a site traditionally picked out as his home, in the traditional period, with resources on a traditional scale, playing at least a part of the traditional role; a person big enough for the legends to have gathered round him. Nowhere else but at Cadbury does Britain supply an archaeological trace of such a person.

But though it could well have been 'Camelot', the argument for it being Mount Badon is unconvincing.

Many credible candidates exist. The historical author and researcher Don Carleton in a recent work concurs that the site must be somewhere in the south-west.[16] He supports the connections to Glastonbury, but he proposes that the battle was fought in the Avon Gorge outside Bristol. Dyrham in Gloucestershire has local traditions, as does Badbury Rings (note the prefix *Bad*). Another is Liddington Castle, which lies within 15 miles of Cirencester or Caer Cerin, a functioning if impoverished town in the period. Liddington stands astride the Ridgeway, the same highway into the west used by the Vikings in the ninth century. Aelle, with a similar sized-force, needed to keep his troops tightly compacted, where they could overlook the plain below for any hostile forces sent to intercept them. But these precautions were unnecessary, because Arthur would have anticipated such an attack long before, and knew precisely

16. Carleton, D., *Arthur: Warrior and King* (Stroud, 2018)

where to block their advance. Although Gildas calls it a 'siege', Badon seems more like a three-day stand-off, rather like the later confrontation between Owain Glyndwr and Henry IV of England at Great Witley in 1405. Aelle would not have completely encircled the hill fort; this would have stretched his line too thinly on the perimeter. Nor would he have risked a frontal assault, which would have been too costly. Instead, the Saxon army pitched camp and waited for Arthur to make his move.

Inside the hill fort and on its flanks Arthur's small force waited for three anxious days before committing themselves to an all-out attack, possibly because they were waiting on reinforcements from more distant British warlords. We know nothing more about the engagement, other than that 'Arthur carried the cross of our Lord Jesus Christ on his shoulders for three days and nights'. What is meant by this is unclear. Perhaps it was a religious fast and purification before the battle, but the Old Welsh word *scuid* (shoulder) may have been mistaken by a scribe for *scuit* (shield). An assault on a Saxon 'war-hedge' or shield wall was a daunting prospect, and a great deterrent to all but the best-trained horses. To smash into and break such a formation required courage, determination, skill and speed. The Roman cavalry called *cataphractarii* and *clibanarii* were based on the heavy cavalry which had annihilated their own infantry in Persia. These men wore heavy mail and helmets, and their main weapon was a long lance. The horses wore mail too, and were trained to kick and bite. Alongside the horses and their riders, vicious war dogs, with a taste for human flesh, deterred any attackers. Geoffrey Ashe was convinced that the men Arthur commanded were analogous to these models:

Whether they, or for that matter horsemen of the Empire, charged and fought in the saddle like medieval knights is an unresolved question. It is uncertain whether the stirrup, or any comparable device, was known in Europe so early, and how much a man on horseback could do without it. But even 'mounted commandos' (the phrase suggested by Robert Graves) would have given Arthur's Britons two advantages. As to the first, mounted men undoubtedly could strike panic into superstitious barbarian mobs. Constantine the Great is said to have routed an army with only twelve, a feat hardly less amazing than Arthur's alleged onslaught at Mount Badon. Tactical mobility, the capacity for swift movement and surprise, might also have made a decisive difference under a bold leader.

And so, on Arthur's command, five hundred British cavalry hurtled towards the Saxon shield wall. Seeking out Aelle's position, they hacked their way to the enemy commander. He is not mentioned again in Anglo-Saxon records, and a tradition states that he died in the battle or in the chaotic retreat afterwards, and is buried on Highdown Hill in Sussex. Once the Saxon line broke, panic spread all through their ranks. It is quite possible that 960 men were slain in the aftermath of this furious assault, but as many must have been killed in the relentless pursuit, with no mercy shown.

In the space of no more than an hour, the fate of the island had been decided. There is so little to tell after such a long preamble, but the event is no less significant for that. This small battle in the West Country was perhaps the most influential in all British history. The barbarian threat had been lifted. A whole generation of enemy warriors and leaders had been slain. Those Saxons brave enough to remain in the island were on a slow trajectory to becoming 'British' themselves. In one small corner of the former Roman Empire, the legacy of civilisation was not snuffed out but extended and preserved. The darkness had briefly lifted in the western half of Britain, and a glorious legend was born. It still endures to this day.

5

'THE LAST DIM WEIRD BATTLE IN THE WEST': CAMLANN (511–537)

In British legend, the period after Badon was an oasis of peace, justice, order and spirituality just before the bleak desert of the 'Dark Ages'. There is no reason to doubt that this was the case – peace after a protracted conflict is always all the sweeter. Lovers are reunited and children follow. The effort and industry wasted on war can be put to more productive uses and new structures take the place of ruins. People are free to enjoy life and to treat their neighbours with hospitality and kindness, instead of suspicion and hostility. These are the fruits of peace and order, but this idyllic interlude cannot last forever. A time comes when those who fought the war become old, and a new generation succeeds, for whom war is no more than 'foreign policy by other means', and so the wars begin all over again.

We know very little about Arthur's glorious reign, except for the extraordinary legendary corpus which it birthed. But however romantic and splendid it was, the Celtic 'Golden Age' could not last. In the Welsh annals, a brief entry for AD 511 simply records 'the fight at Camlann, in which Arthur and Medraut (Mordred) were killed'. These few words have given birth to some of the greatest literature in the history of mankind, but the information contained in the sentence is virtually useless in historical terms. We do not even know if Arthur and Medraut were killed fighting as enemies or as comrades-in-arms. Camlann has been identified with Camboglanna on the River Irthing, which means 'crooked glen'. This is near the Roman fort at Birdoswald close to Hadrian's Wall, but there must have been many hundreds of places called 'crooked glen' in Britain besides this. There is a River Camlad near Priestweston in Shropshire, near to Mitchell's Fold stone circle, a site associated with Arthur. There is the River Cam in Somerset, close to the site of his famous victory. The poet and chronicler Layamon in his *Brut* located the 'fight' on the River Camel in Cornwall – and it was Layamon who was responsible for the demonization of Mordred, 'wickedest of men', as he called him. But we must not allow ourselves to become distracted by legends.

As to the battle, there is very little that can be said. It is even unclear if there ever really *was* a battle. All leaders, however mighty, grow older, weaker, less keen for the fight. Younger, stronger men scheme and plot. Old comrades pass away, and the empty chairs at the Round Table gape at those still left. Eventually, one of the Young Turks sees his chance and makes a challenge – it was ever thus. By tradition this challenger was Medraut or Mordred, who is said to have been Arthur's nephew. Such treachery within royal families was traditional, and there is a story which says that Arthur slew his own son, Anir, in such a strife, or *gueith* – a Welsh word which signifies something different to a *bellum* or battle proper. Camlann sounds like one of the bitter clan wars between countrymen that have featured throughout all Celtic history. A small, insignificant skirmish, then, in which the embittered, careworn and senescent Arthur is mortally wounded, and the darkness falls once more. Yet, like Badon, its significance goes way beyond the curt sentence in the annals. It stands for something beyond history – the final battle we all must fight.

Geoffrey of Monmouth, writing in 1136 or thereabouts, considerably embellished the bare entry in the annals. He has Arthur leave Britain to fight overseas, but he foolishly entrusts the kingdom to the traitor Mordred, his nephew and regent. Mordred abducts Arthur's queen, Guinevere, and Arthur immediately returns to Britain to take her back. Arthur confronts Mordred in the battle and spears him through, but Mordred holds his uncle in a death embrace. Arthur survives, but has a grievous head wound, and is carried away on a barge into the west by fairy women so that his wounds may be tended. He never returned – at least he hasn't yet. Curiously, when Arthur's supposed skeleton was unearthed at Glastonbury Abbey in the twelfth century, the skull featured just such a wound. So, we come to the end of the Arthurian affair – but perhaps not:

> Yet some men say Arthur is not dead but had by the will of our Lord Jesus Christ into another place: and men say he shall come again and win the holy cross. I will not say it shall be so: but many men say that there is written on his tomb this verse: 'Here lies Arthur: once and future king.'[17]

The man called Arthur had passed away, but his legend gave him an immortality which will endure for as long as men and women dream. His example gave the Britons a desperate hope that, in the hour of their most dire need, he would return – *Arturus Redivivus*, 'Arthur re-born', literally reincarnated to save his people. The memory of his glorious reign gave hope that the Saxons could be beaten, and religion and culture still thrive – in short, a magic germ of forthcoming national redemption as they steeled themselves for centuries of bitter warfare.

But in the Anglo-Saxon lands, news of his death brought an infusion of energy as confident new warriors under ambitious kings searched for fresh territory. According to Gildas, within a few years the British kingdoms fell into anarchy, and a deadly plague spread in the western half of the island. The darkness had returned, and with it a terrible era of bloodshed.

---

17. Malory, T., *Morte D'Arthur* (London, 1485)

6

CATRAETH/CATTERICK, NORTH YORKSHIRE (598–600)

The Anglo-Scottish border country has always been a notorious warzone. This 'debatable land' was fought over for centuries by the ill-famed Rievers (from whom we derive the word 'bereaved') – such clans as the Armstrongs and the Elliots, those 'roving reckless names', families which could raise private armies well into the late medieval period. In the times we are considering, such men were far more than the border outlaws they eventually became. Indeed, they were kings, many of whom claimed descent from a mysterious Roman officer named 'Paternus of the Red Cloak'. One particular king of these border statelets was, however, destined to be remembered in folklore with such enduring affection that every schoolchild knows the rhyme about him, even in these days of the internet:

Our auld King Cole was a jolly old soul
And a jolly auld soul was he
Our auld King Cole fill'd a jolly brown bowl
And he ca'd for his fiddlers three
Fidell didell, fidell didell quo' the fiddlers
There's no lass in a' Scotland
Like our sweet Marjorie.

These famous lines from the Bard of Ayrshire may prove useful to set the scene, for this border region became the focus for some of the most savage battles in British history during the late sixth and early seventh centuries. But was there really an historical character called 'Old King Cole'? If we can decipher the rhyme, perhaps we may uncover that precious treasure – forgotten history, and some more 'lost' battlefields.

The author Charles Kightly in his *Folk Heroes of Britain* tells us that after the Romans relinquished control in about 410 the military zone around Hadrian's Wall split into 'a mosaic of independent princedoms whose land extended both north and south of the now abandoned wall'. In his chapter entitled 'The Real King Cole' Kightly makes a clear case for an historical personage behind the nursery rhyme – and a very important personage he was. For this real Cole's descendants came to rule the entire area between modern Edinburgh and Yorkshire – 'the whelps of Coel Hen' or Cole 'the old'. The nursery rhyme possibly developed out of the ancient practice of orally reciting long and complex regnal lists, retained in mnemonic verses sung by bards. These bards would have all been familiar with 'Coel the old' – the progenitor of their royal family trees. One of the first of these nobles connected to 'Old King Cole' was a very powerful warlord of the Gododdin or Votadini tribe called Cunedda (modern Kenneth). Another of his descendants was Urien, who ruled Rheged, a kingdom which extended from Carlisle to Manchester, so that everywhere west of the Pennines remained Celtic-speaking. Urien and his son Owain became such legendary Celtic heroes that they were incorporated into the Arthurian myths as 'knights of the Round Table'. These 'sons of Cole' became the leaders of the British national resistance after Arthur's passing. But we must return to the mysterious Cole if we are to understand the crucial cultural significance of all this – and why it is that one of the most desperate and epic conflicts in our national story has been virtually excised from our collective memory.

As we have seen, the Romano-Britons were very far from being a pushover for foreign invaders. Arthur's triumph was the culmination of half a century of training, planning and investment. But in these northern lands no such rediscovery of a martial tradition had been necessary because the area had always been a militarised zone – or at least as far back as anyone could remember. These *Cwr y Gogledd* or 'the Men of the North' were hard men, bred to war since childhood, and glorying in it. War was their most beloved occupation, all other sports such as hunting mere preparation for the main event. Although their own local culture was special to them, they still remembered that they had once been part of a unified authority which had extended throughout the greater part of the island. They saw themselves as 'fellow-countrymen' or *combrogi* of their Celtic cousins in Wales, the West Midlands, Devon and Cornwall, and realised that it was vital to keep all these lands as a contiguous unit if they were to survive, recover, and finally reclaim sovereignty of Britain.

The Anglo-Saxons (in the northern part of Britain they were mainly Angles) were, by contrast, deadly enemies of their blood, whose growing settlements of Bernicia, Deira and Lindsey represented an existential threat. These Anglian tribes regularly raided into the smaller Celtic kingdoms for slaves and loot, or demanded tribute in exchange for refraining from their thieving ways. The sons of Cole were not content to tolerate these incursions, and believed that it was their inherited duty to expel the invaders.

According to John Morris, whose research on these matters was a lifelong passion, 'King Cole' was a man named Coelestius. He was the very last *Dux Britanniarum*, a Roman military officer directly accountable to the emperor, left in command of the military base at York and the entire zone on either side of the wall. When Rome fell in 410, these peripheral areas at the edge of the empire were left to their own devices and many local commanders used their military muscle to seize control of the areas they occupied and pocket the revenues from those regions, which were very rich in resources. Little wonder that Cole was remembered as *Coel Hen Guotepauc* or 'Old Cole the

Magnificent'. We cannot know if Cole's authority was genuine, or if it was a revival of an old Roman military title to dignify a local pretender as Arthur perhaps had done. Whatever the case, Cole's descendants ruled in the former frontier zone until 573 when his great-great-grandson Gwenddolau died in the Battle of Arthuret. So devastated was Gwenddolau's bard, Myrddin, at the death of his patron – the last of the 'whelps of Coel' – that he ran off into the woods where he went insane and lived as a 'wild man'. Myrddin was the prototype for Merlin.

One clue which may suggest that Cole was a native-born Briton, whatever his Roman military rank, is that his territory immediately fragmented into a constellation of smaller kingdoms after his death. This is consistent with the Celtic practice of partible inheritance, whereby all living male heirs received a portion of their paternal inheritance. This was one of the reasons the Celts were eventually subjugated, for it encouraged intra-familial strife which fatally weakened any unified resistance. Each son became the lord of some domain, however tiny and barren – but it was a matter of honour that they should retain their royal dignity, such as it was. There were many such kinglets in the north, all descended from 'Old Cole', such as Cynfelyn, Catrawt, Morcant, Pabo, Guallawc and Dunawt, in addition to the more important ones we have seen already. All these men were fiercely proud and independent, and more likely to war with each other than with the national enemy. But if they could unite with a common purpose under a strong leader, the Anglo-Saxons would be in dire trouble.

The Anglian kingdom of Bernicia had been established in the aftermath of the great Yellow Plague of the 540s. The British statelet of Bryneich around Bamburgh had been left so depopulated and weakened that an Anglian warlord, Ida, soon took over the region between Lothian and the River Tyne. What helped the settlement was the absence of any immediate local military threat, because Cunedda, the son-in-law of Cole, had been resettled from the region to north Wales, where his whole tribe were sent by some powerful authority, very possibly Coelestius himself, with a commission to destroy the Irish settlements there. In Yorkshire, another group established another Anglian colony, Deira, near to York itself, and in Lincolnshire and Humberside there was another Anglian kingdom called Lindsey. By 570, York itself had fallen and a powerful king called Aethelric combined all the Anglian forces and attempted a surprise attack over the mountains into Rheged. On a bleak Saturday morning, Aethelric's forces were confronted at Argoed Llyfein in the Forest of Leven in Cumbria. Their movements had been monitored until they were well inside British-held territory, where Urien of Rheged awaited them. The Bernician army was heavily defeated, but there were more important political consequences. This obscure victory was all Urien needed to propagate a hero cult among the Celts – and to install himself as the 'New Arthur', the prophesied king who would unite all the 'whelps of Cole' and finally drive the Angles into the sea from whence they came.

Suddenly emboldened, and with a leader to rival the legendary Arthur, the sons of Cole made common purpose together at last. Morcant, Guallawc and Dunawt pooled their forces with Urien's and they invaded Bernicia. The Angles were literally driven into the sea – on to the small island of Metcawt, now called Lindisfarne, where they awaited almost certain death. The final victory was in sight for Urien, when he was tragically assassinated by a traitor acting on behalf of Morcant, who had become jealous of his fame. This was in 590, and the news sapped morale all over Celtic Britain. An elegy sums up the emotional desolation after his death:

> I bear within my cloak the head of Urien most generous of Princes
> On his white breast a raven feeds, great were his deeds
> And far from the fame of Urien from Rhiw I have borne a head
> Whose lips are red with blood, woe to Rheged this day
> His slender white body will be buried this day
> Beneath earth and blue stones, sorrow to me and sad disgrace.

This Celtic melancholia did not last long, however, for Urien's son Owain was, if anything, a greater hero than his father; he became the 'Sir Ywain' of the Round Table in the legends. Owain had proposed a pact of mutual assistance with Mynyddog Mwynfawr, king of the Gododdin, whose royal centre was at modern Edinburgh.

By now the Arthurian legends were deeply ingrained in the warrior culture of the Britons. Mynyddog invited all the most famous warriors in Britain to his palace, 300 elite mounted warriors such as Arthur had led at Badon. These gallant 300 were then treated like living gods for a year and a day, feasting and drinking rich mead – between bouts of training with their weapons and perfecting their horsemanship. They were very similar to the samurai of medieval Japan, and their mindset was the same – for theirs was a suicide mission from which none were expected to return alive. After draining their final mead horns, and a last tender embrace with their lovers, the men donned their mail, saddled their warhorses, and rode south – 300 men against ten times as many Angles – to Catraeth.

So, it was a matter of honour now, and every man had already made his final peace with the world; they had become deathless, immortal, warriors of destiny – and dealers of death, for each man had sworn the sacred oath to 'avenge sevenfold'. Modern historians dispute the numbers involved, and suggest that a large force of infantry must have been involved in the battle alongside the cavalry. Catterick is deep inside England, a long way from Edinburgh, and remains a vast military camp to this day. Aethelfrith, son of Urien's foe Aethelric, was now the overall commander of the Bernician and Deiran forces. Standing on prepared positions he could have amassed a force of between 3,000 and 5,000 men – an overwhelming superiority in numbers. Some have suggested that after a year of mead-drinking binges the Celtic warriors were so drunk they didn't know what they were doing, but this is an extremely careless misinterpretation of the custom of the mead oath.

By now the famous charge at Badon was a legend that every Celtic warrior dreamed of emulating. These men were so brainwashed by the bards that they no longer feared death. Their only goal was everlasting glory, so that they in their turn would be immortalised in the mead hall, their deeds sung to eager youths at the fireside. Theirs was just to 'do or die', and the greater the odds against them the more undying the fame they would win. Those who think no sane military leader would have dreamed of an attack against such unequal odds fail to understand the Celtic mindset.

So, the gallant comrades arrived at the brown River Swale, and the crossing at Catterick. Aethelfrith's comparably huge force awaited them there, supremely confident but unnerved by the insouciance, indeed the euphoria, of the Britons in the face of certain death:

> Men went to Catraeth, shouting for battle
> A squadron of horse,
> Blue their armour, lances poised and sharp
> Mail and swords glinting
> Though they were slain they slew.
>
> None to their homeland returned.
> Short their lives, long the grief of their kinsfolk
> Seven times their number the Saxons they slew,
> Many the widows they made, many the mothers that wept
> After the wine and the mead, they left us armoured in mail.
>
> I know the sorrow of their death
> They were slain and never grew grey,
> Of the war-band of Mynyddog
> Unbounded grief, of three-hundred comrades
> But one returned.[18]

---

18. *The Book of Aneirin*

It was the swansong of the British cavalry. If the numbers of English dead Aneirin suggests are at all accurate, rather than mere poetic device, the attack must have been almost as devastating as that at Badon. But Aethelfrith's men held, and with their horses blown, the British survivors must have eventually dismounted to fight on foot. Owain of Rheged was surrounded, outnumbered and killed. The dogged resistance went on all through the night, until a final attack the next morning annihilated the British force. Only a handful were taken alive, all seriously wounded. Only one – Aneirin, the bard himself – lived long enough to be ransomed. A sad and glorious tale Aneirin had to tell, but his elegy for his fallen comrades meant that the battle was yet to claim its last victim. The poet criticised a British warrior who had failed to respond to Owain's plea for aid, and this was a terrible dishonour. It seems that this man deliberately sought out Aneirin and killed him.

The battle had been glorious indeed, but in military terms it was a disaster for the Britons. Aethelfrith's army now occupied the estates of the slain heroes, and within a few years the combined kingdoms of Bernicia and Deira (together Northumbria) overran Rheged. A regional 'super-state' had been born, and soon a mighty king of that country, Edwin, was to plunge Britain into one of the bloodiest wars in its history.

7

'THE STRIFE ON THE WALL': HEAVENFIELD, NORTHUMBERLAND (633–634)

The suicide of the British cavalry at Catraeth, brave and memorable though it was, had grievous political consequences. York, once one of the mightiest fortresses in the Roman Empire, and for a few years the actual imperial capital, had fallen to the Angles of Deira. Now that the Germanic kingdoms of Deira and Bernicia had united, and Celtic Rheged had fallen, the combined superstate of Northumbria began to have some imperial pretensions of its own. Small, vulnerable British nations nearby were ripe for incorporation into Northumbria, among them Elmet in the Calder Valley of West Yorkshire. Northumbria was a threat to more powerful states too; the Picts, Ulaid (Ulster) in north-east Ireland and Man in the Irish Sea looked askance at the growing menace of an Anglian fleet in their waters – for the Northumbrians were originally a seafaring people, and well used to fighting at sea. But three other nations were also deeply concerned about the rise of the new Northumbrian power: Wessex, Mercia and Gwynedd.

Of these three, the first two were what we should call Anglo-British, which is to say that a Germanic aristocracy had come to dominate a population comprising coexisting Germanic and Brythonic bloodlines, perhaps with occasional interbreeding. The free Britons dreamed of recovering these places and called them 'the Lost Lands'; their name for England, Lloegyr or Loegria, means just that. Bardic prophesies claimed that the day of deliverance was at hand, even in this darkest hour, and that a mighty king was coming, a hero to equal Arthur, who would liberate York and rule all Britain from there as the Roman emperors had. Northumbria was also an Anglo-British nation, though the British there were ascribed an inferior social status. This was probably true to a lesser degree in Wessex and even in Mercia. Into this fractious and fissiparous racial and political mix, the explosive issue of religion was also intruded. Gwynedd was a Celtic Christian nation, but Mercia was still staunchly pagan. The Northumbrians were also pagans, but Wessex was just in the balance between paganism and Christianity. Of the seven original Anglo-Saxon nations, only Kent had been precariously converted to the Roman Catholic faith, commencing with St Augustine's mission in 597.

Of all these countries, Northumbria was clearly the most powerful. It was, therefore, in a position to impose tributary arrangements on lesser kingdoms, which would be paid annually in gold, silver, stallions, cattle, slaves, war dogs, hunting dogs, falcons, wine, mead and delectable foodstuffs. These tributes were extremely onerous, because the lesser kings had no choice but to extract the resources from their own tenants and nobles. Three years after coming to the throne in 616, Edwin's expansionism blew the lid off this simmering cauldron when he fabricated charges against the elderly king of the tiny statelet of Elmet, 'the Elm-forest', in West Yorkshire. Its king, Ceretic ap Gwallog, tried desperately to defend his kingdom in a stand on the River Idle in 619, but, hopelessly outnumbered, he was defeated and forced into exile in Gwynedd.

So began a war of epic proportions. In our times, perhaps less than 10 per cent of the population would have even heard of this war, let alone the battles fought in it – Cefn Digoll or 'Long Mountain', Hatfield Chase, Winwaed, Maes Cogwy/Maserfeld – are not conflicts commonly discussed, except perhaps in some elite schools, military academies and universities. Sometimes, local schoolchildren saunter home through these places, blissfully unaware of the momentous events which occurred there – indeed, their schoolteachers do. But at least regionally, one stands out, and even in these times is yet remembered – Heavenfield.

On 11 April 627, King Edwin of Northumbria took the momentous decision to convert to the Christian faith. King Cwichelm of Wessex, fearing Northumbrian power, had sponsored an assassination attempt on Edwin. The assassin had come very close to killing his target, lunging at Edwin with a poisoned dagger that made contact. Edwin, desperately fighting for his life, made a vow that, should he survive, he would convert to the Roman Catholic faith of which his wife was already a communicant. Edwin lived, and was true to his vow. The chief pagan priest, Coifi, also converted, along with all the leading nobility. Edwin was too ill, however, to personally revenge himself on Cwichelm, and there was, in any case, a much easier way of punishing Wessex without wasting his own precious resources.

Mercia was still a congeries of tribal groupings or clans which had yet to consolidate into a homogenous state. But it was expansionist and aggressive, and ruled jointly by two notoriously violent brothers: Eowa, who ruled the northern Mercians, and Penda, who ruled in the southern Midlands. It was to this latter brother, the most violent and deadly of the two, that Edwin now appealed for assistance. Penda's name is still a byword for savage paganism, thanks in large part to his denigration by the later Northumbrian historian the Venerable Bede. However, it is wrong to portray Penda as a simple villain whose only motives were glory and plunder. In fact, he played a remarkably subtle political game which saw him rise from minor warlord in Worcestershire to lord of all southern England, fabulously wealthy and the sire of a powerful dynasty. His grandfather was Creoda, the first real Mercian king, who claimed direct descent from the father of the gods, Woden, through the legendary King Offa of Angeln in Denmark and Icel, one of the first Anglian warriors to land in Britain. Germanic Wodenism was an essentially military cult, and all other matters were subordinated to war. Penda seems to have settled with his warband in east Worcestershire, at Pebworth, right on the border with the neighbouring Hwicce tribe. These people occupied the entire lower Severn Valley, plus Gloucestershire and Worcestershire. Penda had his eye on absorbing this territory into Mercia. The aristocracy of the Hwicce were Germanic, but the base population were still Celtic. The obstacle to this annexation was Wessex, which also had its eye on the rich and fertile lands between the Severn and the Avon.

Edwin was technically Penda's overlord, and he gave him a commission for a large-scale raid into Wessex to exact tribute. The West Saxons and the Gewissae, their close allies, marched to prevent Penda's marauders from entering Cirencester in 628. Cwichelm and Cynegils, the West Saxon commanders, must have been quite confident in their ability to repel Penda's force, but they received a nasty shock. Penda routed the West Saxons, and the kingdom of the Hwicce was absorbed into Mercia. There was nothing now to prevent the Mercian warbands from plundering far into the south-west; Penda's force was strong enough to lay siege to Exeter. The kings of Dumnonia, who ruled from Exeter, were vassals of the West Saxons, and so Penda was determined to have their tributary payments made payable to him in future. Edwin's shrewd plan seemed to have worked out perfectly – but now, one of the strangest and most mysterious twists in British history occurred. To understand this, we must go back a few years, and consider political developments in another country – Gwynedd.

The Celtic bards, inspired by the *Awen* or 'flowing river of spirit', were not historians in the modern sense. This ancient knowledge, inherited from the Druids, was a synergy of past and future imaginative states, which a skilled seer such as the aforementioned Myrddin could utilise to enter trance states in which not only past but also future events were visualised, to be uttered in prophecy. One such prophecy was *Armes Prydein Fawr*, or 'the Great Prophecy of Britain', attributed to Taliesin, a tenth-century bard. This foretold – incorrectly, as it turned out – the defeat of the English at the hands of the Welsh, Scots and Vikings. But the Celtic prophetic tradition was very ancient. In the early seventh century, a similar prophecy, attributed to Merlin, became particularly significant. Called *Cyfoesi Myrddin a Gwenddydd ei chwaer*, 'a conversation between Merlin and his sister, Gwenddydd', it reveals that a 'great eagle' – a leader of imperial stature, a hero to equal Arthur himself – was soon to be born among the Britons. This warrior king would raise a great army of the Britons, recover the 'Lost Lands', and finally crush the English to reclaim the sovereignty of Britain. Now that Rheged had fallen, the only viable British 'High King' was Cadwallon ap Cadfan of Gwynedd. He was a powerful king in his own right, but he also had an ancient and complex system of alliances with all the Celtic nations connected via the Irish Sea – Ireland, Cornwall, Man, Brittany and Galicia, where there was a long-standing British colony.

Geoffrey of Monmouth tells us that Edwin had been received as an exile at the court of Gwynedd when he was a boy, which seems unlikely; the story was probably a dramatic embellishment to make the rivalry between Cadwallon and Edwin seem like an ancient and eternal personal feud. But there is no doubt that the two men were on a collision course.

Edwin struck first, in 629. While Cadwallon was feasting at his residence at Penmon on Anglesey, a Northumbrian fleet made a surprise attack. Completely unprepared, Cadwallon narrowly escaped to the island then named Glannauc, now called Priestholm. As Edwin's men ransacked Anglesey searching for him, Cadwallon was transferred to a ship and slipped through the English cordon to escape to Ireland. Edwin would have been furious to have missed his man, but in all other respects his operation had been a great success. Gwynedd was soon occupied by Northumbrian garrisons, and the only hope of resurgence for the Britons seemed dead; and yet, in this darkest hour, the prophecy of Merlin still lived.

According to the *Moliant Cadwallon*, an ancient Welsh ballad, Cadwallon was conveyed from Ireland to Brittany, where he raised an army. His fleet sailed to Guernsey, and from that island to Devon where his army, perhaps a meagre force of 1,000 men, landed and raised the standard of the High King. Fortunately for him, the men of Dumnonia were eager to rally to him, because Penda was blockading Exeter at just that moment. What seems most likely is that Penda, far from his home bases and outnumbered, decided to withdraw; Geoffrey of Monmouth, deriving his account from earlier Welsh and Breton sources, states that Cadwallon processed northward. Geoffrey mentions fourteen battles Cadwallon fought, and no fewer than sixty lesser engagements. This 'campaign' could in fact be interpreted as a sort of triumphal procession, but the key test came when Cadwallon's army, perhaps 5,000 strong by now, entered Mercian territory. To fulfil the Prophecy of Merlin, Cadwallon was required to gather his forces at an ancient grove near the River Severn called Onennau Meigion or 'the Ash Trees of Meigion'. Geoffrey's source states that Cadwallon fought Penda here and defeated him, but the conflict might have been a stage-managed affair in which Penda effectively switched sides. This was unprecedented – a British Christian king concluding a pact with a British/Germanic pagan warlord – but both feared Edwin more than one another.

In 630, the combined forces of Cadwallon and Penda crossed the Severn. A Northumbrian army confronted them at Cefn Diggoll or Long Mountain near Welshpool. The Northumbrian force was probably outnumbered, and Cadwallon won a great victory. Gwynedd was liberated after more than a year of occupation. As if by a miracle, the fugitive who had been smuggled off Priestholm only a year or so before seemed poised to do battle for the sovereignty of the entire island of Britain. To the Britons, this turnaround must have seemed truly magical.

Cadwallon spent the next two years trying to consolidate his hold on Gwynedd, but for all that the bards declaimed that he was a Mab Darogan or 'Son of Prophecy' Cadwallon must have been keenly aware of his debt to Penda and his Mercians. Combined, their armies comprised a large force, perhaps 8,000 men, a vast horde for those days. Penda's personal valour and ferocity intimidated all who stood against him – he personally killed many kings and their champions in battle. The Mercian troops, deeply instilled with the warrior mentality of the cult of Woden, and always keen for booty from fallen opponents, were truly terrifying adversaries.

Meanwhile, Edwin was preparing for the battle he knew must soon come. In the autumn of 633, Cadwallon and Penda marched north. On 12 October they confronted Edwin's army at a place Bede called Haethfelth or Heathfield. The sixteenth-century historian John Leland was convinced that this was Sley-Burr Hill, a burial mound on Hatfield Chase outside Doncaster, but there are other possibilities. In 1951, excavations took place near the village church of Cuckney outside Warsop. Over 200 skeletons from the period, all male and many bearing wounds consistent with violent deaths, were exhumed from what was evidently a mass grave. Cuckney is quite near to Edwinstowe, the village which still bears Edwin's name. It is not unreasonable to suppose that Edwin's forces were deployed forward to this area, which is close to several important highways to the north used by Cadwallon and Penda.

The outcome of the battle was a catastrophe for Edwin, who was killed fighting alongside his son, Osfrith, who was also slain. Edwin's other son, Eadfrith, fled for his life but was ruthlessly tracked down by Penda's Mercians and put to death. The Northumbrian army was annihilated, and as Penda's pagan outriders plundered and ransacked far and wide, Cadwallon made straight for York. The impossible dream of a long-dead bard had finally become reality. The Welsh army, with the High King of Britain riding at its head, entered York as had been prophesied.

With winter coming on, Penda's Mercians returned home, heavily laden with loot from battlefields and monasteries. Now that Edwin was dead, Mercia was released from all previous tributary obligations to Northumbria, and Cadwallon recognised him as the undisputed king of all Mercia. But for Cadwallon's forces there could be no triumphant return home, because they must now perforce remain in York as an occupying army. Bede is explicit that Cadwallon's depredations made him a 'barbarian worse than any pagan', and says that Cadwallon intended to 'exterminate all of the English race within the island of Britain'. The Northumbrian state had disintegrated after Edwin's death, and the population immediately reverted to paganism. An exiled prince of Bernicia, Eanfrith, sought parley with Cadwallon, only to be ruthlessly murdered by him. Another pretender, Osric, besieged the Welsh army, but Cadwallon led his forces out and defeated him. As the cruellest months of winter came, the Welsh harried the already starved and wretched population until the moors and woods were full of desperate refugees. These are the bitter lessons for a defeated people – but although they had forsaken their new God, He had not forsaken them.

Edwin had driven the sons of King Aethelfrith, Oswald and Oswy, into a lonely exile on the tiny island of Iona. There, they became converted to Christianity, and in particular Irish-Celtic Christianity. Both boys were exceptionally devout, and also extremely well educated, something of a rarity for rulers of the period. Oswald, the eldest, now gathered an army about him composed of tough Irish clansmen from the kingdom of Dalriada of western Scotland and north-east Ireland. Many Northumbrian nobles and exiles rallied to Oswald, who advanced on York, but as yet his army was too small to confront Cadwallon. Confident that he would easily crush yet another pretender, Cadwallon's army, far superior in numbers, marched out of York to deal with this new threat.

At last, we are able to definitively identify a battlefield, which is at a place Bede called the 'Denis Brook', now called Rowley Burn, about 4 miles north of Hexham, very close to Hadrian's Wall. Oswald's army took up a strong position, which could not be outflanked, facing east, between the wall in the south and Brady's Crag to his north. At the place where the little church of St Oswald's now stands, Oswald ordered his warriors to kneel and pray, declaiming that St Columba of Iona had appeared to him in a dream the night before, assuring him of victory. He then ordered a huge wooden cross to be erected at the centre of his position; today a similar cross still stands there in memory of his famous victory.

Unfortunately, we know very little about the progress of the battle itself. Perhaps Cadwallon's men were surprised in an early-morning attack, or maybe the battle was a bloody strife which went on all day. What we do know is that the Welsh broke and ran. The retreat from such a slaughter, over such unforgiving terrain, and so far from home, was very much the greater part of the defeat for the Welsh, which they called *Cantscaul*, 'the strife beside the wall'. Few of them can have returned to their homeland – certainly not Cadwallon, who was discovered cowering in the Denis Burn and swiftly dispatched. The High King of Britain had met his ignoble end. Northumbria was resurgent, but to the south a more deadly enemy than Cadwallon remained – Penda, the last pagan king.

8

MASERFIELD/MAES COGWY (641/642) & WINWAED (655)

Cadwallon left a young son, Cadwaladr, but the boy was so young that a regent was appointed in Gwynedd until he came of age. Gwynedd had lost an entire generation of warriors, but fortunately for them, Northumbria was also devastated and exhausted. While the two adversaries licked their wounds, Penda embarked on a decades-long campaign of looting and enforcing protection on his most vulnerable neighbours, especially East Anglia, two of whose kings he personally slew. Oswald, meanwhile, spent several years consolidating his control of Northumbria. The long-term strategic aim of Northumbrian policy was, according to Charles-Edwards,[19] to seize control of the territory of the former Cornovii tribe – the plain encompassing Staffordshire, Shropshire and parts of Cheshire. This area comprised two client-states of Mercia which were independent Celtic-speaking areas allied to Penda: Luitcoit, near Lichfield, and Pengwern, near Shrewsbury. Oswald seems to have suborned Penda's brother Eowa, now very much in the shadow

---

19. Charles-Edwards, T. M., *Wales and the Britons, 350–1064* (Oxford, 2012)

of his infamous brother, to switch his allegiance to Northumbria, possibly with the promise that he would be given suzerainty of these conquered areas.

Penda, surprisingly, seems to have been extremely tolerant of these Celtic client kingdoms. Mercian graves of the period end abruptly 7 miles east of Lichfield, and at Yoxall 7 miles north. But in 641 or 642 (we cannot know the exact year, though we know the exact date – 5 August) Oswald, possibly with a Mercian contingent under Eowa, confronted Penda at a place the Welsh called Maes Cogwy or Croesoswallt, and the English Maserfelth or Maserfield. By tradition the battlefield is located at or very near to Oswestry – 'Oswald's Tree' as it was originally named.

Penda requested help from his Celtic allies as soon as Oswald's force crossed the border. Cynddylan ap Cyndrwyn, Prince of Pengwern, was eager to put his forces at Penda's disposal, and Gwynedd also provided a substantial contingent. Oswald's army, with or without Eowa's help, probably numbered 3,000 to 4,000 men, but Penda's allied British-Mercian army may have been larger. A furious assault by the pagan king, then in his prime, smashed Oswald's line. Seeing he was doomed, Oswald sank to his knees and prayed for the souls of his soldiers. It was as well, because most of them died with him on that hot August day. According to the historian Henry of Huntingdon, the plain of Maserfield was 'white with the bones of the Saints'. Penda saw the victory in terms of a triumph of paganism over the Christian God. Accordingly, Oswald's mangled corpse was dragged from the slaughter heap to be ritually dismembered. As an offering to Woden, Oswald's head and limbs were smitten off, and offered up on poles to be hung in the branches of a great oak tree nearby. His torso was crucified and left beside the bodies of his slain warriors. All this was somewhat disconcerting to the Welsh, who were Christians; a later Welsh source compared Penda's gory rites to diabolism, suggesting he was in league with infernal forces. Once again the pagan king had triumphed, and once again Northumbria instantly disintegrated. Penda had become a sort of living legend, even among the Britons, who dubbed him 'Panta ap Pyd' – 'Penda, Son of Danger'. He was now, as Frank Stenton called him, 'the most formidable king in England'. Mercia, a loose coalition of frontiersmen and pioneers just a few years before, was suddenly the most powerful nation in the entire island.

But Mercia's virtual hegemony at this crucial time in the island's history was based on raw military might alone. Each spring, Mercian forces, usually with Penda in the vanguard, raided and pillaged their neighbours, burned and plundered, carried off precious valuables, desecrated Christian holy places, and then withdrew to await later tribute payments. The Mercians were uncouth barbarians with no use for civilising influences, and their dominance was resented everywhere. Oswine, a pretender to the throne of Deira, briefly usurped that kingdom but died as a result of a conspiracy involving Oswy, Oswald's surviving brother. Oswy, a devout Christian, had grown up with his beloved elder brother at his side during their lonely sojourn on Iona. He was incensed at the insult to his brother's body, and arranged for a raiding party to recover the remains and return them for Christian burial at Bardney Abbey in Lindsey. Many miraculous cures were soon attributed to his shrine and he was declared a Saint of the Church.

Penda's reprisal was swift. In 644 he led a vast army, 5,000 strong, into the northern lands. Bamburgh was put under siege and was said to have been saved from immolation only by the prayers of the devout St Aidan. Oswy had no choice but to offer up his remaining treasures to Penda, and to promise his daughter in marriage to Penda's son, Peada. This son was eager to convert to the Christian faith; it must have been very apparent to the bright young man that his father was a being from an almost vanished era, the last of his kind.

It was almost certainly due to the intrigues of Oswy, who had despatched a Christian mission into Peada's sub-realm of Middle Anglia, that Penda decided to re-invade Northumbria in 655. The campaign was a simple repeat of those before – but this time on a truly huge scale. Contingents from over thirty different client nations and allies, both English and British, processed north with Penda, burning and looting in their time-honoured style. Oswy wisely withdrew to a great fortress called Iuddeu, now the Rock of Stirling in Scotland. In desperation, he offered his son to Penda as a hostage and made another enormous payment of treasure, which Penda distributed among his British allies. This was a fatal error on Penda's part; with their saddlebags stuffed with gold, the Britons had no incentive to remain and were anxious to get back to their homeland as soon as possible. It may well be that Penda's operations so far to the north had stretched his lines of communications too far. The time spent besieging Stirling was precious time lost, because now, as the autumn rains commenced, Penda's mercenary warbands turned south for home through unpredictable and hostile country.

Oswy began shadowing Penda's force with his own army as soon as the latter marched south. A network of Northumbrian observers sent runners and riders over the mountains and dales to report on Penda's progress. His vast, unwieldy and heterogeneous army struggled on through the miserable November weather with the grim-faced Penda leading. Oswy was waiting for a sudden heavy rain in the mountains, which would turn the usually small streams into raging, impassable torrents. Oswy promised to build a dozen monasteries and give his eldest daughter up to a nunnery if he were granted victory over Penda, and now his prayers were answered.

The Mercians and their allies are said to have reached a swollen beck called Winwaed, which may have been the River Went. But just outside Leeds, in the suburb of Whinmoor, which possibly means 'the strife on the moor' (Winwaed itself means 'the strife at the (swollen) ford'), there is a stream nearby called the Cock Beck, later to be the scene of another bloody encounter. The housing development nearby is still called Penda's Fields, and this may be our only clue as to the location of the battle, fought on 15 November 655.

Leeds would make sense as the location for the battlefield, because it stood on the junction of an old Roman road from York to Manchester. On the evening before the battle, Cadfael, Penda's Welsh ally, deserted him and took this route home towards Gwynedd. The Welsh had already been paid off, and so the decision was understandable, but perhaps 1,000 warriors left with him. Nevertheless, the dishonour was felt very sorely among the Welsh, especially the warbands of Pengwern and Luitcoit, who had most to lose if Oswy was the victor. Forever afterwards, Cadfael was calumniated among his countrymen as 'the battle-shirker'.

Penda's force was still vastly superior in numbers. His 2,000 Mercians formed the core, with 1,000 East Anglians under Aethelhere and 1,000 Deirans under Aethelwald. Oswy's force was smaller, but stormed forward with such spirit that Aethelwald, the sub-king of Deira, commanded his forces to stand aside – he had little reason to love Penda, who had hacked his father Oswald's body to pieces at Maserfield. The Northumbrians, enraged after months of Mercian depredations, smashed through to Aethelhere of East Anglia and slew him. At last, the Northumbrians broke through to the mighty Penda himself and the old warrior was brought down. His head was smitten off, Bede gleefully informs us, and Henry of Huntingdon tells us that all over England children sang a joyful rhyme to celebrate the pagan king's demise. More Mercians drowned after the battle than were slain in it, and few, if any, made it home.

After decades of bitter warfare, Northumbria had finally triumphed. Oswy consolidated his hold over the western Midlands by sending a party of assassins to massacre the royal family of Pengwern in 659. The Roman Catholic Church soon encouraged Oswy to exert his authority over the entire island, and there seemed to be nothing stopping him from establishing his hegemony.

9

THE FORTUNES OF WAR (659–825)

Northumbria had regained the ascendancy as the most powerful of the Anglo-Saxon heptarchy under Oswy, but it was not to last long. Although the infamous Penda was dead, his three sons Peada, Wulfhere and Aethelred survived him. Peada was allowed to continue as a puppet king of Middle Anglia for a while before Oswy arranged for him to be poisoned by agents working for Peada's wife, Oswy's daughter. While Oswy was on campaign against King Talorgan of the Picts in 658, three powerful Mercian nobles – Eafa, Immin and Eadbert – proclaimed Wulfhere as the rightful King of Mercia. The coup was ruthlessly executed and Wulfhere soon re-established control, driving out the Northumbrian governors. Wulfhere now occupied the formerly independent territories of Luitcoit and Pengwern, and distributed these lands to the patriots who had facilitated his coup or hidden him from his enemies. This ended the long-standing alliance between Mercia and the Welsh border states, and a fixed border was settled at a place on the Severn called 'Wulfhere's Ford' outside Welshpool.

A resurgent Mercia, now ruled by Christian kings, soon usurped the hegemony of Northumbria. Oswy's son Ecgfrith succeeded him, but his misfortune was to be born at a time when both the Mercians and the Picts were growing stronger, forcing him to fight on two fronts. In 679 Ecgfrith was heavily defeated by Aethelred I of Mercia, Penda's youngest son, at a huge battle fought somewhere on the River Trent in Lindsey. Six years later, in 685, Ecgfrith with a large army was lured into the Scottish mountains to subdue the Picts. The Picts gave ground to him, but suddenly sprang an ambush, killing him and most of his army at the Battle of Nechtansmere, possibly somewhere in Angus. Northumbria had lost its preeminent position among the Anglo-Saxon nations, but it retained its regional dominance.

South of the Humber, however, there was now only one nation that could overawe the others, both Anglo-Saxon and Celtic: Mercia. This status ultimately derived from sheer military superiority, but for roughly a century and a half, Mercia began to develop economically, spiritually and politically – and it was in this period that the foundations of a unified nation of the English, with a 'market for many nations' trading with merchants from the Continent at London, was born. Although the Mercians violently punished client states that proved rebellious – Kent was especially unfortunate in this regard, with Rochester and its cathedral burned down in 676 – these reprisals were limited, and somewhat less severe than in Penda's day. As the Mercians were diverted into almost ceaseless border wars and counter-raids against the Welsh, for a few precious years England experienced comparative peace.

Just as the English were beginning to dream of a unified nation, the Welsh were starting to see themselves as one people with a common language, religion and their own laws and traditions. Their constant internecine warfare bred a tough and ferociously military identity which helped them blunt Anglo-Saxon incursions and even to retake territory in some border zones. In 722 the West Saxons were defeated in Cornwall at the Battle of Hehill, now called Hayle. The Mercians were beaten that year too, at Pencon, somewhere near Carmarthen, and a King of Powys called Eliseg 'seized the inheritance of the men of Powys by force from the power of the English'. Another Welsh victory at Garth Maelog saw English settlements abandoned, and a permanent physical partition constructed. Named for a Mercian king, Offa's Dyke was, like Hadrian's Wall, an enduring testament to a mighty ruler. But it also represented a limit. The stubborn resistance the Britons put up had left them a vital enclave in the west, where their culture would survive to the present day.

Offa died at Offley in Hertfordshire in July 796. For eighty years, just two mighty Mercian kings, first Aethelbald (reigned 716–757) and then Offa himself (reigned 757–796), had exercised complete control of southern England. Coenwulf, a cousin of Offa, proclaimed himself 'Emperor of Britain' in grandiose style, but such hubris concealed very real weaknesses. Coenwulf demonstrated his ruthless military might by launching a massive invasion of Wales in the 820s which burned and pillaged the whole country. Gwynedd, Dyfed, Powys and Brycheiniog were all ravaged by the 'Mercian incendiaries'.

This predatory and arrogant attitude towards neighbours ultimately led to the downfall of Mercia. In 825, a new Mercian king, Beornwulf (reigned 823–826), marched into Wiltshire, expecting King Egcberht of Wessex (reigned 802–839) to be in far-off Cornwall fighting the 'West Welsh' with his army. Instead, Egcberht confronted the Mercians outside Swindon, near the village of Wroughton. Here, at a battle the West Saxons called Ellendun, Wessex won a decisive victory which effectively ended Mercian domination. At last, one Anglo-Saxon nation had succeeded in making itself into top dog. The dream of a united English nation was almost within the grasp of Egcberht and his descendants, known as Cerdicings, the descendants of a legendary West-Saxon ruler called Cerdic. But before they could claim the laurels, the kings of Wessex were going to have to fight for their very existence against an enemy more terrifying and deadly than anything the island peoples had faced before: the Vikings.

10

'THE GREAT HEATHEN ARMY'
(865–878)

I was fortunate to have been born during the 'golden age' of historical fiction writing for children in Britain, the 1950s and 1960s. I eagerly devoured all the works of such superb authors as Rosemary Sutcliff and Cynthia Harnett, for instance, but one of my favourites has always been *The Namesake: A Story of King Alfred*, published in 1964 by the writer and illustrator C. Walter Hodges. This genre of writing was, I soon realised, not really 'children's literature' at all. When Rosemary Sutcliff won the Carnegie Medal for *The Lantern Bearers* (1959), the judges were explicit in praising it as superior to 'much adult fiction'. Their raw power to transport the imagination, by a process the Ancient Greeks called analepsis, was a great comfort to me during several prolonged convalescences as a child. But for the purposes of this book I have chosen to confine myself to only the briefest outline of the military challenge posed by the Vikings, and of Alfred's courageous and intelligent attempts to contain them. Alfred's battles are still well-known – Ashdown and Edington, for example, were such famous English victories that they do not qualify as conflicts eligible to be included within the remit of this book. However, a cursory overview of the initial Viking onslaught must be included here – for this invasion by a large and well-organised army numbering in the thousands was the prelude to two centuries of the most savage and relentless warfare, and it forged the nation called England.

These unrelenting wars have marked the English national character. In my last book, I examined how magic and myth came to underpin our national culture, in subtle and sometimes more obvious ways. But the psychical legacy of centuries of violence and bloodshed have left deep and ugly scars – epigenetic traumas which we have yet to face and resolve – in comparison with which the influence of magic pales into relative insignificance. I believe that there *is* some kind of redemptive meaning in all this, if we look for it, and that the failure of our educational system to examine these matters in recent years deprives the youth of an opportunity to commune with vital aspects of the collective imagination. I am not alone in noticing this phenomenon; the eminent and deep-minded British musician and singer P. J. Harvey, for instance, made trenchant and poignant observations along these lines on her 2011 album entitled *Let England Shake*. But we must return now to the onslaught of the *Mycel Heathen Here* as it was known to the Anglo-Saxons – 'the Great Heathen Army' – for in 865 England really was shaken, and but for the miraculous intervention of Alfred the kingdom would surely have fallen.

The 'Great Army' implies a numerous force to our modern minds, but armies of this period were not very large as a rule. Some scholars think that the Viking army was composed of as few as 1,000 warriors. It is true that there were constraints on numbers, because a very large force required a correspondingly large and sophisticated base from which to launch their operations, and because of the limited availability of ships. However, a confederacy of pirates from the Viking settlements in northern France combined with Danish mercenaries from other regions could probably have mustered a considerably larger force, numbering around 3,000 or more.

Norse traditions, notably a saga called *The Tale of Ragnar Lodbrok*, maintain that the invasion was in response to King Aella of Northumbria's execution of a notorious Viking chieftain, Ragnar Lodbrok. When news of his execution reached Ragnar's sons – especially the eldest two, Ivar 'the Boneless' and Halfdan – they resolved to avenge their father by destroying the Northumbrian kingdom and parcelling it out to colonists from the Danish homeland. Aella, at least according to legend, had thrown Ragnar into a pit full of adders, a painful and ignoble death for a Viking warrior. There are other examples of how dishonourable provocations could lead to extreme retaliation from the Vikings. We have seen how the original Anglo-Saxon colonists had erupted in a destructive rebellion which engulfed all of southern Britain in the fifth century; later, in the eleventh century, King Sweyn 'Forkbeard' of Denmark would launch a massive retaliatory assault on England in revenge for the murder of Gunhilde, his sister, by English assassins in the St Brice's Day Massacre of 1002. A concerted project to take down the four main Anglo-Saxon kingdoms now commenced.

Of course, Viking raids were nothing new. Ever since the first recorded encounter, in 787, the 'Northmen' had embarked upon extensive hit-and-run raiding in their superbly crafted and designed longships, which could be beached both at the prow and stern. Their shallow draught meant that they could penetrate estuaries and rivers, lay siege to ports and cities, terrorise the countryside, and steal such precious valuables as they could carry off before being paid to depart by cowed kings and nobles. Even as the first millennium approached they were staunchly pagan, and indeed hostile to Christianity. This militant paganism was perhaps a reaction to the Holy Roman Emperor Charlemagne's campaigns against the pagan Saxons and his intimidation of the Danes. It is true that the Danes became Christianised in time, but during the initial onslaught there was a deliberate effort to target Christian sites, not only because they contained valuables but to strike a blow at the very notion of 'civilisation' itself.

Ireland, Wales, Brittany and the remote islands of Scotland were similarly exposed, but an invasion of England was quite another matter. Very hard fighting lay ahead. To minimise the need for costly pitched battles, a policy of intimidation and terror was adopted. The Viking army was quite different to an Anglo-Saxon army. The 'officer corps', as it were, of an Anglo-Saxon army comprised the thegns, aristocratic retainers of the king who held their lands from him in exchange for military support. Such men were well equipped, kept up a modicum of military training and were usually brave and dependable enough. The levies they brought with them, however, were of poorer quality, and could only provide themselves with more basic equipment – a spear, shield and dagger, perhaps, but certainly not a sword, a helmet, or armour – and most could not have been supplied with a mount. Very few would have seen any serious military action, and were completely reliant on the gallantry and discipline engendered by their superiors – and especially the king himself.

By contrast, the Viking force was composed of experienced professional mercenaries, trained for war since they could toddle. They were superbly athletic, disciplined and highly co-ordinated as ship's crews so often are, well armed with weapons far superior to anything most Englishmen could obtain, and above all they were ferociously aggressive and brave in battle. They were also capable of constructing impregnable fortifications very rapidly, and so hardy and resourceful that to starve them out would usually result in a similar famine among those besieging them. Fear of these 'barbarians' was very real, and they came to be seen as a punishment of God on the English for their sins. No one feared them more than the four Anglo-Saxon kings, for they had a special pagan rite which terrorised the bravest monarch. The rite of the 'Blood Eagle' involved hacking open the living victim and splaying out their lungs so that they resembled an eagle's wings – an offering to Odin, the Norse version of Woden. No wonder that many rulers, unmanned by this terrible fate, chose instead to pack their bags and head for sanctuary in Rome. But we must return to the progress of the war.

Like their Anglo-Saxon predecessors, the Great Army put ashore on the Isle of Thanet in Kent, where they encamped for the winter. The people agreed to pay them in exchange for peace, but this was not agreeable to the pirates; they accepted the payment, called *Danegeld*, but ransacked the area nevertheless. In 866 they arrived in East Anglia and demanded horses from King Edmund, who agreed to provide these in exchange for peace. After spending most of the year at Thetford, the Viking army moved off to Northumbria, perhaps to settle their score with the wicked Aella. According to tradition, Aella was subjected to the rite of the Blood Eagle soon after the Vikings captured York in 867. They set up a puppet-king in Northumbria named Egbert, who soon wisely fled to Mercia.

The resourceful and now very mobile Vikings could strike anywhere at will. Unfortunately for King Edmund of East Anglia, it was his turn next. There was no point in procrastination or further appeasement, and so Edmund made a stand against the heathens outside Thetford. His meagre forces were soundly beaten, but Edmund managed to escape into a wood called Haeglesdune where, tradition states, he suspended himself beneath a footbridge in hopes of concealing himself until nightfall. Unfortunately, a courting couple were strolling that way and they saw the reflection of the king's gilded-spurs in the water. The Vikings were informed, no doubt for a small consideration, and Edmund was taken alive. Tradition states that he was dragged to an oak tree known thereafter as St Edmund's Oak, tied to it and scourged before being used for archery practice until his body was bristling with arrows.[20] Edmund was then cut down and subjected to the grim rite of the Blood Eagle. Finally, his head was smitten off and thrown into a hawthorn bush nearby.

---

20. In 1848 this tree collapsed; curiously, an iron arrowhead was discovered 5 feet from the ground.

What was left of his body was impaled on a stake. His manner of death was humiliating and painful, but he achieved sanctity in the process, becoming known as 'the Martyr'. Now only two English kingdoms remained: Mercia and Wessex.

It was the misfortune of Mercia to feel the force of the Great Army next. In 867 the Vikings set up camp at Nottingham, erecting strong defences. King Burgred of Mercia promptly laid siege to them. A mutual assistance pact existed between Mercia and Wessex, so Burgred appealed to King Aethelred of Wessex for military aid. Aethelred honoured the pact, and with his younger brother Alfred beside him marched the West Saxon army to Nottingham where they reinforced the beleaguered Mercian king and his forces in the oldest part of the town, around St Mary's Church, where the defences are still plainly visible today.

Despite their overwhelming superiority in numbers, the allied English forces made no progress. Eventually, Aethelred and his men left for home. By 869, Burgred had no choice but to pay the Vikings to move on, which they did. Elements of the Great Army then pillaged Berkshire, in West Saxon territory, so it was now Burgred's turn to reciprocate with Mercian aid. Thinking discretion to be the better part of valour, Burgred instead fled to Rome, where he died in ignominious exile. The Vikings, meanwhile, took all of eastern Mercia for themselves. In western Mercia a puppet, a 'foolish king's thegn' called Ceolwulf, was installed to rule on their behalf, so at least the western Midlands remained nominally English. This astonishing success for the Vikings – the conquest of a third Anglo-Saxon nation – was soon celebrated by the *skalds* in the mead halls of Denmark, Norway and Sweden. Wessex would be next.

In 870, a Viking called Bagsecg arrived to reinforce the Great Army with a large fleet known as the Great Summer Army. This must have swollen the Vikings' numbers considerably, with young jarls like Oskytel, Anwend and Guthrum keen for conquest and settlement. The *Life of Alfred* records nine major battles in Wessex in just one year, including Ashdown, where it is claimed the entire plain was littered with Danish corpses after the battle. These losses, in the thousands rather than hundreds, indicate that by now the Great Army was perhaps more than 5,000 strong. At Christmas this vast force seized Reading and fortified it. When their outriders went out on a foraging expedition they were immediately interdicted by Aethelwulf, King Aethelred's ealdorman in the area. At a place called Englefield, he slew many prominent Viking jarls and managed to contain the remaining Vikings at Reading until King Aethelred and Alfred came up to support him with the main West Saxon army. Once again, it proved impossible to storm the Viking defences, and after suffering heavy casualties the West Saxon army withdrew.

The Vikings now made an almost fatal blunder. Sensing that the demoralised English were at a low ebb, they pursued the West-Saxon army along an ancient trackway called the Ridgeway. As a result, January 871 saw the Battle of Ashdown. The Viking army was incomplete because many warriors remained at Reading, but it was probably still larger than King Aethelred's force. As the Viking army massed for an early-morning attack, Aethelred insisted on finishing his prayers before forming up his men. This was an absurd and dangerous delay; the Danes cared nothing for religious devotions and had already seized the high ground. Alfred, showing extraordinary courage and leadership, personally rallied the West-Saxon army and led them forward 'in dense battle-order' – the famous shield wall – uphill towards a stunted thorn tree around which the Danish jarls had raised their standards. Alfred, charging 'like a wild boar', furiously assaulted the Viking line, and the English, seized by a sort of battle madness, slaughtered thousands of Danes, including five jarls and a king. By the time the king arrived with his own household troops, the Vikings were doomed. Leaving thousands of dead on the field, they were forced to retreat.

But the Vikings soon recovered from this shock defeat. At Basing, outside Reading, King Aethelred's army was defeated within a month. In spring the West Saxons suffered another heavy defeat at Merantun. It is very likely that Aethelred was wounded in this battle, because in April he died. With his sons mere boys, his brother Alfred, the hero of Ashdown, was selected as the new king. He was an unlikely hero, weak and sickly, possibly with a wasting disease of the bowel; he was also sensitive, intelligent and prone to bouts of severe depression which afflicted him until his death. But beneath this frail exterior beat the living heart of the Anglo-Saxon race, in the breast of the greatest Englishman who has ever lived.

For all his later greatness, Alfred's position was very weak in 871. After nine battles, including a defeat at the Battle of Wilton in the very heart of Wessex, Alfred had no choice but to capitulate and pay the *Danegeld*. The Danes were only too keen to take his payment and leave West Saxon territory for London, then a Mercian city. Their losses had been very heavy, and for the older warriors (some had been in England for more than six years) the idea of a peaceful life as a country farmer must have seemed rather appealing. But Alfred was no coward, and the Danes knew there could be no final conquest of England so long as he remained alive. It was only a matter of time until the war resumed with a fresh intensity.

In 876, a new Viking leader, Guthrum, made a lightning attack from Cambridge into the heart of Wessex. The Danes continued moving west into Devon, where they shut themselves up in Exeter. Alfred laid siege to the town, and they eventually agreed to leave Alfred's kingdom to move on to Gloucester, without receiving a payment of *Danegeld*. During 877 the Danes seemed placid enough, but 'after Twelfth Night', the *Anglo-Saxon Chronicle* tells us, in early January 878, Guthrum rode out with a large warband and surprised Alfred at Chippenham, where he had been celebrating Christmas with his immediate family and a few bodyguards. The whole West Saxon nation was doing the same, and so Alfred was extremely fortunate to have been alerted just in time to escape into the Somerset marshes. Almost certainly Alfred's whereabouts had been revealed to Guthrum by an English spy.

Wessex was rapidly occupied by the Great Army, and much misery was visited upon the hapless population of Wessex as they burned and plundered at will. Some English nobles chose to escape overseas, but for those who remained there seemed precious little hope that Alfred was still alive. In fact, Alfred had retired with a small band of household warriors and their families to an 'island' in the trackless marshes called Athelney. The Danes knew approximately where he was hiding, and twenty-three shiploads of Danes landed on the north Devon coast with the intention of flushing him out. They bore with them the magical pagan banner called the Raven. They believed that so long as the flag flew in their midst, they were unbeatable; the Raven banner symbolised the entire Great Heathen Army. But the Viking fleet was spotted at sea by the local ealdorman, Odda, and he rallied the men of Devon and attacked. Over 800 Vikings were slain, and the Raven banner was taken in a catastrophic defeat.

Meanwhile, Alfred himself was actively pursuing a policy of savage guerrilla warfare against the Danes, and as spring approached it became clear to the West Saxons that their king was not only alive but also full of fight. News of the Raven banner's capture was spread by word of mouth, and excitement mounted as Easter approached. Eventually, Alfred sent out messengers to summon the fighting men of Somerset, Hampshire and Wiltshire to join him at a landmark known as 'Egbert's Stone' near Mere. His appearance after so many desperate months in hiding was greeted with rapturous cheering, and the army, perhaps 4,000 men in all, marched immediately to confront the Danes at Edington in Wiltshire. The man people greeted as 'one who had returned from the dead' was very much alive.

On 12 May 878, Alfred marched towards Iley Oak, where Guthrum was encamped. Bishop Asser, Alfred's biographer, tells us what happened next:

Then, he attacked the whole pagan army fighting ferociously in dense battle-order, and by the divine will he eventually won the victory, made great slaughter among them, and pursued them as far as their fortress at Chippenham. Everything they left outside the fortress, men, horses, or cattle he seized, killing the men, and encamped outside their gates. After fourteen days the pagans were brought to the extreme depths of despair by hunger, cold and fear, and they sought peace.

This time Alfred meant business, but his response was unusual. Guthrum was taken out hunting and hawking with Alfred at his personal estates nearby, and after three weeks of hospitality the Viking leader agreed to be baptised with Alfred as his godfather. He took the baptismal name of Athelstan. Asser tells us:

Guthrum, their king, promised to accept Christianity ... and thirty men with him, which all fulfilled ... at a place called Aller ... King Alfred raised him from the holy font of baptism, receiving him as his own son; the unbinding of the chrisom on the eighth day took place at the royal estate at Wedmore. Guthrum remained with the king for twelve nights after baptism, and the king freely bestowed many excellent treasures on him and all his men.

What was the point of all this, after such humiliating ordeals?

The Vikings were a superstitious people, and Alfred's comeback – seemingly 'from the dead' – unnerved them. It was known among them that as a child Alfred had visited Rome, where, for reasons no one has yet discerned, the pope anointed the little lad even though he was not yet 'throne-worthy', as the Anglo-Saxons called it. As we have seen, Alfred was hardly the stuff of which medieval military leaders were made – at least on the surface. Yet twice he had bested the most powerful Viking army in history. Guthrum and his thirty compatriots had watched from the palisades of Chippenham as their comrades were dangled from the gallows, and they must have known that their lives were in the hands of a ruthless man who had every reason to execute them too. And yet there was feasting, merriment, camaraderie, sport and talk of a new faith. In short, the Danes were subjected to an exercise to induce what modern psychologists would call 'cognitive dissonance'; confused, and amazed to be alive, they were only too pleased to take their leave of the victorious king.

Guthrum moved on to Cirencester with the remnants of his army, but in 879 they made the decision to return to their earlier conquest of East Anglia. Here, Guthrum (or Athelstan as he was called now) ruled as a Christian or pseudo-Christian monarch, and the Great Army finally dispersed to become peaceful farmers – at least for the time being. In 886 a partition of England was agreed whereby all of the country from 'up the Thames to London, and up to the River Lea, along the Lea to its source and then in a straight line to Bedford, then up the River Ouse to Watling Street' and all points north and east of that line were recognised by Alfred as being under de facto Danish control – the Danelaw, as it became known. Alfred simply did not possess the necessary military wherewithal, the financial and organisational resources or even the inclination to fight the Danes to a finish. That task, he knew, would take several generations to achieve.

For the remainder of his days, Alfred laboured to rebuild his shattered kingdom. He was remarkably successful; his exemplary achievements in the literary, cultural and spiritual fields are beyond compare, but in purely military terms his legacy was extraordinary. He reorganised the army so that the *fyrd*, or militia, could always take the field at short notice, serving designated tours of duty in rotation. He was the founder of an English navy. He initiated the construction of a system of forts serving every shire, all well defended and with a ready water supply. The population would now have a ready refuge in times of emergency, and all Viking movements between these *burhs*, as they were known, could be swiftly interdicted by the garrisons.

The Vikings troubled Alfred for the remainder of his reign. Two more armies arrived, including one under the command of Haesten, a notorious buccaneer who, finding no fortune in

France, decided instead to attack England and Wales. Alfred waited for the Vikings to move away from their base at Mersea Island in Essex, and then attacked the place, taking all the Viking women and children as hostages. The warriors broke through and commenced a campaign of terror which took them across the country to Quatford in Shropshire, then into Wales, and finally to Northumbria, where they dispersed or settled down. This proved Alfred's point; the Danish threat was beyond even his genius to solve. The conquest of the north-east of England was a *fait accompli* – but thanks to Alfred, Wessex, and a new concept of 'England', had survived.

11

TETTENHALL/WEDNESFIELD, STAFFORDSHIRE (910)

As a very small boy I would sometimes walk hand in hand with my grandfather Harry beside the Wom Brook in the village of Wombourne in South Staffordshire. Having been somewhat psychologically scarred by the Great War, he was not inclined to discuss war as a rule, and unlike my walks with my father, which usually involved a continuous commentary about history – especially military history – there were only a few times I can recall my grandfather tutoring me concerning such matters. One day we were waiting for my uncle to return from his shift at the local colliery, sat at a pub called the Red Lion on Battlefield Lane, just off Battlefield Hill, when I casually enquired about the origin of the names. I was very surprised when my grandfather gave me an answer as unequivocal and authoritative as my father's usual responses. He asked if I had ever heard of King Alfred the Great, which, thanks to my father's endeavours, I had, even before I attended any school. I secretly, and incorrectly, suspected that my father must have learned all he knew – which was a great deal – about these ancient matters from *his* father, who now told me about Alfred's son, King Edward 'the Elder' as he is known to history.

Here, in this little lane at the edge of the Black Country, I was told, Edward had trapped a great army of marauding Vikings and slaughtered them to the last man. I still have no idea how this local tradition originated. Many years later, I took my fiancée out to lunch, and we happened to dine at the Red Lion. I had quite forgotten my boyhood experience there, but I happened to glance at a framed account on the wall describing how, on 5 August 910, the Danes had been massacred by King Edward the Elder, and that this place was the site of the so-called Battle of Tettenhall near Wolverhampton, one of the greatest and most decisive victories against the Viking invaders. My father demurred. He thought that the battle had been fought at either Compton or Tettenhall Wood, both to the west of the borough, now the City of Wolverhampton, not far from a place still called the 'Warstones'.

It was not until after many years had elapsed that I realised the huge national significance of this battle – and also discerned why it was that such a notable victory of the English is so strangely obscure, perhaps especially in our own times. In short, I believe my grandfather was wrong, and my father was also wrong – the story of the battle he heard was the invention of an itinerant Irish balladeer, commissioned to produce a suitably 'patriotic' account of the battle on the occasion of the thousandth anniversary in 1910. In fact, Edward 'the Elder' was probably not even present at the battle, even though a primary school in Wednesfield still bears his name. Given that this battlefield was closer to my roots than probably any other, this obscurity was especially frustrating – but as I studied the campaign, over many years, the 'true story' of this conflict unfolded itself until it eclipsed the vague clues supplied by my forebears to reveal a character from history as redoubtable and determined as Alfred: his daughter Aethelflaed, Lady of the Mercians.

Although Edward 'the Elder' succeeded to the throne of Wessex after Alfred's death in 899, he was not actually the eldest child of the great king. This was Aethelflaed, his daughter, but in the macho culture of the Middle Ages there was no scope whatsoever for a woman to secure political power, however illustrious her pedigree, let alone interfere in the peculiarly male pastime of warfare. Even today, when almost all military roles are open to women, the military sphere is still male-dominated and controlled. In the early tenth century this exclusivity was total. But for reasons we will examine shortly, Aethelflaed was destined to prove the exception to this rule, to become a military leader as effective as her more famous younger brother, Edward, and a political operator as shrewd and intelligent as her glorious father.

The realm of Wessex passed to Edward, but like his father he did not have the strongest claim, and had instead been chosen for his military skill, prowess and bravery. He had already deputed for Alfred while his father was still alive, and had shown considerable valour in battle. But the 'true' claimant was actually Aethelwold, the eldest surviving son of Alfred's brother Aethelred. Aethelwold was bitterly resentful of Edward, and his petulance led him to mount a desultory rebellion which had absolutely no chance of success. Piqued, Aethelwold fled into the Danelaw, and intrigued with the Danes to invade Wessex, and to raid into the territory of West Mercia, which was now ruled by a viceroy named Lord Aethelred as an independent English realm staunchly allied to Wessex. This Aethelred had been a very loyal and brave commander who had acted in complete concert with King Alfred. He did not refer to himself as a king, but neither was he a mere 'ealdorman'. His status fell somewhere between the two – and in recognition of this fact, Alfred had arranged that he should take Aethelflaed as his bride, to cement the deep alliance and friendship between the two English realms.

There are reasons to suspect that Aethelflaed was not altogether happy with this arrangement. Lord Aethelred was very much older than she was, and although her own mother had been Mercian, she was a foreigner in a strange country. The couple had one daughter, Aelfwyn, who was destined to become the very last ruler of an independent Mercia, but it is recorded that after this birth Aethelflaed refused to sleep with her husband again. The reasons can only be guessed at, but it could have been a particularly painful and difficult childbirth for her. She may have found intercourse with her husband disagreeable. It was claimed that the decision was made out of piety at the time, but in all likelihood this independent-minded woman had reasons of her own, which we will never know.

In 902, Aethelwold invaded Wessex. Edward easily repelled him, chasing his Danish army into East Anglia, where part of the West Saxon army, greedy for plunder, disobeyed Edward's order to return home. Aethelwold attacked this section of the English army and cut it to pieces, but he lost his life in the process. Edward was now undisputed King of Wessex. The Danes licked their wounds and began to look to alliances with their comrades overseas, realising that it was only a matter of time until Edward and Aethelred invaded in force. The Viking kings of York ruled a military statelet centred on that city, but in Ireland a similar arrangement pertained in the city of Dublin, where a colony of Norse settlers had set up one of the biggest clearing houses for slaves in Europe. Some of these Norse now attempted to establish a similar colony on the Wirral, outside Hoylake. DNA testing has revealed that there is a larger percentage of people with Norse ancestry in that area than in comparable regions to this day.

In 907, Lord Aethelred was forced to refurbish the fortifications of Chester in response to the threat from the Wirral. Edward, however, seemed unusually inactive on the military front. Instead, he attempted to buy off the Vikings; agents were sent out to negotiate with Danes in the border zones to relocate elsewhere. But in 909, Edward and Aethelred combined their forces to attack Lindsey, which had a large colony of Danes. Lord Aethelred removed from nearby Bardney Abbey the remains of King Oswald– which Oswy had rescued from the battlefield of Maserfield – and had them relocated to Gloucester, his own regional capital. Aethelred's royal lineage is somewhat obscure, but it had been his illustrious namesake, Penda's son Aethelred I of Mercia, who had founded Bardney Abbey. In effect, this was a propaganda exercise to emphasise that from now on both Wessex and West Mercia were in the fight against the Danes, and that their ultimate intention was to eliminate Viking York and establish English control over the whole of England. For six weeks, the English harried and plundered Lindsey, inflicting much misery on the population. The allies eventually withdrew, but this punitive expedition galvanized the angry Danes into punitive action of their own.

In the summer of 910, the Viking kings of York mounted a counter-invasion aimed at crippling West Mercia. King Edward was in Kent, so could not immediately help Aethelred. The two Viking commanders, Halfdan and Eowils, struck deep into West Mercia; the *Anglo-Saxon Chronicle* records that they reached the River Avon. Lord Aethelred's forces fell back, either to his capital at Gloucester or to his royal estates near Winchcombe, and sent frantic pleas for help to Edward. The *Anglo-Saxon Chronicle* says that Edward 'sent his army, both from Wessex and Mercia' but does not say Edward was present among them as is often claimed. The Danes, many of whom were freebooters from overseas, were unconcerned; they calculated that there was plenty of time to loot the Severn Valley area before English troops arrived. They crossed the Severn near Upton-upon-Severn and headed north along the west bank of the river until they reached Danesford, just outside Bridgnorth, which their compatriots had used as a refuge a few years before. Loaded down with vast quantities of loot, they decided to make their way home. But Lord Aethelred had not been idle.

Reinforcements from the nearby West-Saxon *burhs* and the men of Wiltshire and Somerset probably reached Aethelred soon after the Danes crossed the Severn. With the river between them, it was now possible to combine these troops with his own Mercian forces and to make a rapid march north towards modern Wolverhampton. It may be that King Edward was indeed at the head of the army, but this is not stated explicitly. Once they had crossed the Severn in early August, the Vikings marched due east. They soon came to a place called Tootenhall, now the suburb of Tettenhall in Wolverhampton.

The *Chronicle* says that the battle took place there, but in Anglo-Saxon times battlefields were recorded as being near to any place of high status or local significance. For many years there has been a lively debate about the location of the battle, because a member of the West Saxon royal house, a great-great-grandson of King Aethelred of Wessex named Aethelweard, contradicted the extant versions of the *Chronicle* and stated that the actual battlefield was at Wednesfield Heath, now Heath Town in Wolverhampton. Now, Aethelweard is to be taken seriously, because not only was he a highly educated royal personage but he was also, in fact, an historian. In his later years he retired to Bridgnorth, which had been at the centre of the action, to write what he called his *Chronicon*, a translation of the extant versions of the *Chronicle* into Latin from the English. Only one, very badly damaged copy survives, which was almost destroyed in the Cotton Library fire of 1731, but it is explicit that the main battle took place further east than Tettenhall, at Wednesfield – 'the plain of Woden' – which was a sacred place of the elder gods and so highly appropriate for the annihilation of the enemy army.

Despite this, I have gathered many stories over the years from people who care deeply about preserving the memory of the battle for posterity. Some of these maintain that Tettenhall, especially the area called 'the Rock', *was* indeed the place where the Danes were annihilated. Wombourne and Compton both have traditions, and one which seems credible is that the Vikings were ambushed while in a long, straggling column near Tettenhall Wood. But Aethelweard's evidence does seem too convincing to dismiss. It seems as if the Danes walked straight into a well-planned ambush. As they neared Tettenhall, the rear of their column may well have been attacked by concealed English forces, who fell upon the Danish wagons and liberated the stolen belongings. The head of the Viking column, with Halfdan and Eowils in the vanguard, reached Wednesfield Heath, near to where New Cross Hospital now stands, on rising ground ideal for a blocking-force to make a stand.

If the Vikings really were trapped between the English in this way, the long-standing confusion and controversy about the exact location may be easily explained after all. In short, this event should perhaps be renamed the Battle of Wolverhampton, even though that town did not yet exist. Desperate Danes may have fled as far as Wombourne, only to be hunted down and slaughtered. The exact details will never be known, but the local pride in this achievement among the folk of Wolverhampton is still very much in evidence. For the Danes, though, it was a catastrophe of the first magnitude. The *Chronicle* states:

> There fell King Eowils, and King Halfdan; Earls Other, and Scurf; Governors Agmund, Othulf, and Benesing; Anlaf the Black, and Governor Thunferth; Osferth the collector, and Governor Guthferth ...

These men commanded large retinues, and all would have died with them. So far from home, there was no hope whatsoever of escape, and no mercy would have been shown to any wounded Danes. The carnage was extraordinary, and so weakened the Viking kingdom of York that it soon fell under the control of a Viking pirate from Dublin called Ragnall. Whether it was Edward who was the overall commander, or Lord Aethelred, we will never know – but of Aethelred's contribution there can be little doubt. Within six months he was dead, most likely from wounds which had continued to fester after the battle. The West Mercian nobles were in no doubt who should succeed him as their ruler: his widow, Aethelflaed, who now became a war leader in her own right as the Lady of the Mercians. How did such an extraordinary situation come about, in such a male-dominated society? Well, not only was Aethelflaed no ordinary woman, but the West Mercians had retained a special type of reverence for women which may have elevated her to the status almost of a deity, and this may partly explain the extraordinary events which now followed.

Archaeological evidence has been unearthed across the Severn Valley area indicating a cult of a goddess named Cuda or Godda. An Oxford scholar and author, Stephen J. Yeates, has made a convincing argument for the survival of this cult from prehistoric times until the Anglo-Saxon invasion of the area in the 570s.[21] What Yeates proposes is that the *Matribus Et Genioloci* or the 'Mother Goddess and Genius of the Place' continued to be honoured in the region long after the Teutonic Hwicce tribe had supplanted the Celtic Dobunni, their more ancient predecessors. The incoming Hwicce accepted the cult of the goddess at that point – and it may *never* have been completely eradicated. Even though Mercia had been Christianised for centuries, the *volkergedanken* – that is, the elemental folk ideas, as the anthropologist Bastian dubbed them – which underlay Mercian society may have been peculiarly receptive to the idea of a female war leader, in her dark aspect as the goddess of destruction and vengeance.

It is true that Aethelflaed left behind no male heir, only Aelfwyn, her young daughter. It is remarkable that after Aethelflaed's sudden death in 918, the Mercian nobles had no reservations about accepting the sensitive and inexperienced young girl as their new ruler – in preference to her mighty uncle Edward. It is just possible that the 'Lady of the Mercians' was nothing less than the final political personification of an ancient goddess. What was even more uncanny was that in Viking mythology, at Ragnarok, the great battle at the end of time, their adversaries would be commanded by a *female* warrior, and so Aethelflaed represented something disturbing to their folk psyche too. Foreigners were astonished at her achievements, and in Irish annals her death was

---

21. Yeates, S., J., *The Tribe of Witches: The Religion of the Dobunni & Hwicce* (Oxford, 2008)

remarked with especial regret. If true, this may account for the faint praise with which the *Chronicle* records these events, for it was essentially a pro-West Saxon collection of annals, designed to legitimate the domination of the *Cerdicings* like Edward. But Aethelflaed was also a *Cerdicing*, though not a male one. In short, the Lady of the Mercians violated many of the preconceptions which it was the job of the chroniclers to uphold. They wanted a hero who was West Saxon and male, but suddenly they were confronted with a heroine who was Mercian (by adoption, and half by blood) and female. It is at least possible that her sudden death on 12 June 918 at Tamworth could have been contrived by West Saxon agents, desperate to prevent the Vikings of York from surrendering to her, as they had promised to do, in preference to yielding to Edward. For this was the historical reality: Mercia, under a female war leader, had begun to intimidate the Danes even more than Edward's Wessex. We will now look at how Aethelflaed's campaign panned out in more detail.

The relationship between Lord Aethelred, Alfred and Edward had been somewhat unequal – Wessex now being very much in the driving seat. The *Chronicle*, though, gives an impression of West Mercia as a sort of vassal state of Wessex, which was very far from reality. Now that a brother and sister ruled in the two nations they were one step nearer to becoming a proto-English state, and Edward was determined that his son, Athelstan, should succeed to him. Alfred had taken a shine to the lad when he was a toddler and had a miniature sword, shield and armour made for him. Athelstan was the 'golden child'. But there was a problem: he was illegitimate, and could not succeed to the throne in Wessex. Edward devised a cunning solution. Although Athelstan was his firstborn and his favourite, with his pale blue eyes and curly blonde hair, Edward had him sent to Mercia to be tutored in statecraft by Aethelflaed, with the intention that he should succeed to the throne of Mercia after her death. Aethelflaed became, in effect, a mother to the boy, and the little lad who would one day become the 'Emperor of Britain' is depicted standing beside her on the monument erected to her memory at Tamworth Castle. Aethelflaed was forced to make other, much more painful concessions to her brother. London and Oxford were both Mercian cities, but it made military sense for Edward to take responsibility for defending them in future. The towns were ceded to Edward so that Aethelflaed could concentrate her limited forces against the main enemy, the Danes of the so-called 'five boroughs' in the east Midlands.

Those nobles who were dispossessed by these arrangements would have been resentful, even if they were compensated, but the overall strategy of the English had changed. For over four decades a bitter war had raged, and the English character had adapted to the changed conditions. What mattered above all was final victory over the invaders, and all other considerations were subordinated to that end. The only issue was deciding which of Alfred's children would finish the Danes off. Aethelflaed was determined that she would be the one to bring the Danes to heel, but a female commander, untried in battle, required a rehearsal for such a grand venture – and now an opportunity presented itself.

Abbot Egbert, a Mercian dignitary, was travelling through south Wales with his retinue when they were set upon by brigands and killed. Egbert was under the protection of Aethelflaed, and she immediately demanded that Tewdr, the petty king of Brycheiniog in the Black Mountains, deliver the heads of the culprits to her. Tewdr failed to comply, probably because he had no idea who had committed the murders, and Aethelflaed invaded within days. She marched to Tewdr's royal crannog, built on an island in Lake Llangorse, and stormed the place. Tewdr escaped by boat, but his wife, children and thirty of his retainers were taken as hostages and the crannog put to the torch. Tewdr soon surrendered, and proved most compliant henceforth. Aethelflaed had demonstrated that she could command expeditionary forces, and had proved herself as resolute and ruthless as any man. Now, she was almost ready to take the field against the main enemy.

Stretching across central England, the 'five boroughs' of the Danes were fortified colonies from which they controlled trade with their comrades overseas. Lincoln, Stamford, Leicester, Nottingham and Derby were the main strongholds, but the Danes had a strong presence in other areas too. At Bedford they were driven out by Edward, resettling in Normandy. He then moved on to Tempsford after defeating three Viking counterattacks, and Aethelflaed immediately saw her opportunity. In the summer of 917, her army moved against Derby. The town was extremely well defended, and Aethelflaed's men took heavy casualties. The *Mercian Register* tells us that 'four of her thegns who were dear to her were killed within the gates'. But at a high price. The first of the five boroughs had fallen, and this was a hammer blow to the Vikings of York, for whom the five boroughs were a defensive screen. In the east, her brother was also taking the war to the Danes. Edward stormed Tempsford and then Colchester, killing the Danish King of East Anglia. But he still had much to do, for Danish forces continued to occupy Northampton, Cambridge and Stamford, and the Fens barred his way to Lindsey. Incredibly, it now fell to Aethelflaed to deliver the killing blow.

The Lady of the Mercians moved against Leicester in the early months of 918, and harried the countryside around so the Danes could not sow their crops. Perhaps mindful of her heavy loss at Derby, she was content to besiege the town and starve the inhabitants into submission. This policy proved effective, and the Danish leaders capitulated. Aethelflaed processed into the town, distributing alms to the poor; she was signalling to the Vikings of York that, should they choose to surrender to her and not Edward, merciful terms were to be had. She knew that the increasingly Christian Danes of York were resentful that their kingdom had been usurped by a pagan from Dublin called Ragnall. These signals were immediately understood, and the Vikings agreed to surrender to her. There was a good military reason for concluding a peace-treaty – Nottingham, 'the key to the North' and her next target, was one of the strongest of the five boroughs. It had defied siege before, as we have seen. But now Fortuna, who spins the wheel of fate, dealt the Mercians a crushing blow.

On 12 June 918, Aethelflaed suddenly died at Tamworth, ancient capital of Mercia. The Mercian nobles convened to confirm her daughter, Aelfwyn, as the new Lady of the Mercians, but within six months Edward deposed her, and had her removed to a nunnery in Shaftesbury for the remainder of her days. The obvious question is, was Aethelflaed assassinated? Any fair-minded historian must face the possibility that may have been the case. But would Edward, eldest son of the great and noble Alfred, really have conspired to murder his own sister? Unfortunately, medieval politics was fraught with such dangers, and no ruler could afford to be too sentimental if the stakes were high enough – and in this case they were. Athelstan, Edward's son, the 'flaxen-haired *aetheling*' who was to become one of England's greatest heroes, was almost certainly guilty of disposing of his rival brother, for instance, and so to discount the possibility of foul play would be naïve.

In late 918, after a prolonged siege, Edward took Nottingham, and constructed a bridge over the Trent there using the Danish prisoners of war. Whether it had been achieved by fair means or foul, Edward 'the Elder' was the undisputed victor of this latest phase of the war, no longer merely King of Wessex but King of the Anglo-Saxons.

12

BRUNANBURH (937)

Sixty years after the arrival of the Great Heathen Army, in 925, Athelstan was crowned king at Kingston-on-Thames following his father's death on campaign. His reign began with an attempt to take him hostage by agents working for Edwin, another of Edward's legitimate sons, who intended to maim and blind him so that he would be rendered unfit for the throne. The plot was foiled, and when Edwin involved himself in further intrigues Athelstan had him cast adrift at sea in a ship with no oars; he soon drowned. This is not intended to denigrate Athelstan in any way. A king who could not deal decisively with such matters was hardly likely to be able to handle the much deadlier threat from the Danes. His ruthless consolidation of power demonstrated to his enemies that he was to be taken seriously. For Athelstan intended that he should be the ruler not only of England, but overlord of Scotland, Wales and Cornwall too – the 'Emperor of Britain'. His splendid coronation was a signal of his grand political intentions, and Sihtric, the Viking King of York, was soon invited to Tamworth to meet Athelstan, who persuaded him to agree to a marriage to Edith (or Eadgyth), one of his sisters. This necessitated Sihtric's baptism in 926, but the Viking soon reverted to paganism. He died the following year, and suddenly all deals were off.

Athelstan mobilised a huge army and marched into Northumbria. His intention was to admonish the city of York and to expel the Clan Ivar, a fraternity of Norse pirates from Dublin who had installed themselves as rulers there. These were fierce, very dangerous and uncivilised heathens, but increasingly those Danes who had been born in the Danelaw identified as Christians and were accustomed to more refined sensibilities. Yet Athelstan was even more abhorrent to them, and the sight of an English army from the south marching resolutely north filled them with dread. Their fears were justified, and York was mercilessly plundered, though Athelstan ordered that no churches should be sacked. The strong Viking defences were pulled down or slighted, and the strategic trade routes snaking across the Pennines were denied to the Vikings, which soon had a knock-on effect in Dublin. No longer would Viking kings mint coins in York with their own image on them, for Athelstan ostentatiously minted his own there, bearing the legend *Rex Totius Britanniae* – 'King of all Britain'. This was no idle boast, but a statement of intent. A charter of 964 makes the scale of Athelstan's achievements clear: 'First king among the English to subdue all the nations within Britain under his arms, though none of his successors extended the boundaries of the empire further than he.' All the nations which he 'subdued' were extremely resentful, but with 15,000 men at his back Athelstan was an ineluctable force. Grudgingly, the lesser kings in the island were forced to accept the inevitable and pay him homage at a deliberately humiliating public ceremony.

On 12 July 927, Athelstan received the lesser kings at Eamont Bridge in Cumbria. Earl Ealdred of Bamburgh, King Owain of Cumbria, King Donald of Strathclyde and finally Constantine, King of the Scots all swore fealty and eternal allegiance to the English king. Constantine's son was presented for baptism, and Athelstan received him warmly from the font, just as his grandfather had done with Guthrum, and with the same implications. Mindful of the possibility of later collusion with the pagan kings of Dublin, an oath was required that they would undertake to abolish the worship of all heathen idols. Rich gifts were exchanged and the kings departed on seemingly friendly terms, but in private their thoughts were of one accord – Athelstan had to be stopped, or they were all doomed to vassalage.

Athelstan's next move only confirmed their fears. His army invaded Gwynedd, whose king, Idwal Foel 'the Bald', had withheld tribute to him. Even though he resorted to the time-honoured Welsh tactic of withdrawal into the mountains of Snowdonia, Athelstan's men forced him to capitulate. As a lesson to the other less rebellious Welsh kings, all five of them were required to submit to the English king at Hereford, as their northern counterparts had done at Eamont Bridge. They were humiliated in like fashion, and even more onerous tribute payments were exacted. From now on, every year Wales would send 20 pounds of gold, 300 pounds of silver, 25,000 oxen, and the finest hunting dogs and falcons in their realms.

This procession of military might had not quite finished, however, for Athelstan made his way into Devon, to Exeter, which was still half-British or 'West Welsh' as the Anglo-Saxons called it. According to the historian William of Malmesbury, Athelstan practised a policy of 'ethnic cleansing' there, because all Celtic speakers were expelled from the city. From now on, the West Welsh were to be strictly Cornish, and the border with Cornwall was fixed at the River Tamar. The clear message was that England was the new island superpower, and the ethnic minorities of Celts and Danes – even in areas long-since anglicised – would be tolerated only on the basis of their continuing compliance. Athelstan became a kind of international superstar, the example for all Christian monarchs – handsome, athletic, extremely well educated thanks to his esteemed aunt, a faithful friend and generous donor to the Church. It is little wonder, then, that many bitter rivals were eager to take such a man down. But how to do it?

There are three reasons why Brunanburh is an especially important battle for the purposes of this book. The first is that it is probably the last battlefield in the book that is still 'lost'. The historian Aethelweard, writing in 975 or thereabouts, says that it was still just called 'The Great Battle'. We know a great deal about the events, but the location is still disputed, with many claimants. The second reason why the battle is important is that precisely this mystery about its exact location points up one of the primary strategic objectives of an invading army we learned from Hilaire Belloc – namely that ingress into the island and successful conquest of it depends largely on several 'gateways' into the hinterland, in this case either the Humber or the Dee. Finally, Brunanburh was the battle that defined the English as a nation, and gave birth to English nationalism (as well as contributing to nascent Welsh and Scottish nationalism in the process).

Towards the conclusion of this book the resurgence of patriotism and nationalism will be examined, but in essence Brunanburh was a baptism of England in blood that produced a latent militarism in the national temperament, which can suddenly flare into life as it would later. While the UK has only small numbers in the armed forces, and has never gone in for 'Prussian-style' militarism or the military parades of the greater powers, because it has been a nation state for *so long* and because that state was born out of a relentless war which lasted 200 years (on and off), the militarism is embedded in the national character at a sublimated level. During Athelstan's reign it was a requirement of every freeborn boy in England to swear to be faithful to him at the age of sixteen, whatever their cultural origin. This deep-seated reverence for the king or queen, at an almost unconscious level, means that patriotic militarism can be invoked easily and naturally, for the most part, by reference to rituals and traditions whose opacity conceals their powerful mythic resonance. The result is that war is the normal state of affairs, not an aberration. This continues today: in the twentieth century there was only one year, 1968, in which no British service personnel were killed on active military duty.

For six years, from 928 to 934, there was relative peace. But resentment against the English power and its 'emperor' ran deep, especially in Wales. A prophecy, attributed to the bard Taliesin and called *Armes Prydein Fawr*, predicted the downfall of the English king and the triumph of the *original* Britons, the Welsh, whom they saw as the rightful heirs to the sovereignty of the island. This prophecy reminded the Welsh that it was they who possessed the real imperial credentials, from Magnus Maximus or 'Macsen'. They saw him as a countryman, a *combrogi*, whereas for all his posturing Athelstan was the descendant of pagan barbarians and a personage of little account. In short, the prophecy was a propaganda exercise to ventilate frustration with the English domination. But such sentiments were dangerous, and no king in Wales could afford to sympathise openly with such views if he wanted to avoid more brutal punishments. They all knew their limitations, and the hopeless odds against them, but there was a limit to how far they could contain the groans of the population. A Welsh cleric appears to have heard of some grand alliance:

> There will be reconciliation between the Cymry (Welsh) and the men of Dublin (Norse), the Irish of Ireland (Gaels) and Anglesey and Scotland, the men of Cornwall and of Strathclyde will be made welcome among us ... the Men of the North (Norse & Danes) will have the place of honour ... the (English) stewards (tax-collectors) at Cirencester (the place tributes were delivered) will shed bitter tears, when instead of taxes, we pay them in death!

Such inflammatory ideas were to be expected among a people so fiery and proud as the Welsh, perhaps, but Athelstan was not worried about Wales. Scotland was quite another matter, though, and when King Constantine proved contumacious (it was a long journey from Alba to Winchester) in 934, Athelstan marched his army into the north again – and this time, his demonstration of military power by both land and sea was simply awe-inspiring.

In May 934, Athelstan commanded his army to attend him at Winchester, the West Saxon capital. Less than a fortnight later this immense force reached Nottingham, where new contingents from Mercia and East Anglia joined with him. It is possible that the army which marched north to Dunnotar, near Stonehaven in Aberdeenshire, was between 15,000 and 20,000 strong – a truly overwhelming force for the time. Athelstan used exactly the same strategy as Agricola almost a millennium before, and the army was supplied by an enormous fleet which shadowed the army as it marched, finally reaching Caithness. At Chester-le-Street Athelstan visited the shrine of St Cuthbert, his grandfather's guardian spirit when he was hiding in the marshes around Athelney. Now, within just two generations, Alfred's illustrious grandson prepared to cross the border into Scotland to claim his inheritance as the undisputed 'Emperor of Britain'. Constantine had no choice but to come to terms. His son, the same one Athelstan had received from the font, was given into his care as a hostage against any further offending, and Constantine himself was taken back to England to be paraded in a humiliating display before Athelstan's court, which included many foreign dignitaries.

Constantine was allowed to return home the next year, and was determined to obtain swift revenge. His only hope of defeating Athelstan was to bring about a coalition of all the non-English speaking peoples of Britain, Norse and Celtic. But his main ambition was to conclude an alliance with the pagan Vikings of Dublin, and the 'Grandsons of Ivar the Boneless'. This was a breach of his sacred oath to Athelstan to refrain from alliances with pagans and to forbid the worship of pagan idols. He knew that this must bring Athelstan's mighty army against him, and so the allies would have to match his numbers. To stand any chance of success the allies would need a minimum of 15,000 men, and a strong defensive position in territory friendly to the Danes – somewhere in the north of England. It is an exasperating fact that we simply don't know where the 'Great Battle' was fought. Despite this, there are two particularly likely locations.

Just as in 1066, everyone knew a storm was coming, but the summer of 937 passed without incident, except that there really were storms – 'terrific winds' according to one chronicler – which prevented Anlaf (or Olaf) Guthfrithson putting to sea with his vast fleet. He had commandeered hundreds of Viking vessels for his venture, but it was late in the year before he put to sea, probably in October. We don't know where he intended to make landfall, but he must have been aiming either for the Humber or the Dee estuaries. If the former was the case, he would have had to sail around the Western Isles, past Sutherland and Caithness, and then down the east coast of England – to meet Constantine's army somewhere on the borders of the Danelaw. The Vikings of York were supportive of Anlaf, and a chronicle dated to about 1000 in York specifically states that the Vikings landed in the Humber Estuary. William of Malmesbury, the first post-Conquest historian, wrote a life of Athelstan, now unfortunately lost, but he reported that the folk of the Danelaw collaborated with the invasion. Irish annals tell a similar story, so the weight of evidence suggests the battlefield may well be somewhere in South Yorkshire. Symeon of Durham, Peter de Langtoft, and John of Worcester all concur with the story of a Viking fleet in the Humber, and a battle near to their encampment there. It is true that they wrote hundreds of years after the events, but they were much nearer in time to the events than we are, all of them were intelligent and eminent men, and, crucially, they had access to sources which have been lost to us.

Some accounts specify that a hill called 'Wendun' was chosen by the Vikings and surrounded with a ditch and palisade. Barnesdale outside Doncaster has been suggested, and Brinsworth nearby. I had an intuition that the small place called Burghwallis off the Great North Road could have been the place on many occasions, but have not established any really credible evidence. Bromford, a village in Cambridgeshire, has also been postulated, but all of these candidates depend on the Vikings having landed in the Humber. But despite all these speculations, there is a very credible candidate on the other side of the Pennines: Bromborough, on the Wirral.

Bromborough, just outside Birkenhead, has a better claim than South Yorkshire if we accept that the Viking fleet entered via the Dee rather than the Humber. At the end of the bloody slaughter, the broken Vikings escaped over a mere called 'Dingesmere', which scholars think may mean 'the sea into which the Dee flows'. A Viking fleet from Dublin, sailing so late in the year, would surely have favoured the shorter route over the Irish Sea, rather than the long and winding journey around Scotland to the Humber. Bromborough seems to have actually been called Brunanburh, and Professors Stephen Harding and Judith Jesch of the Centre for Viking Studies at the University of Nottingham have offered good academic evidence that Bromborough is the battlefield. Much has been made of the fact that the invading armies received active support from their Viking cousins in the Danelaw, supporting the Humber theory, but there was also a colony of Vikings on the Wirral, around Hoylake, quite near to Bromborough. The Scots and Strathclyde Welsh could have just as easily marched south through Cumbria (friendly territory for them) as through Northumberland, Durham and into Yorkshire. Exasperating though it is, no definitive site for the battlefield can yet be identified, but as to its progress and outcome, we have abundant and detailed evidence.

Athelstan lost no time in responding to the invasions, despite the opinion of William of Malmesbury, who alleged that he dithered too long before calling out his army. We know this is not true, because by the time Athelstan confronted the allied forces, his army was not yet fully concentrated. To fool the Scots and Vikings, he ordered tents for twice as many men as he had with him to be pitched, while his remaining forces from all over England followed a few days' march behind. He also doubled the campfires at night, and sent messengers to ask for a parley with Constantine, Anlaf and Owain of Strathclyde. These negotiations were a ruse to gain three days before his entire force was assembled.

Once backup arrived, the Mercian and West Saxon divisions were drawn up before the fortified hill of Wendun, perhaps 20,000 heavily armed troops supplemented by many hundreds of professional Viking mercenaries in Athelstan's pay. Opposing them, the combined allied force was probably almost as large, perhaps 15,000 strong. The English attacked at dawn, Mercians against the Vikings and West-Saxons fighting the Scots and Welsh. It was a truly titanic struggle, which went on all day (some traditions say two days). The Irish chroniclers described it as 'immense, lamentable, and desperately fought'. No quarter was asked or given by either side and thousands of men were killed. As the sun dipped the Strathclyde Welsh finally broke ranks and fled. The furious English smashed through the gap thus made in the allied line, causing a general retreat into the woods and meres nearby. Athelstan's forces pursued them through the night to their ships, slaughtering any found hiding with 'cruel blades whetted on grindstone'. Only a few Vikings ever made it home to Ireland, including Anlaf. They left five other kings, seven jarls and Constantine's son dead on the battlefield. Constantine himself managed to escape somehow. The death toll among the English was just as high, certainly into the thousands slain. But the victory was a triumph for Athelstan, and for the entire English nation. The *Anglo-Saxon Chronicle*, usually quite a dry record, was ecstatic about the battle:

> In this year (937) King Athelstan, lord of warriors,
> Ring-giver of men, with his brother, prince Edmund (the Magnificent),
> Won undying glory with the edges of swords,
> In warfare around Brunanburh,
> With their hammered blades, the sons of Edward,
> Clove the shield-wall and hacked the linden bucklers,
> As was instinctive in them from their ancestry ...

All through the day the West Saxons in troops
Pressed on in pursuit of the hostile peoples,
Fiercely, with swords whetted on grindstone,
They cut down the fugitives as they fled.
Nor did the Mercians refuse hard fighting ...
To any of Anlaf's army who invaded our lands
From across the tossing waters,
In the ships bosom, they gave death in battle.
Five young kings, stretched lifeless by the sword
Lay dead on the field, likewise
Seven of Anlaf's Jarls, and a countless number of
Vikings and Scots ...
The chief of the Norsemen, compelled by necessity,
Was forced to flee to the prow of his ship
With but a handful of men. In haste the ship
Was launched, and Anlaf fled hence,
Over the waters grey, to save his life.

The *Chronicle* is exultant, too, at the traitor Constantine's
misfortune:

No cause had he
To exult in that clash of swords,
Bereaved of his kinsmen, robbed of his friends
On the field of battle,
By violence deprived of them
In the struggle.
On the place of slaughter he left his young son,
Mangled by wounds he received in the fight ...

Finally, the panegyric gets to the point. The long battle for
the sovereignty of Britain is now over. The English 'the Welsh
overcame' to win the land, over centuries of struggle, and then
for three generations they had been forced to defend their new
homeland against the heathen Northmen. But at Brunanburh the

West Saxon royal bloodline, the *Cerdicings*, have won the whole island, and established the power of the English throne over all peoples in it:

> Likewise the English king and the prince,
> Brothers triumphant in war together
> Returned to their homeland of Wessex.
> To celebrate the carnage, they left behind
> The horn-beaked raven with dusky plumage,
> And the hungry hawk of battle,
> The dun-coated eagle with white-tipped tail
> Shared the feast with the wolf, grey beast of the forest.

The Vikings were pagans, and so their dead were left on the field of battle to rot, along with the Scots and Welsh, who were oathbreakers:

> Never before in the history of this island
> As the books of ancient scholars tell us,
> Was an army put to greater slaughter by the sword
> Not since the days when the Angles and Saxons first landed
> Invading Britain from across the wide seas
> From the east,
> When warriors eager for fame,
> Proud forgers of war, the Welsh overcame,
> To win for themselves a kingdom.

Aethelweard's *Chronicon* intimated that the battle was as convincing a victory over the Danes as Badon had been for the Britons over the Saxons: 'The barbarians were overcome on every side and held no superiority anywhere ... all parts of Britain were consolidated into one, so that there was peace and abundance of all things everywhere.' The battle was celebrated all over Europe, and all other monarchs looked to Athelstan as their model, he who 'instilled terror into all the enemies of the fatherland'.

So why, over 1,000 years afterwards, do all English schoolchildren know about the Battle of Hastings, but virtually none about Brunanburh? My own suspicion is that the later Norman historians were obliged to downplay Athelstan and his achievements, especially Brunanburh. His was just the kind of story to inspire his countrymen and tempt them into rebellion. After 1066, Anglo-Saxon heroes (with the exceptions of Alfred the Great and Edward the Confessor, who were 'special cases') ceased to exist. A conquered English people would have to make do with renegade heroes like Robin Hood and Edric 'the Wild'. Yet, despite the attempt to airbrush Athelstan and Brunanburh out of history, ironically his great victory was the very pinnacle of English military might and international political prestige. It was too good to last, of course. On 27 October 939, Athelstan died at Gloucester without an heir. There was probably a private compact that he would be succeeded by his brother Edmund 'the Magnificent', who had fought gallantly alongside him in the battle. Fortune is fickle, as we will presently see, but for the time being England was at the peak of its powers, and all its enemies were cowed.

But given time, all things pass away.

1. Caer Caradoc hill fort, overlooking the tiny village of Chapel Lawn outside Clun. Tradition relates that this was where Caratacus was finally defeated. (Photograph by S. Rae)

2. Caratacus and his captive family in Rome, where he was to plead successfully for their lives to be spared. (Courtesy of the Library of Congress)

3. Boudicca, the avenging goddess who almost ended Roman rule in the island. (Photograph by Luke McKernan)

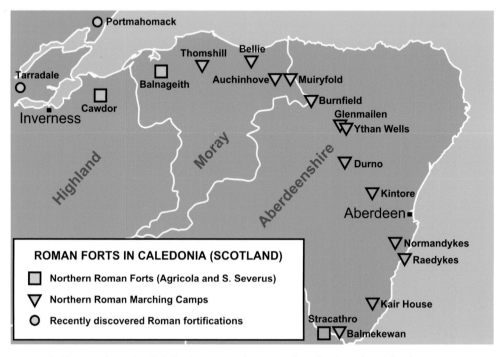

ROMAN FORTS IN CALEDONIA (SCOTLAND)

◻ Northern Roman Forts (Agricola and S. Severus)

▽ Northern Roman Marching Camps

◯ Recently discovered Roman fortifications

4. Roman forts in Caledonia. Somewhere nearby, the last free islanders were defeated by Agricola.

5. Badbury Rings, a potential candidate for Mount Badon. (Photograph by Jim Champion)

6. Cadbury Castle. Tradition states that Arthur's Camelot may once have stood here. (Photograph by Hugh Llewelyn)

7. River Swale at Catterick, N. Yorks. Here, the last British heroes made a suicidal cavalry charge against the Anglo-Saxon foe. (Photograph by Colin Gregory)

8. St Oswald's Church, Heavenfield, Northumberland. Oswald smashed Cadwallon's Welsh army and liberated Northumbria. (Photograph by Mike Bishop)

Above: 9. Oswestry from the air. The Welsh mountains loom in the background. Oswald was traditionally killed nearby, and his army slaughtered by the pagan king Penda of Mercia. (Photograph by John Mc Linden)

Left: 10. Repton Church, Derbyshire. The Great Heathen Army fortified the church during their lightning invasion of England. (Photograph by Paul Dixon)

11. Anglo-Saxon carved cross in Wolverhampton city centre. Within miles of this place, the Battle of Tettenhall was fought – probably at Wednesfield. (Photograph by Elliot Brown)

12. The ancient Coronation Stone at Kingston upon Thames, where Athelstan was finally crowned as king. (Photograph by Loco Steve)

13. Athelstan's tomb in Malmesbury Abbey. In his reign, England reached the zenith of its military power. (Photograph by Hugh Llewelyn)

14. Statue of Byrhtnoth at Maldon, Essex. The gigantic warrior still guards the narrow causeway he defended to the death. (Photograph by Shirokazan)

15. St Andrew's Church, Ashingdon, Essex. Cnut built the church to commemorate the thousands of fallen on both sides. (Photograph by W. J. Prior)

16. Stamford Bridge Battlefield monument, N. Yorks. The glorious last victory of Anglo-Saxon arms in 1066. (Photograph by Shirokazan)

Above: 17. The battlefield of Hastings. The Anglo-Danish army lined up in a shield wall where the abbey now stands. (Photograph by Jim Linwood)

Below: 18. A typical Norman castle of the motte-and-bailey type. William I quickly dominated England with a network of these fortifications. (Photograph by John Fielding)

Above: 19. Lewes Castle, where Simon de Montfort routed the forces of King Henry III and his son Prince Edward. (Photograph by Richard Gailey)

Right: 20. Evesham, Worcestershire. The narrow medieval streets became the scene of 'the murder of Evesham – for battle it was not'. (Photograph by Dr Bob Hall)

Below right: 21. Bryn Glas battlefield, also called Pilleth. At last, this famous Welsh victory is properly commemorated. (Photograph by Gwenddolen)

22. The 'field of peas' upon which the Battle of Shrewsbury was desperately fought. The church was built as a memorial to the 7,000 men who died. (Photograph by Andrew/ARG_Flickr)

23. Blore Heath, Staffordshire. Where sheep quietly graze today, 4,000 men lost their lives as the Wars of the Roses resumed in deadly earnest. (Photograph by Chris/cr01)

24. Kingsland, Herefordshire. At Mortimer's Cross nearby, the Yorkists turned the tide of the war in their favour. (Photograph by Amanda Slater)

25. Tewkesbury Abbey, Gloucestershire. Here King Edward IV defeated Queen Margaret and her son in a vicious contest. (Photograph by Alistair Rae)

26. King Richard's Well memorial at Bosworth Field. Henry Tudor was crowned king on the battlefield, but the climax of the Wars of the Roses was yet to come. (Photograph by Amanda Slater)

27. The River Teme at Powick Bridge, Worcestershire, 'where England's sorrows began' at the outbreak of the First English Civil War. (Photograph by Iain Cuthbertson)

28. View of Edgehill battlefield. (Photograph by Feathering the Nest)

29. Roundway Down battlefield, where the 'Royalist Summer' reached its climax. (Photograph by Sarah J. Dow, A.R.P.S.)

30. Marston Moor Memorial, N. Yorks. Prince Rupert's defeat here doomed the Royalist cause. (Photograph by Shirokazan)

31. River Cherwell at Cropredy, Oxfordshire. This small victory emboldened King Charles I to confront the New Model Army. (Photograph by Rob Glover)

32. Naseby battlefield monument. The battle developed almost exactly as at Edgehill, ending in catastrophe for the king. (Photograph by Shirokazan)

33. Oliver Cromwell. His protectorate was under constant threat from English rebels – and the Scots. (Photograph by Judy Dean)

34. King Charles I. His constant intrigues with Scottish and Irish sympathizers finally sent him to the scaffold. (Photograph by Ann Longmore-Etheridge)

Above left: 35. Charles II. His brave attempt to avenge his father's execution was thwarted at Worcester, where his Scots army was brought to bay by Cromwell. (Photograph by Ann Longmore-Etheridge)

Above right: 36. Monument at Fort Royal, Worcester, where the Royalist artillery overlooked the city walls. (Photograph by Elliot Brown)

Above left: 37. The Commandery, Worcester. Charles escaped through the packed streets of the city only by the skin of his teeth. (Photograph by Andrea Vail)

Below left: 38. James Scott, Duke of Monmouth. An illegitimate son of Charles II, he sought to depose his uncle, King James II. His army of farm labourers acquitted themselves manfully. (Courtesy of Yale Center for British Art)

Below: 39. The King's Sedgemoor Drain, Somerset. In a stiff contest fought in the darkness, Monmouth's army was overcome by professional soldiers in what was hopefully the last battle to be fought on English soil. (Photograph by Jeremy Halls)

MALDON, ESSEX (991)

It is a measure of Norse resilience that when Athelstan suddenly died just two years after his famous victory they were immediately emboldened to conspire with Anlaf Guthfrithson yet again. Anlaf met with initial success, recaptured the five boroughs, and marched as far south as Northampton. He turned north to pillage Tamworth, and took many important English hostages there. King Edmund had no choice but to make a temporary peace with Anlaf, and fortunately for the English king he was killed while campaigning against Oswulf, a Northumbrian ealdorman. This gave Edmund the opportunity he needed to restore his authority over York, and eventually the emergency passed. Edmund was unfortunately killed in a brawl by a man named Leof at Pucklechurch, and was succeeded by his brother, Edred. Archbishop Wulfstan of York, who seems to have spent more time intriguing with the Vikings than ministering to his archdiocese, immediately invited a notorious Viking freebooter, ominously called Eric 'Bloodaxe', to become the new ruler in York. Eric was a Norwegian who had been exiled for various misdemeanours from his homeland. He was a vicious pagan, and uncivilised, but Wulfstan arranged for Eric and his family to be baptised so that he could quickly take up residence at the 'King's Garth' in York.

In 948, Edred invaded with a large army and 'overran all Northumberland'. Ripon, with its beautiful basilica and cathedral built by St Wilfred, one of the glories of Europe, was deliberately burned. While Edred was devastating Northumbria, Eric discovered a small detachment of his force at Castleford and destroyed it. The main English army threatened York, and to save the city from Ripon's grim fate the citizens surrendered. Edred, who was perhaps in ill health, and certainly ill tempered, withdrew his army, but as soon as he did so the crafty Wulfstan invited another Viking chieftain, Olaf, to become king in Eric's place. Meanwhile, Eric 'Bloodaxe' was still at large, and returned to claim the throne of York. He immediately cleared the Scottish border region of bandits but was killed in an ambush at Stainmore in the Eden Valley alongside his brother and his son. With the death of this archetypal Viking character, the age of the 'old-fashioned' Vikings was over. They would return in time, but from this point it will be more accurate to describe them as 'Danes' than 'Vikings' – and increasingly as 'Anglo-Danes'. In this relatively quiet period, England experienced something which must have seemed very strange – not only an absence of war, but actual peace.

Edred died just a year after Eric 'Bloodaxe'. The new English king, Edwy, was young and headstrong, and alienated key courtiers sufficiently that plots were hatched to replace him with his brother Edgar. When Edwy suddenly died, Edgar 'the Peaceful', as he became known, succeeded him, and the inchoate nation of England, free from external enemies, experienced a flowering of its spiritual, economic and indeed military potential. He had no need to flex his military muscle; an ostentatious display of his supremacy was all that was required. Shortly after his (second) coronation at Bath in 973, the *Anglo-Saxon Chronicle* records that he 'led all his marine force to Chester; and there came to meet him six kings; and they all covenanted with him and took him for their lord and swore to be his faithful allies by land and sea'. The six kings were then required to row Edgar out to his waiting ship as a sign of their inferior rank.

Edgar's fleet was massive, and its ships were state-of-the-art, depriving the Vikings of their long-held supremacy at sea. English ships intimidated Continental and Scandinavian powers, and Flemish and Viking mercenaries were hired as Edgar's own bodyguards. These were full-time professionals, but Edgar could also call upon an army of 20,000 at will – meaning that the English army and navy were probably the most numerous and effective in northern Europe at the time. Three separate fleets, each of 120 ships, were on continuous patrol each summer when Viking raids were most frequent.

Suddenly, in 975, Edgar died aged just thirty-two. The 'golden years' were over, and great national troubles seemed imminent when, shortly afterwards, a great comet appeared. The Anglo-Saxons took this for an ill omen, and their instinct proved correct when the next harvest failed and a terrible famine ensued. The new king, Edward, was a rather petulant teenager, and difficult to advise. When he exacerbated the famine-stricken population's woes by decimating the monastic system, many looked to his younger brother Ethelred as an alternative.

Eventually, Edward 'the Martyr', as he became known, was murdered by his stepmother Elfrida while visiting her residence at Corfe in Dorset. In 978, the ten-year-old Ethelred 'the Unready' began a reign which was to last for thirty-eight gruelling years. This was an invitation to the Vikings to test the English defences with sporadic raids – they no longer intended settlement. Their motive now was to turn the English king and the civil service Edgar had created into their tax collectors. The *Danegeld* was a tax levied on land which was used to buy off the Danes – protection money, in effect. But much of the silver collected was creamed off by corrupt English officials, and this eroded trust in national institutions, including the Church. The people of the Danelaw particularly resented English domination, and were eager to reassert their previous autonomy.

All this could perhaps have been contained, or even made satisfactory, had it not been for Ethelred's character. As he grew older it became clear that Ethelred was not fated to be in the glorious company of Alfred, Athelstan and Edgar. He was lazy, indecisive, cowardly, vengeful, cruel and, above all, impossible to advise – 'unready' actually means 'ill advised'. In 981, seven shiploads of Danes appeared off Southampton and left it in flames, slaughtering the men and taking the saleable women as slaves. The blissful years of peace were well and truly at an end.

The proud martial spirit or *ofermod* of the Anglo-Saxons had been fostered over generations of bloody conflict with the Danes. These were men such as are rarely to be found in our days – literal giants. When the skeleton of the hero of this chapter, Byrhtnoth, was exhumed at Ely Cathedral in 1769, his *headless* body was estimated to have been 6 feet 9 inches in height. These were the kind of men who had kept the Viking threat at bay for so long, and Byrhtnoth was their last great representative. An impressive statue of him now stands over the battlefield. In 991, a fleet of Danes, Norwegians and other Baltic pirates ravaged the east coast in a fleet of ninety-three ships. The *Chronicle* says:

> In this year Ipswich was harried and very soon afterwards ealdorman Byrhtnoth was slain at Maldon … it was decided to pay tribute to the Danes because of the great terror they inspired all along the coast … on this occasion it amounted to 10,000 pounds in silver. This course was advised by Archbishop Sigeric …

Maldon was a bitter and terrible defeat for the English and ushered in three decades of such unrelenting chaos, misery and distress that the foundations of the state never recovered. Paradoxically, this humiliation was not deliberately downplayed or forgotten, nor was Byrhtnoth's memory execrated. For Maldon was, like Dunkirk in 1940, a glorious defeat, and became the subject of probably the most celebrated Anglo-Saxon battle poem, *The Battle of Maldon*.

Olaf Tryggvason, the Norwegian king, took the combined Viking force of roughly 4,000 men to Northey Island outside Maldon, intending to cross an extremely narrow causeway to the mainland when it emerged at low tide. Byrhtnoth, despite being well over sixty, was a wily commander, and knew that his force of about 2,500 men must fight a defensive battle. Not only was he outnumbered, but only his personal household troops were of high quality, perhaps 300 men in all; the rest belonged to the part-time *fyrd*. These yeomen were brave, but ill equipped and inexperienced. Their only hope of success lay in holding the Vikings on the narrow causeway itself, and as soon as the pirates moved on to the thin strip they were targeted by English arrows and spears to great effect.

Despite his superior numbers, there was little Olaf could do to break the deadlock. He had already appealed to Byrhtnoth to end the bloodshed by paying tribute, which the old ealdorman contemptuously rejected. Next the Vikings appealed to Byrhtnoth's *ofermod*, his sense of honour. A messenger cried out that the fight was not a fair one because the two armies could not face up to each other man to man. If he would let the Vikings cross, then a proper battle could be fought with an honourable victory for one side or another. Seeing that it was only a matter of time until seaborne Viking reinforcements outflanked him, Byrhtnoth acceded to the Viking request, and the grim-faced warriors filed over the causeway to draw up opposite the English ranks.

It was a fatal blunder, of course, but it was no disgrace. A disgrace would have been to accept the Viking peace terms – blackmail – as Ethelred was to do for the remaining years of his miserable reign. The Viking tactics were simple. The giant ealdorman, over 7 feet tall, stood among his elite household troops in the centre, resplendent in the finest armour, beneath fluttering pennants – an easy target. He was quickly overwhelmed and killed, but his kinsmen, faithful friends and hearthside troops refused to leave their lord's body to be desecrated. As the *fyrd* broke and fled to the rear, the guard stood firm, faithful to their *beots*, the mead oaths taken in exchange for receiving weapons. The poem says:

Thought shall be the harder, heart the keener, courage the greater, as our strength lessens. Here lies our leader, all for hewn in the dust, that valiant man; may he lament forever who thinks now to turn from this battle-play. I am an old man, too old to flee, but instead purpose to lie here beside the body of my stricken lord, he who I have dearly loved!

The surviving English were soon overpowered and slain, but their deaths had not been in vain. The old giant Byrhtnoth was a last wistful glimpse of the days when the English offered 'spears for tribute; you will not gain treasure so easily here; point and blade shall bring us together first, grim battle-play before we pay tribute!' It was comforting for the immiserated English people to remember the deeds of such men as Byrhtnoth, for Ethelred henceforth chose the more cowardly policy of buying the Danes off with silver. First it was 10,000 pounds later that year; in 994 it was 16,000 pounds; in 1007, the tribute rose to a staggering 30,000 pounds in silver. Eventually, the Archbishop of Canterbury, Alphege, was taken hostage and a tribute of 3,000 pounds in silver demanded as his ransom. When there was a delay in delivering this, the archbishop was brutally murdered. The Danes now saw that it lay within their power to depose the cowardly English king and seize control of the entire kingdom.

Year by year, Ethelred's pitiful reign dragged on. English fortunes sank. Archbishop Wulfstan II, who had replaced the murdered Alphege, spoke for the entire English people when he groaned that the Danes 'humiliate us daily, despite our payments. They ravage and pillage and burn, plunder and steal and take everything we own to their ships. And lo! What other thing can be clearer, and more evident from these events, than that God is angry with us!' England, once so mighty, had indeed fallen very far from grace. Only a hero, a man of the old school, could save them now – but could such an Englishman still be found in such fallen times? Could a new Alfred, a *Cerdicing*, rescue England again in its darkest hour? The answer, of course, was a resounding yes – but only for a brief season.

14

ASSANDUN/ASHINGDON, ESSEX (1016)

The Danish onslaught intensified just at the time of maximum psychological vulnerability for the English. Although Abbo of Fleury, a leading churchman of the time, condemned the millenarian notion that the Devil would be unleashed in the year 1000 as had been prophesied by St John, the common people came to see the Danes as servitors of Satan, a malicious visitation on them for their sins. These sins were manifold and obvious in the early eleventh-century English state, from the king downward. Archbishop Wulfstan II was so concerned that he felt moved to write a sermon to the English people as a whole called *Sermo Lupi Ad Anglos*, 'the Sermon of the Wolf to the English'. This was read out in every important church in the country, and amounted to a rebuke to Ethelred's corrupt and treacherous regime. But Wulfstan was not content to imply that the king and his wicked advisors – such as one Edric Streona, of whom we will hear more shortly – were at fault; the whole rotten edifice of the English state was to blame for a widespread breakdown in the traditional moral order.

The Danes, it should be said, were *not* the only target for Wulfstan's complaint. They had by now become Christianised, though many still venerated the elder gods in private. Indeed, they were probably more respectable citizens than their Anglo-Saxon neighbours by this time – certainly they were wealthier, living in prosperous trading ports and towns – but their pagan ancestors had generally coarsened the culture. It was largely thanks to the influence of the Vikings that the English learned to swear so well, for example. There was also a lively sex trade, and English (and Irish) women were shipped all over Europe by Viking slavers. Prostitution became rife as well as drunkenness and, most pernicious of all, black magic. Wulfstan was particularly disgusted at the practice whereby men clubbed together to buy a woman for their collective use as a sex slave. Moreover, despite heavy taxation to appease the Danes, they roamed around the country at will, usually unopposed by English forces. It was the same story at sea, with Danish and Baltic pirates appearing on an almost annual basis. Ethelred was powerless and feeble, regularly taking to his bed during the periods of most pressing crisis. But there was one way he could retaliate against the Danes and turn popular opinion in his favour; he wouldn't even have to go to war to do it.

Ethelred sent out sealed instructions to the king's deputies and tithing officers in all his domains south of the Trent. On Friday 13 November 1002, St Brice's Day, the church bells would ring for early Mass. This would be the signal for death squads to gather and attack the Danish quarters of the large towns. Some stories say that the mobs broke in on them while they were taking their traditional weekly bath. In Oxford the Danes managed to barricade themselves into St Frideswide's Church, where Christ Church Cathedral now stands. They were burned out, and seemingly executed – a mass grave recently found nearby may have contained the remains of some of these unfortunate victims. The pogrom engulfed London, where fleeing Danes were trapped on London Bridge and slain or drowned by jumping into the Thames. During excavations to build the London Olympic Stadium for the 2012 games, forty headless skeletons were discovered, seemingly unfortunate Danes whose heads were buried separately nearby. There were important victims among the dead, including Gunhilde, sister of King Sweyn Forkbeard of

Denmark. Sweyn swore an oath on the 'bragging cup', that he would kill Ethelred and take England for his own. His revenge was truly terrifying, as we will see.

But how had Ethelred been so foolish as to make such a catastrophic mistake? According to tradition, the idea of a pogrom, the 'St Brice's Day Massacre' as it became known, was first mooted by one of the great 'villains' of English history, Edric Streona. When Ethelred was forced to make restitution for the rebuilding of St Frideswide's Church and central Oxford, he described the Danes as being 'cockles among the wheat', a pestilence to be exterminated. Streona was a minor nobleman from the Shropshire border with Wales. He was wily, ambitious and shrewd; moreover, he was absolutely ruthless in his pursuit of political power. He intruded his brother Beorhtric as admiral of a new English fleet which was under construction, and eventually rose to become the Earl of Mercia – a virtual viceroy. For some reason Edric seems to have been immune from criticism so far as Ethelred was concerned, and as Streona schemed to arrange a royal marriage to the king's daughter, a mere girl, the former thegn's star continued to rise despite his brother wrecking the English fleet in a storm.

With leaders such as this, England was doomed. Finally, in 1013, Sweyn invaded with an army of 10,000. He landed in the north, in the Danelaw, where as many men again joined him, and then this huge host marched south. Sweyn gave explicit orders that every town and village south of the Watling Street was to be burned if it did not submit to him as the rightful king of all England. Only London, safe behind its ancient walls, stood out against him. The desperate Ethelred sent his wife and sons to Normandy by ship. He joined them but disembarked at the Isle of Wight to see what would happen next. At Christmas, he was given the news that he had been deposed. The English nobles had offered the throne to Sweyn. Seeing that all was now lost, the hapless Ethelred took ship for Normandy. After so many centuries, the dynasty of the *Cerdicings* seemed to be over.

The next few months in English history proved so extraordinarily dramatic that an Elizabethan play was written about them.[22] The author was anonymous, but stylistic similarities to later works by one William Shakespeare led several experts to conclude that this was indeed an early work of the Bard himself. Sweyn returned to his son Cnut at Gainsborough in Lincolnshire where he was guarding the Danish fleet. He was preparing to march his army in triumph into London when Sweyn suddenly collapsed and died in early February 1014. Many Englishmen saw this as a miraculous intervention by St Edmund, whose shrine Sweyn had threatened. Cnut, Sweyn's son, was young and inexperienced.

Seeing their chance, the English nobles immediately wrote to Ethelred in Normandy, promising that he would be restored without recriminations if 'you will only agree to rule us better than before'. Ethelred sent his son Edward to England to test the waters, and sometime before Easter Ethelred returned to a rapturous reception in London. On this solitary occasion Ethelred proved as good as his word. He gathered an immense army which he personally led into the Danelaw. The area around Lindsey, which had supported Sweyn, was devastated. Vastly outnumbered, Cnut wisely put to sea with his fleet. As a retaliation for the treachery of the English nobles, all his English hostages were put ashore at Sandwich with their noses slit and hands cut off among other mutilations. There was another fleet of Danish and Baltic freebooters blockading the Thames at Greenwich, but they were content to withdraw on payment of 21,000 pounds in silver.

Within months, this most unfortunate of kings had achieved a dramatic turnaround. But character, as they say, is fate, and it was not long before Ethelred returned to his old ways.

By now, Edric Streona's influence over Ethelred was so insidious that he was king in all but name. Edric advised the king to call

---

22. *Edmund Ironside, or War Hath Made All Friends*

a great national council at Oxford, where the representatives of the Danelaw could put their case for reparations for Ethelred's devastation of the region the previous year. Two of the most powerful representatives of the Danelaw, Sigferth and Morcar, were also political allies of Ethelred's handsome and dashing young son, Edmund, called 'Ironside' because of his prodigious martial strength. Edric, who opposed Edmund's succession, had the two men abducted and then murdered in a tavern. Edmund, who was a popular hero among the common people of England, raised an ill-equipped but militant army of rebels. Streona panicked and went over to the Danes with forty ships of the fleet. Cnut raced to besiege London, and with the Danes hammering at the gates, and surrounded by dykes to prevent incoming supplies, the news came that after thirty-eight long years Ethelred the 'Unready' had died on St George's Day 1016. The English nobles endorsed Edmund 'Ironside' as the new king, but it was now clear that a bitter and bloody civil war was inevitable.

Edmund gathered a small army of Anglo-Danes from the five boroughs and invaded West Mercia, Streona's stronghold. Cnut immediately retaliated by harrying into Warwickshire, and during the winter of 1016 many of Edmund's northern allies, such as Utred of Northumbria, deserted his cause and went over to Cnut. In spring Cnut and Edric confronted Edmund's peasant army at Penselwood near Gillingham. The English were by now full of fight, and Edmund was a leader to compare with Alfred and Athelstan. The shocked Cnut had to settle for a bloody draw, and gathered his forces for another attempt. In June 1016, at Sherston just outside Malmesbury, Edmund's army faced Cnut and Edric again. In an epic struggle, the enraged English, including a giant yeoman named 'John Rattlebone' who fought with a huge club, smashed the Danes after two days of continuous fighting. Seeing that Edmund's men were about to break through the Danish line, the dastardly Streona killed one of his own men who bore a remarkable resemblance to Edmund. He then hacked off the man's head and held it aloft, claiming that Edmund was dead.

But it was too late to fool the triumphant English, and at last, after so many years of humiliation, an English king had decisively defeated the Danes.

Dismayed, Cnut withdrew to protect his fleet, and to tighten the ring around London, still defiantly besieged by his forces. Cnut was wisely advised by his experienced commanders Thurkill 'the Tall' and Eric Hlathir of Norway to draw Edmund's army into a prepared confrontation outside London. Because of the considerable barrier posed by the Thames, it was supposed that any attack must come from the south bank of the river, but Edmund cleverly forded the river upstream with his forces and marched them swiftly east along the north bank. When Edmund's army suddenly appeared at Clayhill Farm (now Devonshire Hill) just north of the city, the Danes immediately panicked. In their haste to cross the river, many hundreds drowned.

London was at last relieved, but Edmund's strategic priority was to pursue Cnut's army and destroy it. Cnut's fleet landed his army in Essex to reprovision and await reinforcements from Denmark. A Danish fleet harried the coast of Kent, but Edmund prevented a further landing there. At Otford, the sight of the famous English king proved enough to panic Cnut's previously superior army, and they withdrew to the Isle of Sheppey rather than face him in battle again. Seeing that the tide was turning, the perfidious Streona met Edmund at Aylesford and offered to abandon Cnut and fight alongside his fellow countrymen once more – in exchange for a royal pardon. Desperately short of men, money and horses, all of which Streona could supply readily, the king agreed to reinstate him. As the *Chronicle* observed: 'No greater error of judgement was ever made than this.' But Edmund seemed to the Anglo-Saxons to be a kind of superhero, gallant, virile (his new wife quickly bore him twins) and faithful to the *ofermod*. He was, in short, everything his father was not, and the whole English nation looked to him to liberate them after generations of defeat and misfortune. The battle could not wait, and both sides now prepared for the greatest military confrontation in England since Brunanburh.

The Battle of Assandun, almost certainly modern Ashingdon, near Southend in Essex (although several other credible candidates exist), took place almost exactly fifty years before the Battle of Hastings, on 18 October 1016. The battle proved to be a similar debacle for the English, despite Edmund's charisma and the most concerted military effort by the Anglo-Saxons since Athelstan's day. Three separate divisions – one from Wessex, one from East Anglia and another from Mercia, the latter under the command of the notorious Edric Streona – drew up in front of the Danish army, which was defending the high ground of Assandun, or 'the hill of ash trees'. Cnut's army was probably about 10,000 strong, but Edmund's force probably numbered 15,000 or more. However, the Danes dominated Beacon Hill and were well prepared and resolute. According to an account from 1035, Cnut had every reason to be confident despite Edmund's apparent superiority; he knew that Streona, who commanded one-third of the English forces, was actually a double agent in his employ.

Edmund ordered the entire English host to kneel before the relics of the holy St Wendreda, which were carried in a casket to the battlefield all the way from Ely. In the English ranks stood the famous hero Ulfkytel, who had defied Sweyn's army and fought them to a standstill as long ago as 1004. After prayers, the English assaulted. After savage fighting, they were repulsed. Edmund rallied his men, leading another furious assault on the Danish line. At a crucial stage, Streona called out to his men that the Danes were too strong and ordered his third of the army to retreat. The wily Earl of Mercia had sold his country down the river for his own personal gain, and the exhausted Danes now went on the offensive. Ulfkytel was slain, along with many other English noblemen like Wulsy, Ednoth, Godwin of Lindsey, Aethelweard and Aelfric. As the moon shone over the field of carnage, thousands upon thousands lay dead alongside them – including Danes. Cnut built a church, St Luke's (the battle took place on St Luke's Day), as a memorial to the thousands slain on both sides. But it was the English who suffered most grievously. The chroniclers wrote that 'all the flower of the English race perished' and that 'Cnut was the victor and won all England by his victory'. There was only one last desperate hope for the English as a cruel winter approached: their gallant king had escaped. Could Edmund, like his illustrious ancestor Alfred, defy all odds and return to lead his people to victory?

Edmund was left with only a small band of hardcore followers, who retreated with him into the Forest of Dean in hopes of eluding the Danes until spring. Streona's lands lay nearby, and it was not long before Edmund was trapped on all sides. At this point he made an extraordinary appeal to Cnut to settle the matter of the war by means of a personal duel, a tradition whereby the two combatants fought each other to the death on an island to preclude treachery. Traditions state that Cnut foolishly accepted the challenge, and that the men fought for the fate of England on the Isle of Olney in the River Severn. Cnut is said to have cried out for mercy to Edmund, but in all likelihood these traditions are either false or gross embellishments. Cnut had nothing to gain by accepting the challenge of the *Holm Ganga*, as the Vikings called the ritual combat, but everything to lose. The two men really did meet, though, and it was under more peaceful circumstances. At Deerhurst in Gloucestershire, Edmund and Cnut met to agree a treaty, exchanging rich gifts and embracing one another as Christian brothers. Edmund would retain the kingdom of Wessex, and the dynasty of the *Cerdicings* would live on, but Mercia, East Anglia and Northumbria went to Cnut. If either man died without heirs, then his portion was to pass to the survivor. Streona was, according to tradition, deeply involved in these negotiations, and we should not be surprised to learn that what seemed like a fairly good deal for Edmund was actually too good to be true.

By the terms of the treaty, Edmund was allowed to visit his former domains providing he brought only a few armed followers. During late November 1016, Edmund seems to have visited Headington outside Oxford. On St Andrew's Day 1016, two household servants installed by Streona murdered Edmund as he sat on the privy. Elaborate tales grew up suggesting that a crossbow had been set up beneath the lavatory, and fired an arrow into Edmund's rectum. Other, more likely tales state that the deed was done by an accomplice lurking beneath with a 'very sharp knife'. Cnut was an obvious suspect as an instigator, and it was probably to deflect this suspicion that he arranged for Streona to take the blame. Cnut promised the English traitor that he would 'set (him) higher than any man in all England' as a reward for his collaboration. The new Danish King of England was as good as his word. On Christmas Day 1016, during an acrimonious game of chess, Cnut had Streona arrested. He was garrotted, flayed alive and decapitated, his body hacked into pieces to be thrown to the stray dogs of the city. His head was indeed raised higher 'than any man in England', spiked atop the highest house on London Bridge – a salutary lesson to all traitors. Final defeat at the hands of the Danes was now a grim reality for the English as they became part of a powerful new Scandinavian empire ruled by Cnut. But the story of Anglo-Saxon independence was not quite finished.

15

'THE LAST VICTORY': GATE FULFORD AND STAMFORD BRIDGE, NORTH YORKSHIRE (1066)

England paid a very heavy price – 80,500 pounds in silver – to Cnut, who now had the authority to dismiss the majority of his army and fleet. He retained forty ships' crews of elite huscarls as his personal bodyguard. Thurkill 'the Tall' and Eric of Hlathir were given the earldoms of East Anglia and Northumbria respectively. An English collaborator named Godwin was given the newly created earldom of Sussex as his reward. At the same time, Cnut immediately made two extremely wise political moves. Wulfstan, whose Sermon of the Wolf had been such an excoriating condemnation of Ethelred's regime, was chosen to be the king's chief advisor and tutor in the arts of English kingship. At his instruction Cnut deliberately projected a humble persona, visiting the tomb of his old adversary Edmund at Glastonbury. He knelt and publicly prayed there, leaving a richly embroidered cloak on the tomb depicting peacocks, the symbol of resurrection. This symbolism was calculated, for although the Danes had conquered England the West Saxon royal line continued. Edward and Alfred, both *Cerdicings* and Ethelred's sons – were still alive in exile in Normandy under the protection of the duke.

A story grew up, that Cnut had mocked his fawning English courtiers, who had obsequiously declared that his power was so mighty that even the tides obeyed his command. Cnut, according to the historian Henry of Huntingdon in his *Historia Anglorum*, ordered his followers to carry him to the beach, where he sat enthroned and commanded: '"I therefore order you (the sea) not to come up onto my land, nor to presume to wet the limbs or clothes of your lord!" But the relentless tide came in, and Cnut declared, "Thus may all the inhabitants of the earth see how vain and worthless is the power of kings. I am not worthy to bear the name of king before Him at whose bequest heaven, earth and sea obey eternal laws." Therefore ... he would never afterwards allow his golden crown to be placed upon his head ... but rather placed it on an image of Christ hanging on the cross.'

This was an astonishing turn of events. After almost two centuries of continuous conflict, an impoverished, emasculated, corrupt and lawless country found that the foreign conqueror, the 'barbarian', was actually morally, spiritually and politically superior to their own native dynasty. Cnut was persuaded to abandon his first wife, Aelfgifu, and take as his bride the much older Emma of Normandy, Ethelred's widow. Emma jumped at the chance, for the young Viking was handsome and kind unlike her previous husband, but she nonetheless insisted that her sons, Edward and Alfred, remain behind in Normandy. Order and justice were gradually restored, and with them came a steady increase in trade with Scandinavia and the Baltic which benefited economic recovery. The previously hostile Viking fleets stopped coming, and Cnut even went on an expedition to conquer Sweden with an English army. Cnut also went on a pilgrimage to Rome in 1027.

After so many years of anarchy, England began a recovery from the long ordeal of Ethelred's reign. But all these positives were threatened by the difficulties that must inevitably ensue over succession, and it was Emma of Normandy, a dominant player in English politics for half a century, whose policy mattered most in that regard. She had left her sons behind in Normandy, and the elder boy, Edward, never forgave her. For her part, she best loved Harthacnut, her son by Cnut.

When Cnut suddenly died on 12 November 1035 at Shaftesbury, Emma immediately urged Harthacnut to return from Denmark with all speed before he could be usurped by his half-brother Harold 'Harefoot'. Harold was Cnut's son by Aelfgifu of Northampton, and therefore had the advantage of being half-English. He was also favoured simply for being present, and the English nobles duly offered the crown to him before Harthacnut could react. Emma disputed Harold's *bona fides*, claiming that he was not Cnut's son and that his mother had been a concubine. Alfred, Emma's second son, impetuously set sail for England, but upon landing on the south coast he was immediately arrested by agents of Earl Godwin. He was handed over to Harefoot, now King Harold I, who had him blinded with hot irons before being thrown into a dungeon to starve to death.

By 1040 Harold I was dead, and Harthacnut returned to become king. His first act was to have his half-brother's corpse exhumed and thrown into a cesspool. The rest of his two-year reign was of a piece with such behaviour. He taxed his subjects with grinding *gelds* which brought the English to the verge of insurrection. The citizens of Worcester defied him, and Harthacnut burned the city and wasted all the shire around. The oppressed and miserable English did not grieve him when he died during an excessive drinking bout in 1042, and the whole nation looked to Normandy where Ethelred and Emma's surviving son, Edward, last of the eligible *Cerdicings*, was still in exile. On Easter Day 1043, Edward 'the Confessor', as he later became known, was crowned. The line of Alfred and Athelstan had finally been restored, and there were high hopes for the new English king.

Except for a brief visit during 1016, Edward had been in continuous exile in Normandy for almost twenty-seven years. All Edward's close friends were Norman, and despite being half-English he was to all intents and purposes a Norman, uncomfortable with the cut-throat politics and unrefined manners of the English court. A magnificent ship had been sent to convey him to England, a gift from Earl Godwin, the most powerful political player in the country. Godwin, however, had been directly implicated in the mutilation, imprisonment and death of Edward's beloved brother Alfred. The new king had neither forgotten nor forgiven this.

Edward was desperately torn. However much he despised Godwin, the man was key to re-establishing the dynasty of the *Cerdicings* in England. Edward's mother Emma hated Godwin but was shrewd enough to realise that such a powerful man had to be bought off. Godwin's five sons were all powerful earls in their own right, giving them great combined military potential. The most dangerous of them was the eldest, Sweyn, who was reckless, boastful and violent. A drunkard, he often claimed that he was in fact the son of Cnut, and that Godwin was not his real father. He would erupt into furious Viking-style berserk rages, and on one occasion slew a man in a brawl at the royal court. Intimidated, Edward opted to leave matters of policy to Godwin while he retreated into his grand plan to rebuild Westminster Abbey in the Romanesque style then fashionable in Normandy. A great many Norman craftsmen and masons were imported to London to help with the project, and a coterie of Norman favourites gathered around the king, especially eminent churchmen such as Robert of Jumieges, who was made Bishop of London. Although his political authority was constrained, Edward was determined to restore England to spiritual health, and unlike most kings of this period he abhorred violence and war, devoting himself to religion and learning. He began to be revered as a sort of living saint, and it was said that his royal touch could cure scrofula. But he could not ignore the governance of the realm entirely, and he was content for key Anglo-Danish noblemen to be pushed into exile.

His policy towards the Welsh was also stern. It was Edward, not William the Conqueror, who was responsible for introducing the first Norman castles into England. Richard Fitz-Scrob led one of the first Norman garrisons into what they called Marche, the Welsh Marches. Emma of Normandy still held the keys to the Royal Treasury at Winchester, but she proved so parsimonious that Edward lost his temper and rode with three earls to seize the vast treasures.

Soon afterwards, and inevitably, Edward was married to the handsome and refined young Edith, Godwin's daughter. Edith was crowned queen in 1045, and remained Edward's wife until his death in 1066, but the union was not blessed with children. The reason traditionally given is that Edward had taken a vow of celibacy at some point shortly after the wedding. His resentment of Godwin did not extend to Edith, and although he sent her to a nunnery and attempted to divorce her when her father and brothers were later exiled, he retained her as a member of his inner circle following her reinstatement. She wrote a detailed life of her deceased husband in her widowhood, and continued to revere him almost as a saint. It is impossible to guess what thoughts went through the king's mind, but it is certainly possible that he would rather be celibate than mix the royal blood of the *Cerdicings* with that of the parvenu Godwin clan. The situation was complicated by the fact that Edmund Ironside's son, known as Edward 'the Exile', was still alive at the Hungarian court. There were other claimants too. William, Duke of Normandy had a claim, as did the Norwegian king, a ruthless giant called Harald III, or Hardrada.

These foreign interlopers were resented, and sometimes it showed. When Edward's brother-in-law Eustace of Boulogne visited Dover in 1051, he was attacked by an angry mob. Edward was incensed, and Eustace immediately demanded that the people of Dover be punished. But they had misjudged the situation. The French knights had provoked the incident, perhaps deliberately, and when Edward ordered Godwin to expedite punitive reprisals against the town he flatly refused. At last, Edward had his excuse to act against the Godwin tribe. Edward called out the *fyrd* under royal proclamation and acted swiftly to deprive Godwin and his sons of their earldoms. Godwin went to Flanders to see Count Baldwin, a powerful and wealthy ally. Harold, Godwin's second son, and the most intelligent of his progeny, sailed for Ireland in hopes of hiring a fleet there. Edith was removed to a nunnery while her fate was considered. Edward did not want to make the same mistakes as his father; he wished to be his own man, not the prisoner of scheming ambitious political players. But the king had overplayed his hand, and as the true story of the events at Dover unfolded it was Godwin who had the public's sympathy.

For his part, Godwin had been busily plotting his return. Tostig, his third son, was with him in Flanders and was married to Judith, daughter of Count Baldwin of Flanders, one of the wealthiest men in Europe. A fleet was provided to Godwin, and messages were sent to Harold in Ireland to rendezvous with him with his fleet in the Thames estuary. In 1052, Harold and Godwin's combined fleet dropped anchor in the Thames to intimidate Edward into granting them a royal pardon and reinstating their earldoms. The public mood was now very febrile, and a reaction against foreigners recast Godwin as a loyalist patriot who had been persecuted for the crime of standing up for his countrymen.

Edward was grudgingly persuaded to capitulate, and the Godwin family were reinstated, including Queen Edith, who was recalled from the nunnery and allowed to reoccupy her rooms in the royal bedchamber. Archbishop Robert of Jumieges, Edward's close personal friend and advisor, was required to leave England, to be replaced by the Englishman Stigand, Godwin's ally. Many Norman and French knights, fearing retribution by patriotic mobs, fled to Scotland. Godwin controlled the south coast ports from which the English navy operated, and acted swiftly to prevent any interference from Normandy.

Edward found himself in the very predicament he had struggled to avoid, all but a hostage of a man he loathed. But in 1053, Godwin suddenly died. He was succeeded as Earl of Wessex by

Harold Godwinson, his second son, and Harold's two brothers, Gyrth and Leofwine became earls of East Anglia and Middlesex. On the death of Siward, Earl of Northumbria (of *Macbeth* fame) in 1055, Tostig was given that huge earldom, meaning that the Godwin family controlled large swathes of the country.

While Harold was intelligent, handsome, valiant and enormously popular, Tostig was a mean-minded thug who ruled his earldom through a combination of intimidation and violence. He murdered several important local rivals, and ruled in the manner of an autocratic potentate. He became friendly with the Scottish king, who was hated in the north of England, but treated Edward with utter contempt and refused to attend court. Despite Tostig's unpopularity, however, Edward was powerless to move against the earl, who surrounded himself with a large army of Danish and Viking mercenaries. By now increasingly exhausted, bewildered and depressed, the king relied on the sensible Harold to keep his brother in check, and this was a de facto recognition that he was now the *Dux Anglorum* or 'chief man of the English'. It seemed that nothing could prevent one of the brothers eventually becoming king – even though neither had a drop of royal blood in his veins. To prevent this, Edward finally resorted to one last desperate measure to ensure the line of the *Cerdicings* was not extinguished.

The king's namesake, Edward 'the Exile', son of Edmund 'Ironside', was still alive and apparently well at the court of the King of Hungary. In 1054, much to the chagrin of Harold Godwinson and Duke William of Normandy, who also had designs on the English throne, King Edward sent Ealdred, Bishop of Worcester to Hungary in hopes of persuading the exile to return to his homeland. The exile had made himself at home in Hungary, and was married with children. Greatly fearing assassination, he rebuffed Ealdred's entreaties. It was clear that his fear of Harold Godwinson was the sticking point, and so in 1056 Harold was sent on a personal mission to reassure him. In 1057, Edward and his wife and young children finally arrived in England, but his fears proved to be fatally accurate. Little is known of the actual circumstances, but in April 1057, just days after his arrival, Edward died before his royal audience with the king. He left behind a young son, Edgar, who was also a *Cerdicing* and an *Aetheling* or 'throne-worthy', but a young boy was hardly likely to prevail against such mighty warriors as King Harald 'Hardrada' of Norway, Duke William of Normandy and Harold Godwinson – all of whom coveted the English throne. By now elderly and infirm, the king, worn down by cares, delegated more and more authority to Harold, who may well have been implicated in the Exile's demise (although William's agents also operated in England). From this point on, conflict was inevitable.

In 1063, in a campaign calculated to ingratiate them with the king, and to enhance their popularity among the common people, Harold and Tostig invaded Wales. Harold quickly overcame the Welsh, and Gruffydd, their king, was murdered by his own retainers, who sent his head to Harold. Taking responsibility for the subsequent political settlement, Harold installed two brothers, both his loyal allies, as kings of Gwynedd and Powys – Bleddyn ap Cynfyn in the former, and Rhiwallon in the latter. Gruffydd's gory head was sent on to King Edward. The elderly king was now so despondent that, in a slight to Tostig, he mistakenly attributed the English success entirely to Harold. As Harold prepared a banquet in the king's honour, an incensed Tostig showed up and slew all the cooks and stewards in an appalling but typical outburst of violence. In 1065, the Northumbrian nobles finally acted to depose him, and Harold agreed to his banishment from the realm on behalf of the king. Two brothers, Edwin and Morcar, were set up as earls of Mercia and Northumbria respectively, and in order to ensure cordial relations with them Harold repudiated his lover, the beautiful Edith 'Swan-Neck', to marry another Edith, sister of the two northern earls. As the elderly King Edward's life drew to its close, Harold had positioned himself as the natural and obvious choice to be the next King of England – but overseas, the storm clouds were already gathering.

During Christmas 1065, King Edward was taken ill. He was brought to Westminster Abbey, the magnificent church whose construction symbolised his reign, or rather his piety, and died there on 5 January 1066. Within hours, Harold moved ruthlessly to secure the throne. Edward had given the realm 'into his care', as a sort of Lord Protector rather than as king. Edgar 'the Aetheling', Edmund's grandson, was king by right but was overlooked. The bigger issue, however, was what had happened in 1064. Harold had the misfortune to be shipwrecked off the French coast that year. He had been taken to the court of Duke William of Normandy, who now claimed that while there Harold had sworn a sacred oath to support the duke's claim to the throne of England. When William heard the news of Harold's coup, he was incensed, and immediately ordered the construction of a vast fleet. He also summoned the combined knighthood of Normandy, Brittany, and parts of France, as well as volunteers from other areas – for an invasion of England. Nor was this the only danger to Harold's new regime. In Norway, one of the most feared warriors of the age, the 7-foot King Harald 'Hardrada', also had a claim to the English throne. Harthacnut had promised King Magnus, Hardrada's predecessor, that should he die childless his claim would pass to the Norwegian king. This was dubious to say the least, but no more so than Harold's own claim.

Realpolitik dictated that the English king should be an Englishman, preferably one with tried and tested military capabilities. That man was indisputably Harold, and in the coming months he would have need of all his considerable martial talents. The signs were ominous when, on 24 April, a great comet was observed for a whole week. This 'hairy star', a 'portent such as men had never seen before', greatly disturbed the superstitious Anglo-Saxons as they waited for two vast fleets, each under the command of a feared military commander, to descend on their coasts – but which would come first?

Trouble started in the south. The banished Tostig had gathered a fleet and anchored in the Solent off the Isle of Wight. He then tacked along the coast to Sandwich, and Harold reacted by ordering his fleet to sea. A large army, potentially up to 20,000 strong, was mobilised, and seeing there was no hope of prevailing against such a force Tostig sailed for Scotland, in hopes of conjoining with Hardrada's fleet. But in these anxious summer months, it was the more formidable threat from William which preoccupied Harold's thoughts.

The Norman duke was constructing a vast fleet at enormous expense – virtually all the great trees of Normandy were felled to provide timber for the project. This armada was sheltered in the estuary of the River Dives, at Dives-sur-Mer, for William feared a pre-emptive strike by the English fleet. Unfortunately for Harold, this option was denied him by the most appalling weather in the Channel. Northerly gales damaged the English naval patrols so badly that the ships had to return to port for a refit. William's ships were stymied, and could only hug the coast as far as St Valery-sur-Somme, where all his warhorses and supplies were waiting to be loaded aboard. Nothing was left to chance; a prefabricated castle had even been prepared. The whole enterprise was quite literally a crusade. The pope had blessed the expedition, and William's army marched under the papal banner. Harold was excommunicated for the alleged breach of his sacred oath to William. We can only speculate about the size of the Norman and allied army, but it was probably somewhat larger than Hardrada's – perhaps 12,000 men, with 3,000 heavy destriers, armoured warhorses trained to kick and bite. Transporting these dangerous and unpredictable beasts was a considerable challenge in itself.

It began to look as if William's fleet would never head into the open sea, and so on 8 September Harold was forced to dismiss his troops so that they could gather the harvest. The contrary winds pinning William down were a gift to Hardrada, whose huge fleet put to sea and met with Tostig off the Orkneys. On 15 September, after a campaign of raiding along the coast of Northumberland, the Norwegian king disembarked his army in the River Humber, at Riccall by the River Ouse within a day's march of York. King Harold II of England was hundreds of miles away in the south, and so it fell to the northern earls, Edwin and his brother Morcar, to organise a defence of the city.

Hardrada's fleet had sacked Scarborough on the way to Riccall, and so Edwin and Morcar were already on alert with a combined army of 5,000 men. Morcar, the new earl, was advised to confront the Norwegians just outside the city at the village of Gate Fulford. Edwin's forces drew up along a small beck or stream, which flowed into the River Ouse, and this anchored the English right flank. Morcar's forces, somewhat more numerous, drew up in front of an area of fen or marsh along the north bank of the stream. Hardrada had left 3,000 men, under his son Olaf, to guard the ships, and the remaining 7,000 marched on York in three separate columns, with Hardrada himself bringing up the rear, on the morning of 20 September 1066. The leading columns soon ran into the English, and seeing they were outnumbered they formed up a shield wall until Hardrada arrived with his own elite troops. Morcar, keen to make a breakthrough before Hardrada and Tostig joined the fray, attacked and began to make progress, pushing the Vikings back up the ridge they had just descended. Meanwhile, Hardrada had been alerted, and brought up 2,000 men who were ordered to conceal themselves behind the ridge to observe the outcome of the battle on the English flanks. Edwin's forces failed to make any progress at all, and so Hardrada ordered troops from his left flank to attack the English centre.

After many hours, Hardrada sensed that the struggle was in the balance. He was one of the craftiest and most experienced warriors in all Europe. He had been a commander in the famed Varangian Guard of the Byzantine Emperor, and had been paid with an ingot of gold the weight of a man. This treasure, along with many others, was always carried with him on campaign, and he regarded it as his personal trophy. As a young man, besieging a city which proved difficult to capture, Hardrada once ordered sparrows to be trapped. Flaming tapers were tied to their legs, and the creatures flew back to their homes in the thatched roofs of the nearby town, which burned to the ground. He was also said to have slain a polar bear in single combat.

As soon as he could see that Edwin's flank was faltering, Hardrada charged the English right flank with his own concealed force. The panicked English could now see that the water level in the little stream was dropping, and now the Vikings, at last all 7,000 of them committed to the fray, went on the offensive. Edwin's forces broke and fled back to York, but Morcar's men were in a much more dangerous position. Behind them, the marsh obstructed their retreat, and soon the beck itself became fordable – the Viking account states that it became possible to cross the bed of the stream over the trampled bodies of hundreds of English dead and wounded. Both Edwin and Morcar managed to escape the battle, but played no part in the Battle of Hastings a few weeks later. Hardrada's army surrounded York, but probably due to Tostig's influence (he did not want the capital of his earldom burned down) Hardrada agreed to withdraw his army to Stamford Bridge, a village a few miles to the east, for a victory feast. After promises of vast tribute and many hundreds of important hostages were made to him, the giant Viking leader departed to celebrate what he must have regarded as a costly – but quick and lucrative – campaign in England. It was to prove his final such victory revel, for, unbeknown to him, the main English army, commanded by King Harold II himself, was on the march against him.

Only two days after the Battle of Gate Fulford, on 22 September, the wind changed direction. William of Normandy immediately ordered his ships to foregather, and he put to sea at last. William's fleet anchored at Pevensey Bay on 28 September. The Norman fleet calculated that a landing near Harold's personal estates in Sussex, around Bosham, would tempt him into an immediate reaction against their landing – but no English opposition supervened. The reason was that the English king, and his 12,000 strong army, had already departed for the north, to oppose Hardrada and Tostig in Yorkshire. The historian Michael Wood postulated that Harold's rapid reaction to the crisis in the north relied not just upon fleet messengers but on a system of beacons which conveyed the news of Hardrada's invasion to him within hours, rather than days.[23] This seems eminently reasonable – the same system was utilised in the emergency of 1588 with the Spanish Armada, and no doubt a similar network of signals spread the news of the Roman invasions in their day.

Harold immediately sent his messengers north to gather troops as he marched speedily up the Great North Road to Yorkshire. Even as Hardrada's men were celebrating the Viking triumph, Harold was 'riding day and night' (according to the *Anglo-Saxon Chronicle*) towards Nottinghamshire. Here, the levies of Cambridgeshire and Nottinghamshire joined his main army, consisting of the men of London, Sussex and the shires around. His own elite troops, many of them hired Danish mercenaries trained to wield the Danish great axe – a heavy, razor-sharp axe with a foot-long cutting edge wielded on a 5-foot wooden helve – were in the vanguard. Four frantic days after leaving London, Harold's army arrived at Tadcaster in Yorkshire – a march of 180 miles. Considering that these men had to convey all their armour, equipment and supplies with them, this remains one of the most astonishing achievements in all military history. Harold rested his army for a few hours before ascertaining the position of his enemy. At first light on 25 September, 12,000 heavily armed English troops advanced on the tiny village of Stamford Bridge. These weary men were resolved to annihilate Hardrada come what may, and they knew that the element of surprise lay with them.

The Icelandic historian Snorri Sturluson gives an account, albeit a dramatised one, of the battle from the Viking point of view, which was probably derived from oral evidence taken from the few Norwegians who survived. Only twenty-four of the original

---

23. Wood, M., *In Search of the Dark Ages* (London, 1981)

three hundred ships in Hardrada's fleet were needed to take the survivors, under Hardrada's son Olaf, back to their homeland. Harold was magnanimous in victory, and allowed Hardrada's body to be taken home for Christian burial, although the slaughtered Norwegian warriors were left where they fell. Over half a century later, the area near the bridge over the Derwent was still called 'Battle Flat' and was covered with the whitened bones of over 5,000 Viking dead. Florence of Worcester, an English chronicler, states that they were formed into a cairn, which became a significant local landmark.

Sturluson claimed that as the Vikings were enjoying the unseasonably warm sunshine, sprawled about eating and drinking, awaiting the delivery of the hostages, some of the warriors guarding the west end of the bridge noticed a dust cloud rising on the old Roman road to York. It was such a hot day that the Vikings had left their mail shirts at their encampment for so far as they knew no English force constituted any further threat to them. Only King Harold himself was capable of deploying a large army, and it seemed inconceivable that it could be him. But then, to their horror, the warriors noticed the glinting of sunlight on mail shirts, helmets, and spear points – 'like ice'.

Instantly, Hardrada and Tostig formed up their army on a hillock overlooking the River Derwent and the vital bridge. Three riders on the fastest horses were sent to Olaf at Riccall, but even as they spurred their steeds on the first elements of the English army arrived. The Vikings on the west bank were swiftly overwhelmed, but Hardrada selected a Viking berserker, a giant even taller than himself, to defend the bridge alone, armed with a Danish great axe. This hero proved a considerable obstacle, and forty men lost their lives in single combat against him before an ingenious solution was devised. Some sort of tub or meal ark was discovered (some traditions state it was a barrel), and a lone English warrior paddled it beneath the bridge. Otherwise preoccupied, the Viking did not notice the threat beneath him until a spear was thrust up between the wooden slats of the bridge into his groin. The English army immediately raced over the corpse of the gallant man to form up on the east bank of the Derwent opposite Hardrada and Tostig, who had formed their 6,000 men into a shield wall. The English army, twice as numerous, and with the advantages of full armour, archers and even, perhaps, some cavalry, prepared to assault the Norwegians. According to Sturluson, though, Harold was overcome at the last minute by a desire to spare his brother from the forthcoming massacre.

A lone English rider approached the Norwegian line, under a flag of truce, and requested parley with Tostig. Hardrada, playing for precious time, consented, and Tostig rode out to speak with the messenger. Although he had his helmet down, Tostig soon recognised his brother Harold's voice. The king offered to spare Tostig's life, and even to reinstate him to his former earldom, if he would agree to switch sides. Tostig gestured to the gigantic Norwegian king, asking what Harold's offer was to him. Harold contemptuously replied, 'He shall have 6 feet of English earth for a grave – nay, 7 feet, for he is taller than most men!' Tostig rode back to Hardrada, who requested to know the identity of the brave man who had boldly approached an entire army alone. Hardrada's wrath with his answer was soon overcome by his need to defend himself, for the English army now advanced in a shield wall, and swiftly closed with the Vikings.

The English troops were by no means fresh, having marched almost 200 miles in five days and 16 miles that morning. According to Marianus Scotus, an Irish chronicler in Germany, Harold's army attacked in seven divisions. He seems to have interspersed mounted spearmen among the infantry, probably hoping to exploit any fragmentation in the Norwegian ranks. The brave Vikings, with only their shields for protection, soon took very heavy casualties, and Hardrada, in the finest Norse tradition, took a sword in one hand and a battle axe in the other and charged forward to rally the line. This was a fatal error, for he was soon targeted by archers and fell with an arrow through his throat. Tostig took up the Norwegian royal standard and rallied the Vikings to him, defiant to the last. A Norse saga of the thirteenth century says that Harold made one final attempt to save his brother. The King of England blew his horn and shouted out to Tostig to surrender and spare more pointless bloodshed. The Norwegians all shouted that they would rather die than yield: 'No truce! We will conquer or die!' Within minutes, Tostig fell too, 'gloriously, and covered with honour'.

Harold ordered his men to finish the Vikings off, but just as the Norwegian main force had been all but annihilated a fresh force of Vikings joined the fray. According to the *Heimskringla*, almost 3,000 Norwegians under Eystein Orri, one of Hardrada's favourite commanders, literally ran the 17 miles from Riccall in sweltering heat and full armour in just three hours. Such a feat was truly remarkable, and many of the men dropped as soon as they reached the battlefield. But those who remained were at least wearing their full armour, and they smashed into the English right flank, and incredibly drove it back – 'Orri's Storm', as the *skalds* called it. But it was a desperate, heroic last effort, and when the English rallied Orri and his men were pushed back. Orri was killed, and the last surviving Vikings threw off their armour and fought like berserkers in the place called Battle Flat. By dusk, the entire Norwegian army had been exterminated. Only Olaf, with just over 1,000 men, remained at Riccall. Swearing oaths never to return, he sailed for the Orkneys minus Hardrada's vast treasures, including his massive ingot of gold.

On 27 September Harold celebrated his victory with civic dignitaries in York. The next morning, while the English army were still nursing their hangovers, William's fleet landed his army at Pevensey Bay. It took several days to convey the news to Harold, and he first heard of William's invasion on 1 October. The king was full of confidence, justifiably, for he had just defeated Hardrada, 'the Thunderbolt of the North', in a lightning campaign. The Normans had already begun plundering and burning Harold's personal estates in Sussex, and the responsibility to defend his own retainers weighed heavily on him. Before there was time to distribute the treasures taken from the Norwegian king, Harold immediately rode south with all speed to London. His own household troops followed, but many of the hired Danish mercenaries were annoyed not to have been paid their bonus from the treasure – and many did not reenlist. The victory at Stamford Bridge had not come without cost, either. Harold lost at least 2,000 men, and the men of Cambridgeshire and Nottinghamshire, having served their terms of duty, returned to their shires. It would be a mistake to think, as many people still do, that Harold simply marched the same army he had deployed at Stamford Bridge to fight William. For the forthcoming contest, Harold needed to call out an entirely new army, which contained only an elite core of veterans of the former conflict in its ranks.

The Battle of Hastings, fought on Saturday 14 October 1066, is so well known that it falls outside the remit of this volume. There are many books about that fatal day, and so a few brief comments about the battle and its momentous consequences will suffice to conclude part two of this history. Harold reached London on 7 October, just one week before the battle. He immediately instructed the shire reeves south of the Thames to call out the *fyrd* by royal proclamation. He left London on the evening of the 12 October to rendezvous with the new army at Caldbec Hill, 7 miles north-west of Hastings in East Sussex. Atop the hill, a lone 'hoar apple tree' was the landmark towards which the English levies marched through the night. The army was smaller than that which destroyed the Norwegians at Stamford Bridge, and of poorer quality. Morale was poor, on the whole, because the *fyrd* had already been on duty all through the summer, and so the sudden call-up at short notice was resented. Harold's force consisted of 10,000 such men, supplemented by his own elite bodyguard.

Harold intended to storm the Norman encampment in a dawn attack, but William's sentinels were quickly alerted to English infiltrators in the night. Harold, seeing that he was discovered, ordered the English troops to concentrate for a defensive battle on a 1,000-yard-long ridge just south of the 'hoar apple tree'. As they lit campfires and sang hymns, the Norman pickets assumed they were all drunk, but the explanation may be that the English army, strung out on the London road, had not fully formed up, and was trying to make its position known to those comrades still trying to find the king in the dark. Florence of Worcester lamented that only a third of Harold's army were in battle-order when the action commenced at about 9.00 a.m, and that only half of the English army actually took part.

William was determined to attack as soon as possible. Before daylight, he had already donned his hauberk, or mail shirt, and ordered his army to form up in three divisions. Opposite Harold's royal standard, at the centre of the English position, were William's Normans, the core of his army, with most of the heavy cavalry. The French were concentrated on William's right flank, and the Bretons on his left. In all, about 12,000 allied troops gave the duke a slight numerical advantage. But William had many other advantages. His Norman knights, in particular, were superbly brave and well disciplined, as well as eminently reliable. He had many archers, including Genoese crossbowmen. Nevertheless, the English position was strong, and Harold would be no pushover.

Harold had only one hope – the intervention of the infamous autumn rains, which would have the effect of turning the slopes of the ridge into a mud bath, impeding William's cavalry attacks. Unfortunately, the morning of 14 October proved to be dry. William's first attack smashed into the English shield wall shortly after 9.00 a.m., and the Normans failed to break the shield wall. William's first horse of the day was killed under him by a Danish axeman, while on his left flank the Breton cavalry and men-at-arms took a severe mauling. Seeing their difficulty, the English militia charged down the hill after them. William saw this development, and his opportunity. He wheeled his own cavalry around and charged roughly 1,500 English troops who had gathered on a small hillock to defend themselves. These ill-disciplined part-timers were rapidly dispatched by the Normans, and suddenly Harold's right flank was hopelessly vulnerable. There was other bad news for Harold: his brothers, Gyrth and Leofwine, had both been killed in the first stages of the battle.

William's next attack involved a co-ordinated assault by all arms, cavalry, infantry and, vitally, archers, who were ordered to loose their arrows over the English shield wall on to the less well-equipped English rear ranks. Many of these men were farm labourers wearing straw hats, with pitchforks and bill hooks as weapons, many of them without shields. Once again, William's horse was killed under him, and a rumour went through the Norman army that he was dead. Despite his injuries, William quickly mounted up again and removed his helmet, shouting, 'Look here! I am alive, and with God's help, this day we shall have the victory!'

This prediction proved fatally accurate for the English people. The Norman infantry, panicked and fleeing down the ridge, saw William alive and turned to face the oncoming English, who, maddened by hours of relentless attacks, had once again set off in an impetuous pursuit. To Harold's despair, William's cavalry quickly annihilated those who had broken ranks, and now William moved his archers much nearer to the English ranks, which were now broken by the armoured knights and men-at-arms. The losses on both English flanks had been so serious that the army concentrated around the king's standards and his elite huscarls. William ordered his archers to concentrate all their efforts on the tight knot of warriors around the king, and shortly afterwards Harold was hit in the face by an arrow. He fell, and was supported by his bodyguards, but a group of four Norman knights supported by infantry broke through to him. Harold was hacked into pieces, and his body mutilated, and within minutes the news spread through the English ranks. The rear ranks soon fled into the woods behind the English position, and alerted any latecomers to the situation. Harold's bodyguard remained stubbornly resolute around the king's body, and fought on until nightfall. They all died to a man defending the body of their lord, true to their oaths, and around them, lying in gory heaps in the moonlight, lay 5,000 other slain or mortally wounded Englishmen. William's losses were also very high, so much so that he had to send for immediate reinforcement of men and horses from Normandy.

The consequences of the Norman Conquest for the English were catastrophic. In short, it was the end of the Anglo-Saxon civilisation which had dominated in the island since the disintegration of the Roman scheme over five hundred years before. The Norman invasion was not gradual but accomplished quickly, with ruthless celerity and brutality. Even the Vikings had gradually succumbed to Anglo-Saxon mores and institutions, but the Normans, on the whole, initially refused to mix with the conquered English, and held their customs and traditions – even their language – in contempt. The huge castles with which they held down the resentful population were not constructed using their own labour, like the Roman fortresses, but were built using impressed English labour. Often, entire quarters of important English towns were simply demolished to make space for them. Although one last large-scale Viking invasion was yet to come, so tight was the Norman grip on England that, for almost a thousand years, no major invasion of this island has succeeded – though there have been many attempts.

While England had fallen to the Normans, however, the Celtic nations of Scotland, Wales and Ireland still retained their stubborn independence. As great lords and barons took control of large swathes of England, the potential for civil wars and regional conflict was always just beneath the surface. As the new regime entrenched itself, a whole new era of bloody warfare was about to commence.

PART THREE

16

A NEW ORDER (1066–1264)

Before dawn on 15 October 1066, Harold's lover Edith 'Swan-Neck', reputedly the fairest woman in England, came to William's tent to plead for Harold's mangled body. She was allowed to search the corpse heap the next morning. The four Norman knights who had first reached the mortally wounded Harold had dishonoured themselves by hacking him to pieces and removing his 'leg', which they gleefully waved in the air as they rode to the duke with the news (it seems the word 'leg' is a scribe's modest cypher for Harold's vital member). Nevertheless, Edith found her beloved, recognising it by 'certain intimate marks, known only to her'. His body was taken for burial at Waltham Abbey, his own foundation. His tombstone simply reads '*Hic iacet Haroldus infelix*', 'Here lies the ill-fated Harold'. Below, someone has added a verse:

In this tomb brave Harold rests
Who once famed King of England was
On whom renown, men, character and authority
Conferr'd power and a kingdom
A sceptre and a crown as well
Until he strove, a famous warrior
To defend his people
But died; slain by the men of France.

Harold was fortunate if the story of his burial is true, for the rest of the English dead were left to decompose where they lay. It was unclear to William whether or not the war would continue, and so his policy towards the English was callous and hostile. The English were still in arms, and the young Edgar 'the Aetheling' was king by right. As winter came on, William's troops suffered a crippling outbreak of dysentery. His sickened army, now less than 10,000 strong, was surrounded by a hostile host population with the potential to raise a force twice as numerous. The key to the realm was London. William attempted to storm London Bridge from Southwark, but the citizenry rallied around Edgar 'the Aetheling' and the Norman attack was driven off. In a typical fit of rage, William burned Southwark to the ground before he led his army in a circuit around London, destroying every village in his path. All routes into London were blockaded, and as Christmas approached it was clear thousands would starve and, in the cramped city, pestilence would follow.

Harold's widow Edith, sister of Edwin and Morcar, the earls who controlled the Midlands and Northumbria, was holding out in Winchester with the Royal Treasury of England. When she surrendered, and the vast fortune fell into William's hands, English hearts sank. Archbishop Stigand met with Edwin and Morcar, Archbishop Ealdred of York, and Edgar 'the Aetheling', and decided to offer the throne of England to William on certain conditions. At Berkhamsted, where William was encamped, the delegation finally gave the duke the thing he had dreamed of achieving since he was a young man. On Christmas Day 1066, as riot and fire spread through Westminster, William 'the Conqueror' became King William I of England, crowned by Archbishop Ealdred in Westminster Abbey. He swore a sacred oath to 'so well-govern this nation as any king before him best did, if they (the English) will be faithful to him'. William trembled as he spoke the words, as well he might – for the regime he inflicted upon the English made his words sound very hollow.

Within a few years, many English nobles were forced to seek refuge in Scandinavia, Scotland and Ireland. The royal standard of Wessex was salvaged from the carnage at Hastings and was taken to Ireland by Harold's surviving sons. By the 1070s, an entire fleet of 300 ships, over 10,000 people, all refugees from William's tyranny, left England bound for the Black Sea, where they were allowed to settle in the Crimea by the Byzantine Emperor, founding small settlements with nostalgic names such as 'New York' and 'New London'. The Varangian Guard to the Byzantine Emperor was originally composed of Viking mercenaries, but after the Norman Conquest it was English exiles who filled its ranks.

The Norman occupation was brutally harsh. One reason for this was their sheer lack of numbers. Only 8,000 Normans actually settled on a permanent basis in England. Even though he was now indisputably king, William spent most of his time in Normandy once the English resistance had been crushed after the rebellion of 1069. They were foreigners who understood very little English and were disinclined to learn any. As such they were an aloof elite, not unlike the later British Raj in India. They were, of course, in constant danger from guerrilla fighters, outlaws and renegades. It was essential that they protect their small groups from attack, and soon the Normans extended an innovation which King Edward had already introduced: the Norman castle, the mighty fortresses which have come to symbolise the conquest.

Alistair Moffat described the Normans as 'natural colonisers',[24] and the instrument for colonization was the castle. The combination of a small retinue of knights, a core of mounted troops numbered in the dozens with perhaps another 100 men-at-arms, and an unassailable strategic base – the castle – meant that Norman military influence was out of all proportion to their tiny numbers. In 1017 the pope granted a commission to a consortium of Norman knights just a few hundred strong to clear

---

24. Moffatt, A., *The Sea Kingdoms* (Edinburgh, 2008)

Apulia, Calabria and Sicily of Saracen troops. The operation was accomplished with ruthless efficiency, and perhaps it was this astonishing success which inspired William's early dreams of a similar conquest of England. A system of castles had developed in France before the Norman settlement. Charles 'the Bald' prohibited their construction in 864, but the independent Norman duchy continued to build them in large numbers. Wace, the chronicler from Jersey who wrote a history of the Norman invasion, said that a prefabricated timber castle was loaded aboard William's ships, ready to erect as soon as they landed in England. These timber constructions, to begin with, were assembled atop a steep hill or mound called in Norman-French a *motte*. At the summit, a stronghold called a keep was enclosed within a timber palisade. The keep was two stories high, and overlooked the entire area around for some miles. Approaches to the castle were also cleared, to prevent concealment and surprise attack by enemy forces. A narrow wooden stairway descended the motte where a gatehouse defended a deep ditch, with a bridge into the outer area, called the bailey. This larger area contained all the domestic buildings, animal pens, farm buildings such as barns, sometimes a chapel, and most importantly the lord's great hall. All this was also surrounded by a deep ditch and a palisade, with gatehouses and watchtowers. Every large English town was immediately dominated by a castle, and as the Normans rapidly advanced to the Welsh and Scottish borders, large numbers were built in the Marches. By 1086, more than a hundred large castles (by this time increasingly massive stone fortresses) kept the English realm in an iron grip.

The reason the Norman castles were initially built in timber rather than stone was that it took some years for them to establish enough local control to compel serf labour – that is English slaves – to build them under the supervision of Norman overseers. But timber is too vulnerable to fire to serve for the purposes of defence adequately. A rag doused in pitch attached to an arrow was all it took to set the whole complex ablaze. Each castle then, of necessity, had to have a good reliable water supply within. When the castles were rebuilt in stone, the keep became a massive, usually rectangular, stone building. The old timber palisades were replaced by high stone walls with intervening towers.

Fearful of the proliferation of these mighty fortresses, following the so-called 'anarchy' during the reign of King Stephen, his successor, Henry II, eliminated the old private castles, and only granted licenses under very strict conditions, with all local lords ultimately accountable to him. In fact, each local dignitary, whether they were a mighty baron or a humbler Norman lord, saw themselves as the instrument of the king's authority, dispensing summary jurisdiction and taking responsibility for local security. The lord of the castle, in his *donjon* (a word which morphed into the English 'dungeon'), exercised dominion as if by divine right. To emphasize this point, the English were all but ethnically cleansed from the English Church, with only one English bishop still secure by 1075. Alongside the great new stone fortifications, magnificent and robust stone churches were built as the Normans saw themselves quite literally as soldiers of Christ, with the pope's blessing on their enterprise. The pope was not pleased when he heard of the virtual genocide in the north of England following the 1069 rebellion there, but for all the despair of the lesser clergy the conquest was a *fait accompli* after 1070, and all subsequent warfare was strictly insular – either between the Anglo-Normans and the Celtic peoples, or among the various island peoples.

Before we return to individual battlefields, a brief resumé of military developments in the first centuries after the conquest will prove germane to what follows.

In 1067, after many months on campaign, William I returned to his duchy of Normandy to visit his wife, Matilda of Flanders, now Queen of England. England was left in the care of his most trusted commander, William Fitz-Osbern, the new Earl of Hereford. The two client kings set up in Wales by Harold, Bleddyn of Gwynedd and Rhiwallon of Powys, were suddenly vulnerable to Norman invasion. An English thegn, a relative to the infamous Edric Streona bearing the same name, initiated a guerrilla war in the Shropshire Hills, becoming Edric 'the Wild' in legend. In the Fens around Ely, another guerrilla resistance fighter, Hereward 'the Wake', defied many Norman attempts to storm his island refuge in the trackless wastes, but was finally betrayed to William. In the great forests of the Midlands and the north, a movement known as the *Sylvatici* or 'savages' lived as forest outlaws, launching attacks on Norman (or as the English called them 'French') convoys. Any Norman travelling alone was fair game, so they could only move in heavily guarded groups from one place to another.

A new law was enacted, called *Murdrum*, from which we derive our modern word 'murder'; whenever a Norman was murdered, the whole local area or 'hundred' in which they were found was treated as guilty and punished accordingly unless the culprit was identified. Soon, from being heroic resistance leaders, men of high rank and renown, the English resistance fighters came to be seen as a liability, and outlaws were shunned, forced to become woodland desperadoes like 'Robin Hood'. Although such people continued to defy the authorities for hundreds of years, the cruel and vicious Forest Laws, enforced by a notorious militia known as King's Foresters, meant that no serious resistance continued after about 1070.

The only region with any hope of asserting its independence from William's new regime was the old Danish-occupied region of the north. York, in particular, still had strong Scandinavian links, and the only plausible hope of shaking themselves free of Norman rule was to invite their Danish cousins with a Viking army. Soon the Bishop of Durham began to conspire with Malcolm Canmore, King of Scotland, to support a bid by Edgar 'the Aetheling' (who was in exile in Scotland) for the English throne. Durham was then occupied by a Norman garrison under Robert de Commines, but he and his men were slaughtered while they slept, and York erupted in rebellion too. The Norman garrison retired to their castle for a long siege, but King William arrived in time to save them. As soon as he marched north to the Scottish border, other insurgencies flared up in Staffordshire, Shropshire, and in the south-west. Harold's sons returned from Ireland and raided along the coast. William immediately turned his army around and marched to put down each rebellion in turn. But now William's fears were realised.

In 1069, a huge Viking fleet of 240 ships entered the Humber under the command of King Sweyn Estrithson of Denmark. An army of 10,000 Danes, Poles, Norwegians and pagan Lithuanians had combined with the northern rebels, and William's exhausted army was too small to face them in open battle. In the end Sweyn withdrew on payment of a considerable geld – the last of its kind ever to be paid to them by an English king. William's reprisals against the northerners were a war crime. He had always bitterly resented his sobriquet 'the Bastard', but even his own men were appalled at his deeds. Orderic Vitalis, a Norman chronicler himself, simply said, 'On many occasions I have been free to extol William according to his merits ... but I dare not commend him for an act which levelled both the bad and the good in one common ruin by a consuming famine ... such barbarous homicide should not pass unpunished.' Over 100,000 people – the equivalent of well over one million on these isles today – perished in the famine. Those who could sold themselves into slavery in Scotland, but there was to be no return home. Yorkshire and Durham were 'waste', with all villages destroyed, ploughs smashed, beasts slaughtered, and even the soil sowed with salt so that no crops would grow again. It was an act which demonstrated the contempt in which the Normans held the English, and which survives to this day in the notoriously complex 'class' system.

What can be portrayed as a quaint anachronism of English culture has much more significant origins. Almost a thousand years after this painful transition, a system of socio-economic stratification originally based on racial and linguistic principles is still alive, though not necessarily well, in England. The same perhaps cannot be said of the Scots, Irish and Welsh, who stubbornly retained their own distinctive cultures. It has been postulated that the enormous resentment towards the 'Norman' elite was one of the underlying psychological causes of the English Civil Wars in the seventeenth century – the notion of the 'Norman Yoke'. We will look at these matters in due course, but my own view is that the Norman Conquest fundamentally changed the English national character – and introduced habits of deference which have never really been lost, except for a few brief years in the 1640s.

England had now been forcibly incorporated into a larger Continental feudal system, and the Norman kings were usually preoccupied with their overseas affairs. The exception was when civil wars, usually between powerful Norman barons, threatened the English holdings. The first intimation of these wars came in a rebellion against William by the earls of Hereford and East Anglia in 1075. William's son Henry I also had to deal with a baronial rebellion when in 1101 Robert de Belleme and his brother Arnulf rebelled against him with Welsh aid. The border country with Wales, the *Marche*, was clearly a potential threat to the Norman kings, and Henry mounted several campaigns against the Welsh. In one campaign he was actually hit by an arrow, but his armour saved his life. Eventually Henry overcame the Welsh, but they rejoiced when soon after his death England was plunged into a bloody civil war between Stephen, Henry's nephew, and Matilda, his daughter. These were the years when, an English monk wrote, 'Christ and the saints slept.' This war, in which the hapless civilian population was harassed and slaughtered by both sides for almost twenty years, was the prelude to a consolidation of Norman power under Henry II, Matilda's son. The mightiest warrior in all Europe, he ruled an empire extending from Scotland to the Pyrenees. Yet in his attempt to invade Wales, Henry was frustrated by the wily Welsh leader Lord Rhys, who united the whole nation against him – and also by the notoriously awful Welsh weather.

In 1199, Henry's youngest son, John, became the new king of England. By now, over 130 years after Hastings, some degree of intermarriage and other significant social interactions had taken place between the Normans and the English. John actually spoke some English, and had a deep love of the country. Unfortunately, he was a psychopath whose legendary cruelty has overshadowed his keen intelligence and learning. But John's most significant failure was his loss of Normandy, which fell to the French king in 1204. From now on, the Norman kings of England were forced to focus much more on their English domains than hitherto. In 1215, the powerful barons of England forced King John to affix his seal to a document known as the *Magna Carta* or 'great charter' (to differentiate it from the separate 'Forest charter'). Although this event is celebrated as a precursor of modern democracy, in fact it was very limited in its scope, and was anyway disregarded by the king within a few months. But the baronial wars seriously weakened England; the entire kingdom was placed under a papal interdict, which prevented Christian baptisms, weddings and burials from taking place. John hired an army of mercenaries, called *routiers* composed of Aragonese and Brabancon cutthroats, whom he deliberately unleashed in a campaign of terror against rebel areas. Fortunately, John's young son Henry became a devout, meek and learned man as unlike his father as could be imagined. King Henry III reigned for fifty-six years, but for all his noble intentions Henry allowed himself to be intimidated by powerful barons, and by one in particular: Simon de Montfort.

17

LEWES, SUSSEX (1264) AND EVESHAM, WORCESTERSHIRE (1265)

The Second Barons' War, as it became known, was fought between 1264 and 1267, by recalcitrant barons led by the French-born Simon de Montfort and the royalist forces led by King Henry III and his son Prince Edward (later King Edward I). Two great soldiers, Simon and Edward, came to the fore during this conflict, which, though brief, was exceptionally bloody and eventful. The background to the war was extremely complex, but reveals the dark unconscious forces which lurk in the human psyche awaiting the conditions necessary to generate bloodshed. Notoriously, economic hardship has always been a breeding ground for such hatreds, and foreigners can all too easily be turned into scapegoats, as we saw in the case of the St Brice's Day Massacre of 1002. During Henry's reign just these influences of famine and foreign immigration conspired to bring about an awful civil war that saw many atrocities against foreigners, and particularly Jews. Amid this febrile atmosphere, an element of personal animosity soured relations between Henry and Simon.

De Montfort was a charismatic, dominating personality, a religious fanatic who saw himself as a popular messiah. He had inherited his French father's fanatical hatred of the Jews; as soon as he became Earl of Leicester, he banished Jews from the city and cancelled all debts due to them. When he secretly married the king's sister, Eleanor, without the permission of the other leading barons, there was much disquiet. Eleanor had sworn a vow of celibacy after the death of her previous husband, William Marshal, and the Archbishop of Canterbury pronounced the union with Simon invalid. Although the decision was overturned on appeal to the pope, royal resentment at Simon's impertinent pretensions festered. Fearing royal retribution, he fled to France and took the cross, travelled to Syria and the Holy Land on Crusade.

Meanwhile, as a series of poor harvests caused severe famine in England, and Henry's expensive foreign policy made him look for increased revenues, royal demands on the Jews (who were legally the property of the king, in exchange for his protection) increased exponentially. So heavy were Henry's financial demands that the Jews were forced to call in loans made to the wider population. The consequences were felt most keenly among the lower gentry, who were always vulnerable to predatory lords and barons who could seize their tenancies. In turn, these knights and yeomen appealed to the barons to exert more control over the king, as their ancestors had done in the First Barons' War with King John. In 1258, Henry was constrained by the barons to agree to the terms of the Provisions of Oxford. Henceforth, a council of fifteen members elected by the barons would formulate domestic and foreign policy on behalf of the king, and this in turn would be subject to scrutiny by a parliament summoned every three years. Henry appealed for arbitration in the matter to the French king, Louis, and at Amiens Louis found in favour of King Henry, who was personally present.

Simon, however, was back in England, and rapidly gathered an army. Appealing to popular xenophobia against Poitevin and Savoyard courtiers, but especially to resentment of the Jews, Simon's followers initiated a series of vicious pogroms against the small Jewish communities and synagogues in Worcester,

Winchester, Canterbury, Lincoln, Northampton, Cambridge and London, where over 500 were brutally murdered. The supposed murder of a small boy known as 'Little Saint Hugh of Lincoln', allegedly by Jews as a ritual sacrifice, fuelled mob violence and massacres. The true objective was to destroy the records of any loans made to gentiles, and since so many were in such debt the disorders spread rapidly. The situation soon drifted towards all-out war.

As soon as he returned to England, Henry raised an army of loyalists against the rebels and the two armies pursued each other around the country, seizing castles and strongholds but avoiding a pitched battle. Simon was enormously popular in London, and enlisted a body of troops, called trained bands, from the city. Combined with his own experienced and very professional contingent, and the retinues of the other rebel barons, he managed to muster a small army of 5,000 men, 500 of them elite cavalry under his own command. Learning that the royal army had concentrated in Lewes, in Sussex, Simon bravely sallied out to force a decision by confronting Henry and his son Edward there – even though he was outnumbered two to one.

On 13 May, the eve of battle, Simon drew up his forces a mile from the king's army, between Offham and Lewes, on high-ground with his right flank under the command of his sons Guy and Henry. In the centre the Earl of Gloucester stood to await the king's onslaught, and on the left the inexperienced but militantly anti-royalist Londoners under Nicholas de Segrave anchored his flank alongside marshland near to the River Ouse. At dawn, Simon ordered an attack on royalist foragers who could be seen returning to camp. Prince Edward, seeing the action, formed up his cavalry stationed by Lewes Castle to charge de Segrave's Londoners. The young prince valiantly pressed his attack, leading from the front, but he was too eager. The panicked trained bands turned and fled a full 4 miles, but Edward's cavalry were so elated that they disappeared from the main battle for two vital hours. The king and his brother Richard, Earl of Cornwall now had no choice but to attack Simon's rebel force, advancing their infantry uphill. Richard's forces soon began to take extremely heavy casualties, and the king 'was much beaten with swords and maces' and had two horses killed under him. The desperate battle raged on, until at last Prince Edward returned with his exhausted cavalry. He immediately saw that his father was having the worst of the battle, and charged Simon's personal battle litter, around which he perceived a knot of armed men. Edward's men took this to be Simon's bodyguard, but actually they were royalist hostages taken by Simon. Edward massacred them in error; he had not noticed that they were not wearing the distinctive white crosses worn by the rebels.

The rebel army led by Simon's experienced personal contingent had, meanwhile, forced the king's men down Offham Hill into the nearby town, and as the action moved to the ancient streets the town was engulfed in flames. Richard, Earl of Cornwall had taken refuge in the upper storey of a windmill, but was surrounded by the mocking rebel troops who beckoned him with the words, 'Come ye down ye wicked miller!' The losses among the royalist army were immense. Henry took refuge in the Priory of St Pancras just south of the castle. Edward anxiously sought him out, and after a brief conference the king sent messengers offering to make peace with the rebels.

The terms were excruciatingly harsh. In effect, Henry was to rule as a puppet king, and remained Simon's prisoner for fifteen months. The 'Mise of Lewes' agreed that a parliament of knights from the shires and two representatives from each borough should meet on a regular basis, and this formed the basis of our own democracy today. In 1265, Simon took Henry and Edward into the Welsh Marches as his virtual prisoners. On 28 May 1265, while out hunting at Tillington in Herefordshire, Edward made a daring escape. He made straight for Wigmore Castle, the stronghold of the staunchly loyalist Mortimer family. From there Edward made for Ludlow, and entered into negotiations with the Earl of Gloucester, Simon's principal ally, who agreed to switch sides in exchange for a royal pardon. Now Edward was to show the precocious military skill that would make him the most feared warrior of his age.

Seeing that the Marcher Lords were deserting his cause, Simon sought to conclude an alliance with the Welsh prince Llywelyn ap Gruffydd. On 19 June, at Pipton-on-Wye, Simon officially recognised Llywelyn as Prince of Wales. If he was to confront Edward, it was vital that Simon's son, also called Simon 'the Younger', should march his forces from London to conjoin with him in the west. But before the younger Simon could reach him, Edward captured the vital city of Gloucester at the end of June. The elder Simon was at Hereford, and to prevent his small army being boxed in west of the Severn he made a rapid march to Kempsey, just south of the City of Worcester. He took King Henry with him as a hostage, and he was forced to borrow armour and livery from Simon, which was to lead to almost fatal consequences later on. Edward had intercepted Simon's son at Kenilworth in Warwickshire, the family seat, but the castle was too small to contain all of his force, and those who could not find refuge within were wiped out by Edward. Many of the banners of the De Montfort party were captured, and Edward devised an ingenious use for them.

When news came that the elder Simon had crossed the Severn, Edward made a rapid march to intercept him. On 3 August 1265, Simon's 5,000 strong army reached Evesham, where the soldiers encamped for the night beside the River Avon. On the following morning, a barber who was posted on the high church tower to keep a lookout for the younger Simon's forces reported that he could see the De Montfort banners on the Alcester road. Simon observed other forces approaching the town, one of which crossed Offenham Bridge to the east, and another blocked the route out of the town on the London road to the south. The alarmed Simon suddenly realised that his son's banners had been captured and used as a deception. Edward quickly occupied the high ground of Green Hill, while the Earl of Gloucester, Gilbert de Clare, blockaded the road to Alcester. Mortimer had trapped Simon by closing his escape route to the south. Edward was determined to avoid any repetition of the disaster at Lewes, and Simon's position looked hopeless. With 10,000 tired but determined and vengeful men, Edward had trapped Simon beneath him with his back to the river. Simon knew as much, and declared, 'May God have mercy on our souls, because our bodies belong to Prince Edward!'

Edward had achieved his deception by an extraordinary forced march from Worcester, where his troops told those in the town that they were heading for Bridgnorth in Shropshire. According to Hilaire Belloc, Edward forded the Severn at Grimley under cover of night, then marched all night to Kenilworth, where he worsted Simon's son – and then marched all night again in order to capture the high ground overlooking Evesham and catch the rebel army quite literally napping. Undaunted, Simon formed his army into three ranks. His own cavalry, many of them veteran crusader knights, were with him in the front rank, with his English infantry behind them and Llewelyn's Welshmen in the rear rank. The weather was awful, and his only hope was to smash through Gloucester's men barring the way to Alcester and escape.

Simon's charge was a desperately valiant effort, but Edward's numerical superiority was overwhelming. He moved in on Simon's flanks and forced him back into the town. The Welshmen, seeing that all was lost, panicked and jumped into the river to swim for their lives. The English rebels, however, were massacred to a man – no prisoners were taken. Edward's men were crazed with bloodlust, and now they repaid the slaughter at Lewes by massacring the entire rebel force. At the time, men called the battle 'the murder of Evesham – for battle it was not'. Simon's son Henry died fighting beside his father before he too was dismounted. Surrounded by enemies, he fought bravely but was overwhelmed and hacked to pieces. His head, limbs and private parts were cut off by the bloodthirsty royalists. The same fate almost befell the king, who was discovered wearing rebel armour and livery. He only saved himself by crying out, 'Slay me not! I am

Henry of Winchester, your king!' Along with de Montfort and his son Henry, eighteen barons, 160 knights and 4,000 (mainly rebel) soldiers died. Although Kenilworth Castle held out for many more months, Evesham was effectively the end of the rebellion. Simon, one of the greatest soldiers in English history, had met his match in the ruthless Prince Edward.

Edward went on to hone his military skills by joining the Crusade, in which he was almost fatally wounded. Returning home by ship in 1272, Edward learned that his father was dead and he was now king. He was not crowned until August 1274, and was extremely annoyed that Llywelyn ap Gruffydd did not attend the ceremony as was normally the case. Llywelyn had been betrothed to Eleanor de Montfort, Simon's daughter, and the couple were deeply in love. As Eleanor was returning by ship to her beloved, Edward had the ship intercepted by pirates from Bristol. Eleanor was taken to Windsor and placed in confinement. Finally, Edward simply gave up these provocations and invaded Wales. With an immense army, of a size not seen since the days of Athelstan, Edward made an inexorable advance into the mountains of north Wales. Eventually Llywelyn was forced to capitulate, and the Treaty of Aberconwy in November 1277 reduced Gruffydd to the status of a minor Welsh lord.

But in 1282, Llywelyn 'the Last' rebelled again. After a brave campaign, he was finally killed in December 1282 when he was lured, unarmed, into a false parley. Wales was reduced to a vassal state, and in 1296 King John of Scotland, was humiliated in a similar fashion. In 1297, William Wallace led a Scottish national rebellion against the English. While Edward was overseas on another campaign, Wallace massacred an entire Anglo-Welsh army at Stirling Bridge, slaughtering 5,000 men. In July 1298, King Edward invaded personally, and 10,000 brave Scots were massacred in their turn at the Battle of Falkirk. Edward became known as 'the Hammer of the Scots', and even in 1307 the sixty-eight-year-old king rode into Scotland to put down yet another rebellion. Before he reached the border, however, he died.

Although his constant military campaigns and the construction of some of the most complex and mighty castles in the known world almost bankrupted England, it was now indisputably the most powerful of the island nations, and the Celtic peoples had been ruthlessly subjugated.

In June 1314, Robert the Bruce defeated Edward's hapless son Edward II at the Battle of Bannockburn, ensuring Scotland's freedom from English dominion. In Wales, meanwhile, the example set by Wallace served as a reminder that one hero could set an entire country ablaze. As Welsh resentments grew, all that was needed was a minor spark to ignite the powder keg. Eventually, the 'Son of Prophecy' – an expected Welsh messiah – came out of obscurity to lead his people to freedom.

18

BRYN GLAS/PILLETH, RADNORSHIRE
(1402)

So long as there is oppression and injustice in the world, then there will be war. This statement seems to radically contradict my assertion in the opening chapter that we may stand on the brink of a new kind of consciousness which will see war as a barbarous anachronism. Ultimately, this is a philosophical rather than a military issue (of which more in the afterword), but lest it be thought that I underestimate the ancient hatreds, the dehumanisation, the bitter feuds – all the evils that men do to one another – let me assure the reader that this is not the case. This chapter concerns a small but intense and bloody conflict in the Welsh Marches in the first years of the fifteenth century. For many years, the battlefield was not even marked on Ordnance Survey maps, and no official memorial existed there – though thanks to the efforts of campaigners an information board and direction signs to the battlefield are now thankfully in place.

But there is another kind of memorial of that fateful day, 22 June 1402. On top of Bryn Glas, 'Green Hill', a stand of Wellingtonia trees were planted near to the ancient church of St Mary's with its Celtic holy well, which unfortunately stood right in the middle of the battlefield. These trees mark the site of at least one mass grave for the bones of the English dead. Even today, human bones are found in the area. As is often the case, the scene today couldn't be more different, almost the epitome of peace. But this greensward was once soaked in blood, and the bucolic calm was shattered by the agonized screams of dying men. The splendid little church was set ablaze as men hacked and stabbed each other to death in the churchyard. When it was all over, the English claimed that Welsh women came to the carnage and mutilated the English dead by cutting off their private parts and stuffing them into their mouths or cutting off their noses and inserting them into their anuses. The dead English bodies, more than 1,000, were left to rot on the hillside in the midsummer heat. The stench was so disgusting that people deliberately avoided the area for months. Once the corpses had decomposed, the bones were buried in large pits, including the one marked by the distinctive trees.

It was very poignant for me to stand on that hill, and to remember that day, for some of my ancestors were of Welsh origin. It is fitting that a memorial has now been installed, for this battle was a spectacular Welsh victory which completely upset the political status quo not only in Wales but in England too. Few English people, I think, would have heard of the battle, with the exception of historical specialists. But of all the battles in this book, for me, this is the hardest one to deal with emotionally. For I must now face the ugly fact that I inherit certain prejudices, hatreds, and vendettas – just as anyone else does. In fact, I am heir to 1,500 years of such rancour and contention. So, if the atrocities committed by the Welsh women were true – which I doubt very much – I would be the first to condemn them as dishonourable.

In fact, when I stood overlooking the battlefield, my thoughts were mainly of those poor souls who died, the rural yeomen of Herefordshire slogging uphill in the heat of summer in full armour under a storm of arrows; they didn't have an earthly chance. Of all the ancient feuds and resentments among the peoples of these islands, perhaps none has been as enduring and intense as that between the Welsh and the English. It seems almost incredible that two peoples, living for the most part 'next door' to each other, until recently Christian and with many common cultural and commercial interests, have often been so incredibly hostile to one another. I wish that it had not been so, of course, but if we are to move beyond war and ancient vendettas, and live at peace with one another, we must each examine ourselves and try to expiate our own part in the cycle of conflict.

It is true that no major battles have been fought in Great Britain since 1746 – though of course Ireland is another story – but we must not become complacent about domestic peace. As I write, Britain is in the midst of the worst political crisis since the English Civil Wars of the seventeenth century. Mob violence, civil disorders and perhaps even worse are anticipated, and some irresponsible politicians seem almost to encourage extremism. For most people, they accept this sad situation as a terrible reminder of human sinfulness and wickedness – and the inevitability of conflict between peoples and nations, which is simply 'the way of the world'. I do not think such an insouciant attitude will do if we are to eradicate the threat of war for the next generations, but if we are to understand why people (usually male) become so angry as to risk their lives in mortal combat, we need to examine the misery of the oppressed peoples, 'the wretched of the earth' – and in the fourteenth century, none were more wretched and miserable than the conquered Welsh; treated like second-class citizens in their own country, under occupation by an English army which held down the population from some of the mightiest castles ever constructed. If we are to understand the significance of Owain Glyndwr's national uprising, and his astonishing initial successes, we need to first examine the extreme conditions, and cruel indignities, which fuelled the insurgency.

Wales is a land of castles, more of them per square mile than in any other country in the world – over 600 were built, of which more than 100 survive. Some of the most famous, like Conwy, Caernarfon and Harlech, were modelled on the massive Crusader strongholds Edward I had seen in the holy land. Their chief vulnerability was continuity of supply – provisioning parties could easily be ambushed in the mountains – but Edward had his castles placed on the coast so that they could be supplied by sea. Within the 'Iron Ring' of these castles, the native population were assigned a lower social status than the English and Flemings who colonised boroughs, walled towns from which the English exercised a sort of cultural imperialism. Welshmen were forbidden to speak Welsh in the 'Welsh Boroughs', and usually required to leave by a designated hour. In some border towns the penalty for infraction was decapitation. In Bishop's Castle, Welshmen could expect to be targeted by archers after curfew. The wandering Welsh bards, heirs of the ancient Druids, were deliberately targeted since they could serve as mediators of sedition.

The arrogant contempt of the English garrisons stoked bitter resentments, and in the halls of many minor Welsh lords there were eager audiences for wandering bards who recounted ancient prophecies of a coming liberation for the Welsh people under a mighty leader, a new Arthur – the *Mab Darogan* or 'Son of Prophecy'. The Welsh royal lineages stretched back to almost unimaginably ancient times – to Arthur, and Magnus Maximus or 'Macsen'. What the English saw as petty barons and princes of obscure territories were much more to the Welsh people, whose folk-culture included reincarnation of the souls of famous kings and heroes of old. Such a hero could be born at any time, and a newborn boy in a rural country manor house could be the chosen one. Because they had such small respect or understanding of such matters, the English authorities failed to realise that they were sitting upon a powder keg which could explode beneath them at any moment.

In 1399, Henry Bolingbroke, a grandson of Edward III, usurped the English throne. The deposed king, Richard II, was starved to death in a dungeon. The regime of Henry IV proceeded to antagonise those who had served the previous king, and one such was Owain ap Gruffudd Fychan, of Glyndyfrdwy, Merionethshire. Owain Glyndwr, as he is known to history, was a retired lawyer and sometime soldier who had served in King Richard's army. He was modestly prosperous for a Welshman, and lived in a splendid fortified manor at Sycharth, Powys, where he was a generous patron of wandering bards. One of the most influential bards was Iolo Goch ('the Red'), who composed *cywydd* or verses which implied that Owain was the prophesied one – the *Mab Darogan*. Glyndwr was thought to be 'the third Owain', the last of three Celtic heroes to bear that name. Owain of Rheged, patron of the bard Aneirin, whom we encountered earlier on, had been the first; the mighty Owain Gwynedd, who contended with Henry II, had been the second. Before he died, Iolo established that Glyndwr was a direct descendant of the kings of Powys, and of the Lord Rhys, who had united the country against Henry II. And it was true that strange portents had accompanied Owain's birth. Shakespeare, whose schoolmaster was a Welshman, evokes these strange omens in his *Henry IV*:

> At my birth ... the frame and huge foundations of the earth shaked like a coward ... the goats ran down the mountains and the herds were strangely clamorous to the frightened fields, and all the courses of my life do show ... I am not in the roll of common men.

There were other strange events. When the earthquake had subsided Owain's father went to the stables to comfort the whinnying horses, and had a sensation of wading through blood. For his part, the little lad was taciturn and withdrawn, and would not be comforted until a sword was put in his hand. There were rumours that he had strange powers, that he could speak with birds, possessing a cloak of invisibility and a stone called 'the Raven Stone' which conferred magical powers. In short, Glyndwr was something much more than his superficial status implied, not only a credible Prince of Wales but a kind of Celtic superhero.

War has a power all of its own, and conflicts escalate very quickly. When Lord Reginald de Grey of Ruthin, one of Glyndwr's powerful English neighbours, closed off grazing and watering rights to him at Croesau Common, Glyndwr, confident in his knowledge of the law, took the case to court. The matter remained unresolved, but de Grey was determined to undermine Glyndwr with the new king. He craftily intercepted a royal summons to Glyndwr, who therefore failed to respond. De Grey then insinuated that Glyndwr was a traitor, and the infuriated Welshman resolved to punish his treacherous neighbour. On 16 September 1400, Glyndwr was proclaimed Prince of Wales before a motley collection of his own family and tenants. On a market day, Glyndwr infiltrated a few hundred of his followers into Ruthin. Producing concealed weapons they immediately began burning the town so that only the castle and a few houses were left standing.

The uprising soon spread to Holt, Oswestry, Flint, Rhuddlan, Hawarden and Welshpool, all of which were burned and sacked in like manner. The number of insurgents rose rapidly, both because of long-standing resentment of English rule and opportunities for looting. At first, the English authorities dismissed this 'rebellion' as a minor disturbance, and the Welsh as 'bare-footed clowns', but the legend of the 'Son of Prophecy' was so compelling to them that Welsh scholars at Oxford and Cambridge universities suddenly absented themselves to join the uprising. On 24 September, English troops arrived in Wales to restore order. The ill-equipped Welsh force, such as it was, evaporated into the mountains, but this was to be no flash in the pan. The national liberation struggle had begun, and was to last for almost fifteen bloody years.

Gwynedd, and especially Ynys Mon or Anglesey, was the seat of the ancient and illustrious kings of that area. Glyndwr's cousins Rhys and Gwylym ap Tudur spread the insurgency to the island and in 1401, at Easter, they disguised themselves as carpenters and stonemasons, and, with just forty men, infiltrated the mighty Conwy Castle. The native Welsh managed to hold out there for many months. Two of the English garrison were killed in the audacious operation, but the cousins managed to negotiate an amnesty in exchange for relinquishing the castle in June, according to the chronicler Adam of Usk. In themselves these daring raids were only low-level armed resistance, but Celtic culture is very oral. Stories of exciting raids and cunning stratagems by Welsh guerrilla bands thrilled the native population as the bards spread the news through every community. Men flocked to Glyndwr's standard, and he was soon able to blockade the mighty castles of Harlech and Caernarfon.

No English king could ignore such provocation, and soon Henry invaded with a large English army. Glyndwr and his commanders, including his standard-bearer and most able soldier, Rhys Gethin (the 'Black'), retired before the English, observing their every movement from concealed positions in the mountain passes. As the English advanced they burned and looted every village and farm, and Welsh children were taken as slaves to be sold in England. To ensure the boys did not grow up to breed more 'rebels', they were castrated. The little girls' noses were slit and they were scalped to mark them out and discourage potential suitors. Rape was overlooked too, and gradually the Welsh people, including its clergy, came over in numbers to Glyndwr's cause.

Henry had already enacted extreme punitive measures that reduced the Welsh to little more than slave status. The entire Welsh people, not just 'rebels', were liable for reparations to the English Crown. All public meetings, family gatherings and bardic conclaves were immediately proscribed. All weapons were to be handed over to the English justiciars, and Welsh-owned castles and defended manors were to demolish the defences at their own expense. Welshmen were excluded from all public office, and no

Welshman could bring a case in court against an Englishmen unless the hearing was in English, using English law. Any Englishman who married a Welsh woman was deprived of his legal rights. It is not an overstatement to compare the regime to twentieth-century apartheid. These harsh laws, and the contempt they showed for the Welsh people, led to an escalation of the unrest across the entire country. A servant girl in Abergavenny opened a town gate to the insurgents, and English columns were regularly ambushed by deadly archers. Henry Dwn, a powerful Welsh yeoman, received a letter which revealed the extent to which Glyndwr now saw himself as the prophesied messiah who would liberate his countryfolk:

> We inform you that we hope to be able, by God's help and yours, to deliver the Welsh people from the captivity of the English enemies ... who for too long have oppressed us and our ancestors ... and now you may know from your own perceptions that their time draws close and because, according to God's ordinances from the beginning, success turns towards us ... no-one need doubt that a good issue will result, unless it be lost through sloth or strife.

As expectations rose, a sign – two, in fact – appeared in the heavens. In 1402, two very bright comets, so bright that the nucleus and tail could be seen in daylight, appeared in the skies. The first, the 'Great Comet', came in February, and a second equally spectacular one arrived in June, just before the Battle of Bryn Glas. The bards were in no doubt that these signs were divine, indicating success in war, and Glyndwr was almost ready to demonstrate his superb military skills in a major battle.

Almost exactly a year before Bryn Glas, in June 1401 Glyndwr demonstrated his abilities in a spectacular battle fought in the wilds of mid-Wales. At Mynydd Hyddgen, on the western slopes of Plynlimon a force of English and Flemish irregulars about 2,000 strong advanced to trap Glyndwr's tiny army. Another

English force under the command of Prince Hal, King Henry's valiant son, was approaching from the other direction. Glyndwr lured the Anglo-Flemish force into the desolate country around the 'five peaks', boggy broken terrain. The approaching English and Flemish were townsmen, unused to such wild terrain, encumbered by heavy armour – and on foot in intense heat. They were poorly trained and badly led, but outnumbered Glyndwr's force by four to one. Glyndwr's men picked off stragglers by approaching on their nimble little mountain 'hobblers' or ponies, dismounting and discharging deadly volleys of arrows. Near Stag's Mountain, Glyndwr gathered his 400 to 500 men and charged uphill with incredible ferocity and bravery. The panicked enemy scattered and lost 200 men killed, with 500 more taken prisoner. So, Owain was a wily and experienced commander who was as capable of weaponising the terrain against the English as Caratacus had been against the Romans. It was a glorious episode, but it foreshadowed an even greater victory to come – Bryn Glas, or Pilleth as it is known in England.

In June 1402, Glyndwr concentrated his forces near to Knighton in Powys, and raided Maelienydd, a cantref in central Wales, and one of the Marcher lordships of Edmund Mortimer IV, son of the 3rd Earl of March. He was a great-grandson of Edward III and so had a better claim to the throne of England than Henry IV. Other members of the Mortimer family had an even better claim than he did. Glyndwr's men burned churches and settlements in an attempt to lure Mortimer into a trap in the same border country where Caratacus had once faced the Romans. Mortimer raised a small army of 2,000 of his own local retainers and tenants, with many local Herefordshire gentry providing the levy. They mustered at Ludlow, where a 1,000-strong contingent of Welsh archers joined them. Welsh archers were among the best in Europe, and their services were for hire to the highest bidder. But it is distinctly possible that Glyndwr had either bribed these men beforehand to change sides or that Glyndwr's agents had infiltrated the company of archers, who marched and fought as a separate, self-contained body. If this were the case, Glyndwr appears to have planned the battle well in advance.

Mortimer's forces were most concerned to prevent any Welsh attack on Leominster, towards which they seemed to be heading. Mortimer was confident that with 3,000 men to Glyndwr's 1,000, the odds were in his favour. In fact, Glyndwr and Rhys Gethin were being continually reinforced, and by 21 June the Welsh army was about 1,800 strong, a much larger force than the English had anticipated. When they made contact with the retreating Welsh near Whitton in Herefordshire, Mortimer's men suddenly saw what they took to be the main Welsh army, consisting of 1,000 men, drawn up on the slopes of Bryn Glas, just inside Wales. Mortimer advanced his force to the lower slopes of the very steep hillside and prepared to attack. Unfortunately for his men, Mortimer had been lured into a deadly trap.

The Welsh, most of them light troops in little or no armour, easily outpaced the English men-at-arms in their heavy armour and quilted padding. As the weary English came on, the Welsh turned and discharged volleys of arrows to deadly effect. Mortimer's archers returned volleys, but with the gradient against them his archers had little effect on the Welshmen, who were goading the English to advance. Suddenly, and completely unexpectedly, the Welsh came charging down the hill shouting war cries, and to his horror Mortimer saw another force of about 800 Welshmen under the command of Rhys Gethin come careening into his already unsteady right flank. Gethin had cunningly camouflaged his men in a narrow defile, where they lay completely invisible to the English. The sudden shock of being attacked on two sides panicked the English, as the Welsh went at them with daggers, swords, halberds and spiked cudgels. Mortimer gave his Welsh archers the order to loose, but whether out of opportunism or pre-arranged intrigue they turned their volleys on the hapless English, their supposed comrades-in-arms.

By now the English were taking terrible casualties, and their discipline was breaking down. The slaughter around the burning church and on the slopes below was merciless. Mortimer was taken as a prisoner, along with Thomas Clanvow, another powerful local nobleman. Many English nobles were killed, and over 1,000 other Englishmen perished. Glyndwr's casualties were quite light for such a spectacular victory – about 200 killed and as many wounded. The rout of the English as they scattered down the Lugg Valley homeward must have left many hundreds of men dead also.

The responsibility for burying the dead following battles fell on the local parish authorities in the locality concerned. In such a remote place, there were simply not enough people available to complete such a task – and Glyndwr's renegades, having done their work, needed to escape into the Welsh mountains quickly before King Henry was able to respond in person. Eventually, after the decomposition of the corpses, their bones were laid to rest by local people. As the Wellingtonia trees attest, they were not treated dishonourably. A memorial plaque to the brave men who died on both sides exists in the churchyard. As to the stories of the English dead being mutilated by Welsh camp followers, these stories may well have been put about by the Marcher nobles to pressurise the English parliament into taking punitive action. But it is not impossible that women who had suffered dishonour at the hands of the English did allow their emotions to overwhelm them, especially those whose children had been violated, mutilated and taken into English slavery.

Mortimer was worth a huge ransom, but a furious King Henry, suspecting him of treachery, refused to pay it. He did pay the ransom for Glyndwr's long-standing enemy Reginald de Grey, however. Edmund had been wounded in the battle, and was nursed by Glyndwr's reputedly beautiful daughter Catrin; so began a tragic love affair straight out of Celtic myth. Quite soon, the couple were married and Edmund became a fanatical supporter of Glyndwr's cause. The minor uprising of the 'bare-footed clowns' of Wales had become part of a wider rebellion against King Henry's authority. Henry Percy, known as 'Hotspur', and his father, the Earl of Northumberland (also called Henry), joined Thomas Percy, Hotspur's uncle, in a conspiracy. Hotspur was a famous warrior in his own right, but the rebels also recruited Archibald Douglas, a renowned Scottish soldier, into the plot. Henry was now faced with two dangerous enemies: one in the north, and the other in Wales. The objective of the Percy clan was to effect a conjunction of their forces with Glyndwr's, so as to have combined numbers equal to Henry's army. They planned to meet with their armies at Shrewsbury in Shropshire, one of the strongest fortresses in the Welsh Marches.

19

SHREWSBURY, SHROPSHIRE (1403)

The Battle of Shrewsbury, also known as Berwick Field, Hussee Field or sometimes Bull Field, is marked today by Battlefield Church, about 3 miles north of the old town. Shakespeare refers to the battle in his *Henry IV*:

> I did demand, what news from Shrewsbury.
> He told me, that rebellion had ill luck,
> And that young Harry Percy's spur was cold.

The confederacy between the Percy family and Glyndwr was aided by Archibald Douglas, the Scottish soldier who had been sent to his homeland to raise a band of select warriors for the enterprise. The Percy family had previously supported Henry Bolingbroke's rebellion in exchange for grants of territory and monies when he became king. When none of these promised rewards materialised, they immediately charged the king with perjury. The ultimate objective of the conspiracy was to depose Henry IV and replace him with Edmund Mortimer – not the Edmund who had been captured and then induced to switch sides by Glyndwr at Bryn Glas, but another man of the same family and name with an even better claim. This Edmund Mortimer was a descendant of Lionel, Duke of Clarence, a son of Edward III, and so had rock-solid credentials.

The main conspirator, the Earl of Northumberland, claimed to be too unwell to join the march south, but his son Henry 'Hotspur' and Earl Douglas left with such forces as they could muster in hopes of gathering support along the way from nobles who had previously been loyal to the deposed Richard II. Richard's fate had not yet become public knowledge, and the rebels gave out that he was, in fact, alive and in Chester, and their heralds requested the gentry of Cheshire, who had been partisans of Richard, to meet Percy's army there. It was expected that Glyndwr's contingent would march to their support. In fact, 'Hotspur' had proven true to his sobriquet, because he had set out too early. Glyndwr's army was a long way off in Carmarthenshire, and only a handful of vital Welsh archers reached Percy in time for the battle. Unfortunately for Percy, his cause did not attract much support until he reached Cheshire, where a large company of excellent English archers joined him. His only additional support came from his uncle Thomas, Earl of Worcester, who joined him at Stafford. From there Percy marched to Newport in Shropshire, and then on to Shrewsbury, which they reached on 19 July 1403.

Percy's army arrived too late to take possession of the town and found the Castle Gate on the northern side of the town barred against them. Meanwhile, King Henry had been gathering an army for an intended Welsh campaign at Burton-upon-Trent when he heard reports of Percy's movements and probable line of march. He immediately left Burton on 16 July by way of the ancient Watling Street, and by the following evening his army reached Lichfield. The two armies were now in a desperate race to reach Shrewsbury and take possession of the castle and its fortifications. The king's army managed to get there in the nick of time, just hours before Percy's men appeared on the evening of 19 July. Even if Glyndwr's forces arrived to reinforce Hotspur, they now had no way to cross the Severn, for Shrewsbury is surrounded by the river on three sides and the king now controlled the vital bridge. Percy was now faced with a quandary. His skirmishers had already begun to engage the king's forces when he saw the royal standard flying over the town.

The next day, 20 July, saw negotiations between the king and Percy, with the Abbot of Shrewsbury as the intermediary. Percy was playing for time, in the desperate hope that Glyndwr's army may be closing the gap in time to join him. A small company of Welsh archers and insurgents from North Wales did reach him, but by 21 July it was clear that if Percy was to force a decision he was going to have to do so against unfavourable odds. He had only 15,000 men against the king's 20,000. While his army bivouacked 3 miles north-west of the town, unsure if they were to advance or retreat, King Henry forced their hand by marching out his army against them on 21 July. The rebel army were drawn up in a huge field of peas, and observers on the town walls could see the vast dust-cloud rising as the two armies – over 35,000 men in all – took their positions. The battle commenced quite late on that Saturday afternoon, and lasted for just three hours. They were to prove three of the bloodiest and most heroic hours in British military history.

One thing ran in Percy's favour. He was renowned as one of the bravest of the brave, a valiant and determined leader who approached war with a gusto that justified his nickname of 'Hotspur'. In Archibald Douglas and his elite Scottish mercenaries, he had a retinue of men of a like mind, whose ferocity and speed may yet carry the day. Percy's plan was to decide the issue by personally going after the royal standard, locating the king and killing him. But first, an exchange of arrows by many thousands of archers commenced, and the two armies were so close that every arrow found a target. In this bloody forty minutes or so, many hundreds on both sides fell dead, the chronicler Thomas Walsingham writing that they dropped 'like leaves in the autumn'. Percy, unable to restrain his men any longer, decided to personally charge the king and his bodyguard.

Percy, with Douglas beside him, hacked their way to the king's standard and brought it down. Douglas killed the king's standard-bearer, Sir Walter Blount, and three other knights. The king seems to have lost his horse in the melee, after killing several assailants himself. He was taken to the rear while a fresh horse was found for him, but at this vital moment his valiant son Prince Hal was seriously wounded in the face with an arrow. The fortunes of battle seemed to be turning towards the rebels.

The stricken prince was carried to the surgeon general, John Bradmore, who removed the arrowhead without anaesthetic using a specialised surgical instrument. The wound was treated with a solution of alcohol and honey, and the brave young prince – the lad who would one day become England's greatest military hero of the age, King Henry V – returned immediately to the fray. The situation was desperate. Edmund, the Earl of Stafford, who commanded the king's right flank, was killed in Percy's charge, and his panicked men fled. The rebels, among them many of the Cheshire contingent, reached the royal baggage train and sacked it, making off with hundreds if not thousands of horses. At this point the king re-entered the action with his elite guard, and Prince Hal rallied the king's left flank.

Now, in a few moments, the course of the entire battle turned. Percy, searching for Henry across the battlefield, foolishly opened his visor, and was instantly hit in the temple with an arrow which penetrated his brain. He was later speared through, but in the confusion it was unclear which of the two commanders had been killed. A great cry went up among the rebel army of 'Harry Percy king!', but within seconds the king rode before his men, declaiming, 'Henry Percy is dead! Harry Percy is dead!' Seizing the moment, his son charged into the rebels' right flank, and their front rank began to disintegrate. By now it was nearly nightfall and those of the rebel army who could fled the field.

An immense slaughter followed; 4,000 of Percy's men lay dead, and in the relentless pursuit another 3,000 were hunted down and killed, or later hanged at the assizes. The king had taken very heavy casualties as well, about 1,800 killed and 3,000 wounded, many of them fatally – for not many could rely on a skilled surgeon like John Bradmore. Thomas Percy, Earl of Worcester was captured alive. He was taken to Shrewsbury Castle dungeon and beheaded two days later for treason. His head was taken to be set up on the gatehouse of London Bridge. Douglas was also taken prisoner, but was ransomed later.

King Henry IV had won a famous victory, and his son had covered himself in glory, showing great promise for that time when he became a full-grown man. So grateful was King Henry to God for his deliverance that he ordered a fine church to be erected at the spot where the battle had raged at its most intense, and where so many eminent men on both sides lost their lives. Sunday 22 July was the feast day of St Mary Magdalene, and so the church is dedicated to her. Because of the summer heat, the bodies were immediately interred to avoid the problems seen at Bryn Glas.

Although Glyndwr's uprising went on for another twelve years, from this point Henry could concentrate his forces against the Welsh threat, which he had good hopes of eventually containing. He now occupied the throne of England by dint of his own personal valour in battle, and he had shown his determination to cling to power at any cost. His wounded son, proudly bearing a nasty scar, was now a national hero to the English – and at Shrewsbury he had learned valuable martial skills which would reach their zenith at the Battle of Agincourt in 1415.

20

BLORE HEATH, STAFFORDSHIRE (1459)

By 1415, Glyndwr's uprising had petered out. Although the 'Son of Prophecy' was never found, and the Welsh crown jewels remain hidden to this day to await his coming, all practical hopes of sustaining Welsh independence were, for the moment, abandoned. When Prince Hal succeeded to the English throne as Henry V and won a spectacular victory against the French at Agincourt, it was Welsh archers under the command of Master Archer Dafydd Gam, one of Glyndwr's implacable enemies, who tipped the balance in Henry's favour. The longbow had completely revolutionised medieval warfare. The mighty knights in their expensive armour could be brought down by a country yeoman carrying little more than a longbow, his helmet, a buckler and a dagger. At Agincourt, the archers taken together loosed their arrows at a rate of 1,000 per second. No plate armour was protection against the longbow. Arrows were observed to penetrate thick oak doors, and horses were especially vulnerable.

For the first time since Edward III, England had conquered its old enemy France, but Henry V's son, Henry VI, 'lost all his father won'. In fact, Henry VI was in every way unfortunate, and as his father's glories faded England rapidly descended into one of the bloodiest wars in its long history – the Wars of the Roses.

There will be insufficient space in this volume to give detailed accounts of the major actions of the conflict, but the Battle of Blore Heath is not so well known, and is an example (though in this case not a very well-executed one) of that most elementary military tactic – the ambush. In his classic *Polyolbion*, Michael Drayton sang of the battle:

> O! Cheshire wer't thou mad, of thine own native gore
> So much until this day thou never shed'st before
> Above two thousand men upon the earth were thrown,
> Of which the greatest part were naturally thine own,
> The stout Lord Audley slain, with many a captain there
> To Salisbury it sorts the Palm away to bear.

A brief background to the civil war will be necessary before we journey into the Staffordshire uplands.

The Wars of the Roses are so called because they were fought by two parties: Lancastrians, represented by the badge of a red rose, and Yorkists, represented by a white rose. The war had nothing to do with the regions of Yorkshire and Lancashire; King Henry VI was a descendant of John of Gaunt, the fourth son of Edward III, and the third surviving one. Henry was, therefore, of the House of Lancaster, and his partisans were known as Lancastrians. The supporters of Richard Plantagenet, Duke of York, who had a rival claim based on his being descended from Edward III's third son, Lionel, Duke of Clarence, were known as Yorkists. Richard also had sons, and so even after his eventual death Yorkist claimants survived him.

Initially, Richard sought to gain control of the realm through political means. Henry VI was, unfortunately, chronically mentally ill. His condition, perhaps some form of extreme affective disorder, worsened during the 1450s, when he and his wife, Margaret of Anjou, had not produced an heir. When Henry became so incapacitated that he no longer recognised key members of court, Richard convened a great council of state and had himself installed as Lord Protector for the duration of the king's illness. Margaret was incensed, and saw that her husband was being manipulated and undermined. When she became pregnant and produced an heir, Prince Edward, there were high hopes for the king's recovery, but he failed to recognise his baby son when the boy was presented to him. By 1455, however, Henry was lucid and coherent again. With Richard unwilling to relinquish power, hostilities commenced on 22 May 1455 at St Alban's, where in a bloody street battle Henry was seriously injured by an arrow and captured by Richard, who was restored as Lord Protector. Margaret, who now had her son's inheritance to protect, and who feared her husband relapsing into mental infirmity again, intrigued to depose Richard, and after an uneasy truce of four years the war resumed in deadly earnest.

The Yorkist forces were dispersed all over the country, which is a major risk in any military enterprise. The main stronghold of the House of York was Ludlow, in the Welsh Marches. Richard had gathered an army in Herefordshire and the border counties, and the Earl of Warwick, Richard Neville, known as 'the Kingmaker', had also joined the Duke of York's army. Warwick's father the Earl of Salisbury also had a substantial force of about 5,000 men at Middleham Castle in Yorkshire committed to the Yorkist cause. Either of these armies were vulnerable to attack from a larger Lancastrian force, but together they would be equal to or superior to the king's army. Salisbury decided, therefore, to march his army across England so as to link up with his son and the duke at Ludlow.

Meanwhile, the Lancastrians were also making their dispositions. King Henry was in Coalville in Warwickshire, but his wife and young son were at Eccleshall in Staffordshire, and as soon as news came of the Earl of Salisbury's approach the queen conferred with the commanders of the royal army. She ordered Lord Audley to intercept and destroy Salisbury's army as it marched through Staffordshire, with the intention of then isolating Richard at Ludlow, and defeating him in turn. Audley obeyed, and raised 10,000 troops in Cheshire and Shropshire, meaning he outnumbered Salisbury's army by two to one. Not content with this significant advantage, Lord Audley chose to fight a defensive battle with his men drawn up behind a fast-flowing and steep-sided brook, his men hidden from view behind a great hedgerow which extended across his front. Thus concealed, the Lancastrian archers from Cheshire could peer over the hedge across the wide expanse of Blore Heath, just outside Market Drayton and await the emergence of the Yorkist forces from the woodland beyond. Few armies have ever enjoyed such advantages before a battle – but, as we will shortly see, luck, finesse, bravado and courage can often confound such odds.

In the early morning of 23 September 1459, Yorkist scouts emerged from the woods onto the heath to examine the obstacle of Hemp Mill Brook, which ran across Lord Audley's front. They immediately saw Lancastrian banners protruding above the hedgerow, but affected to be unconcerned and withdrew. They immediately reported to the earl that a large enemy force lay ahead. Salisbury took the brave decision to fight. As his men drew up in front of Hemp Mill Brook, just out of range of Lancastrian arrows, they fell to the ground and prayed, fully expecting that they had seen their last sunrise. A parley was arranged, and while negotiations went on Salisbury formed his supply wagons into a defensive circle, into which his men could retire in case of a rout. When the Yorkist envoys returned, the earl ordered his archers to loose at their opponents on the other side of the brook. When the Lancastrians emerged into the open, the Yorkist archers seemed to retreat, and, sensing an opportunity, the Lancastrian cavalry charged them. But in doing so, they were exposing themselves to just the trap which Lord Audley had devised for Salisbury's men – namely the necessity to ford the deadly brook, where the heavy warhorses and their riders would falter.

After all his careful preparations it is extremely unlikely that Audley was responsible for this impetuous charge, but it was to cost him his life – and 2,400 other Lancastrian lives too. As soon as the Lancastrians reached the brook, Salisbury turned his archers around and they discharged volleys at the advancing Lancastrians. A terrible slaughter ensued, and the panicked Lancastrians retreated. Seeing that a possible disaster was imminent, Lord Audley charged again, and this attack was more resolute. After an intense fight, Audley gained the far bank of the stream with some hundreds of men, but was charged by Sir Roger Kynaston, a distinguished knight and a descendent of the Welsh kings. Lord Audley was killed, at the spot where a memorial called 'Audley's Cross' now stands.

This was a crucial turning point, but the king's army was still very much stronger, and occupied a better defensive position. Lord Dudley, Audley's deputy, now took command of the royal Lancastrian forces and ordered his remaining infantry reserve of 4,000 men to advance. But the press on the banks of the brook was by now so dense that the archers could not safely discharge their volleys. As it became clear that the Yorkists intended to force a decision, a body of about 600 Lancastrian archers defected to the Yorkist side and began loosing at their former comrades, as at Bryn Glas. Lord Dudley could not prevent a panicked retreat across the open heath to the south-west, and a terrible bloodbath ensued. The Yorkist cavalry were still capable of a lengthy pursuit of the fleeing enemy, and they did just this for the following twenty-four hours.

Although Salisbury lost 1,000 of his 5,000 men killed, the king's forces sustained more serious casualties: at least 2,400 killed, among them a roll-call of some the most distinguished knights and nobles in the kingdom. As Michael Drayton's verse implies, the most serious losses were sustained by the county of Cheshire. Queen Margaret had gifted the badge of a silver swan to any volunteers for her son's cause (as she had redesignated it) among the gentlemen of the county to induce them to join the Lancastrian army. Thousands had done so, but very few of them returned alive. John Sutton, Lord Dudley, and his son Edmund were captured, Dudley having been wounded. Apart from Lord

Audley, the Lancastrian dead included Hugh Venables, Richard Molyneux, Thomas Dutton, John Legh, John Egerton, Richard Done, John Dutton and William Troutbeck – all irreplaceable and experienced knights. On the Yorkist side, the earl's sons John and Thomas were both wounded. Lord Audley's body was carried away to be buried at Darley Abbey in Derbyshire, but many of the Yorkist dead were given a burial nearby. A local farm contains a tumulus said to be a mass grave.

Having won a most creditable victory against such heavy odds, Salisbury was nevertheless cautious in case another Lancastrian army was nearby. He therefore quickly departed from Market Drayton towards Ludlow, but took the precaution of employing a local friar to remain on the battlefield, where he was paid to discharge a cannon every half an hour so as to make any lurking Lancastrians suppose that the battle was still ongoing. Nothing could now prevent a junction of the Yorkist armies at Ludlow. Once their forces were combined, it seemed nothing could save Henry VI, his belligerent queen or his infant son.

21

MORTIMER'S CROSS, HEREFORDSHIRE (1461)

In July 1460, the Earl of Warwick entered London and took control of the city save for the Tower of London, which he put under siege. As we saw in the introduction, possession of the capital was of the utmost importance during any civil war. A Yorkist army, 25,000 strong, was raised from among the citizenry and from those counties directly adjoining London. Warwick and the Yorkist army immediately marched to confront King Henry at Coventry. The Lancastrian army, meanwhile, made for Northampton. On 9 July, a gruelling battle was fought in drenching rain outside the town. So damp was it that the Lancastrian cannon were rendered useless, and to compound this misfortune a traitor, Lord Grey, colluded with the Yorkist army and allowed them to enter the heavily fortified entrenchments the king had commanded him to defend. Dangerously drawn up with its rear towards the River Nene, the Lancastrian army fled. The hapless king was captured yet again. The redoubtable Queen Margaret, however, managed to escape with her precious young son, the Prince of Wales, and with the Duke of Somerset and a few bodyguards they made their way to the North.

Although her husband was now a prisoner, Margaret was still the heart and soul of the Lancastrian cause, devoted to her son and determined to preserve his rights at all costs. Through her tireless efforts a new army was assembled, and Richard, Duke of York was forced to leave London and march to Yorkshire to dispose of this fresh threat. Richard's handsome young son Edward, Earl of March was sent out to the Welsh Marches with the intention that he should raise fresh troops from the Mortimer family domains, and such Welsh archers as he could hire. The Yorkist party had had the best of the war so far, and it is possible that Richard had become overconfident. His army was quite small – about the same size as Salisbury's at Blore Heath, no more than 5,000 strong. This was wholly insufficient to engage the Lancastrians until his son arrived with reinforcements from the west.

On Christmas Eve 1460, Queen Margaret and the dukes of Somerset and Exeter, with several powerful northern earls and their large retinues, left York at the head of almost 20,000 men. On 30 December, the Duke of York, despite being outnumbered four to one, attacked the queen's army outside Wakefield. This rash and ill-considered offensive action saw Richard killed, along with 3,000 of his 5,000 men – a catastrophe of the first magnitude. Richard's young son Edmund, who was only twelve, was captured and put to death by Lord Clifford, who forever afterwards bore the grim nickname of 'Butcher Clifford'. The Wars of the Roses were bloody and savage to a degree never equalled in this island since. So bitter and prolonged were these wars that personal blood feuds festered, preventing all chance of conciliation or compromise.

This decisive Lancastrian victory completely turned the course of the war. Not only was the leader of the rebel cause now dead, but Lord Salisbury, the victor at Blore Heath, was taken prisoner. He was swiftly decapitated. All that remained was for Margaret to arrange the destruction of Richard's son, Edward, who was at Wigmore in the Welsh Marches. As soon as news came of his father's death and his army's destruction, Edward resolved to take his revenge. The young man was the darling of the borderlands – handsome, dashing, athletic, immensely brave, and gifted with a natural talent for war. Within weeks he had an army of over 20,000 men ready to march against the queen. With this army, Edward marched to Shrewsbury where he intended to gather even more troops, but news came that the earls of Pembroke and Wiltshire had raised an army for the Lancastrian cause in Wales, and it was marching towards the Mortimer family lands on the border. Edward had no choice but to return to address this dangerous threat, for the overall commander of the Lancastrian force was Owen Tudor, father of the Earl of Pembroke and the king's uncle. The operational commanders, however, were Jasper Tudor, Earl of Pembroke and James Butler, Earl of Wiltshire.

The two armies confronted each other at Mortimer's Cross near Kingsland in Herefordshire on 2 February 1461, the holy feast of Candlemas. As the two armies arrived at the field of conflict, a rare and almost magical phenomenon was witnessed by the combatants. This was what is called parhelia, or 'sun-dogs', whereby the rising sun seems to divide into three separate suns, one each beside the actual one – an atmospheric optical illusion. Such signs were considered auspicious or disastrous by many simple folk in the medieval period, and the common soldiery were extremely anxious upon witnessing the parhelia. Gradually, the suns joined into one. Shakespeare's *Henry VI, Part 3* describes the weird scene:

> Three glorious suns, each one a perfect sun;
> Not separated by the racking clouds,
> But sever'd in a pale clear shining sky,
> See, see! They join, embrace, and seem to kiss,
> As if they vow'd some league inviolable,
> Now are they but one lamp, one light, one sun.

Edward reassured his men, declaiming that the display was a propitious sign for victory. Afterwards, he would take the sign of 'the Sun in Splendour' as his personal emblem.

There is, unfortunately, no precise way of knowing exactly which dispositions the two armies took up, or from which direction they arrived, though the area around the Mortimer's Cross Inn at Kingsland in Herefordshire is central, as is attested by many artefacts discovered there over the years by farmers, ramblers and metal detectorists. Sir Richard Croft, from Croft Castle nearby, advised Edward to take the crossroads, where Jasper Tudor's advanced guard would have to gather to cross the River Lugg. A large company of archers was stationed there by Edward. Jasper therefore had no choice but to attack Edward, despite slightly inferior numbers. Edward's army numbered about 5,000 or slightly more, and the Lancastrian force about 4,000.

The Earl of Wiltshire led the assault on Edward's right flank, and managed to push the Yorkists back across the crossroads. Pembroke's division or 'battle' engaged Edward's centre but failed to make any significant progress. By afternoon, with the winter light fading fast, Owen Tudor decided to attempt a flanking movement on Edward's left, but his half-trained and poorly equipped yeomanry lacked the numbers, *elan* or expertise to comply with his order. Owen Tudor's wing of the Lancastrian army, all of them Welshmen, broke and ran, including Owen himself. He managed to get as far as Hereford, 17 miles away, but was captured and beheaded there, along with many other Lancastrian nobles and gentry. The rest of the Lancastrian force followed. The earls of Pembroke and Wiltshire managed to extricate themselves, but virtually the entire Lancastrian army was wiped out. It was an emphatic victory for Edward, and because of the barbarous treatment of his twelve-year-old brother at Wakefield, and stories of the Yorkist prisoners of war murdered after that battle, no Lancastrians were taken alive during the rout.

Once again, the war had taken an entirely new turn. Edward was now in a position to conjoin with the Earl of Warwick at Chipping Norton in the Cotswolds. From there Edward raced to London, where the victorious Yorkist hero was greeted by adoring mobs on 2 March. He was immediately proclaimed King Edward

IV, but King Henry was still alive, and his dangerous wife, with her precious son, was still actively recruiting and organising in the northern counties.

The Battle of Mortimer's Cross was small and obscure but extremely decisive. The Yorkist cause, which only a few months previously seemed doomed, was now very much alive. Unfortunately, apart from the few lines from Shakespeare quoted previously, very little is known about the details of the battle. In 1799, a monument was erected commemorating it on the turnpike road nearby.

22

TEWKESBURY, GLOUCESTERSHIRE
(1471)

The fortunes of war were now running for the Yorkist party, and new king Edward IV was determined to settle matters once and for all. Margaret was still in the field with a large army, and had managed to defeat the army of the Earl of Warwick at a second battle fought at St Alban's. She was a vengeful woman, and she had Lord Bonvile and Sir Thomas Kiriel, Henry VI's former gaolers, executed when they were captured. The vendettas were becoming more and more toxic. This intense hatred was soon to culminate in the greatest slaughter seen in this island since Roman times: the Battle of Towton. Towton can by no stretch of the imagination be described as either forgotten, lost or obscure. Even today, many people know that more people were killed in it – a staggering 28,000 – than in any other English battle. Two great armies were gathering, each intent on exterminating the other; no quarter would be the rule.

The armies met between the villages of Saxton and Towton in North Yorkshire on 29 March 1461, in a blinding snowstorm and howling winds. The Yorkist army was still arriving, and so initially it was outnumbered – only 20,000 of its total complement of 30,000 were present at the start of the battle, which lasted all day. The Lancastrian army was 35,000 strong, and had taken up a defensive position. But the winds favoured the Yorkist archers, and Lord Fauconberg, commanding the Yorkist vanguard, ordered them to loose their deadly 'bodkin' arrows onto the enemy. Their volleys took a considerable toll on the Lancastrians, whose countering volleys fell short, doing no harm to their Yorkist adversaries. This goaded the Lancastrians into a furious and blind frontal assault in which over 50,000 men murdered each other in close-quarters combat over eight hours. The nearby Cock Beck flowed red for three days afterwards with the blood of the slain. Eventually, Yorkist reinforcements arrived under the Duke of Norfolk, and the Lancastrians gave way, many of them being trampled to death in their flight across the Cock Beck or stream.

In all, including the following rout – little more than ritualised slaughter – an incredible 36,776 men were killed. This was the costliest but most emphatic victory of the war for the Yorkists. Edward was now king not just in name but in fact. He had offered an amnesty to any who renounced the Lancastrian claim to the throne, and many were now willing to abandon Henry. Edward IV was left to reign in comparative peace for nine years – but Margaret of Anjou would never relinquish her son Edward's claim to the throne.

With Henry in exile, however, and no powerful supporters left alive, Margaret's cause seemed hopeless. She lost the royal treasures, and was even attacked by a band of robbers – but so fanatical was she that a renewal of the conflict was certain so long as she and her son remained alive. The Lancastrians attempted an abortive rebellion in May 1464 under the command of the Duke of Somerset, but this was defeated by John Neville, whose retribution against the rebel leaders was swift and merciless. Henry toured various castles and country houses still loyal to him, until eventually he was betrayed by a 'black monk of Addington' at Waddington Hall in Lancashire in July 1465. The poor man tried to conceal himself in the woods nearby but was easily discovered. From there, Henry was taken to London, where he was kept as a prisoner in the Tower, estranged from his wife and son and all human contact. In his lonely imprisonment, all seemed lost to him, and he wrote mournful poems to console himself. But the deposed king's cause was still alive in France, where his wife and son were now in exile at the court of the French king.

Before we examine the campaign of 1471, a brief background to the complex political machinations which preceded it will prove useful. In 1470, the Earl of Warwick, who had become disaffected with Edward IV due to his favouritism towards the relations of his new queen Elizabeth Woodville, landed in England. His most powerful ally was Edward's brother George Plantagenet, Duke of Clarence, who had persuaded Warwick to install him on the throne. Warwick had no intention of doing any such thing, but instead made his way to France to intrigue with Margaret to reinstate or 'readept' Henry and his descendants. A marriage was solemnised between Warwick's daughter Anne and Prince Edward, though this was not consummated. Queen Margaret was too shrewd to allow her son to return to England until her husband had first been liberated.

Warwick and Clarence advanced on London, and meanwhile, in the north, Warwick's brother John Neville had raised a Lancastrian force. King Edward had no choice but to accept exile, and took ship at the port of King's Lynn with his younger brother Richard for Flanders. King Henry was liberated from his close confinement in the Tower and 'readepted' at St Paul's Cathedral as king. But now Warwick betrayed his promise to Clarence that he should inherit the throne after Henry's death. Instead, Prince Edward and his descendants would succeed him, the throne only reverting to the House of York if the Lancastrian line died out. The duke saw that he had been duped, and secretly intrigued to reconcile himself with his estranged and exiled brother Edward. With Warwick having cleared a safe path for the return of Margaret and her son, the Lancastrian heir finally prepared to land in England.

Meanwhile, the exiled Edward had received the help of the Duke of Burgundy, the enemy of the French king. Supplied with a tiny fleet and a few hundred men, Edward tried to land at various places along the east coast, eventually doing so at Ravenspurn in Yorkshire. He marched on York, evading Lancastrian forces sent to interdict him. By the time he reached the Midlands, thousands were flocking to his banner. He announced his intention to depose Henry. On 14 April 1471, his army of 15,000 surprised the Earl of Warwick in a night attack in dense fog at Barnet in Hertfordshire. Despite being only half the size of Warwick's army, the momentum was initially with the Yorkist force, but the Earl of Oxford eventually drove back Lord Hastings and a large body of Yorkists. Returning to their own positions, the Lancastrians were mistaken for the enemy in the fog and shot at and fired upon by their own side; they had mistaken the Lancastrian banners for Edward's 'Sun in Splendour' device in the dense mists of early morning. In the confusion, the Earl of Warwick's brother was killed; Warwick attempted to flee but was cut down in the rout, along with 4,000 Lancastrian troops. The Kingmaker was dead.

On the very same day the Battle of Barnet had been lost, Margaret and Prince Edward landed at Weymouth. She was obviously extremely perplexed and upset, for now Edward had control of London – so often the key to victory in the case of civil war. Her only option was to raise an army among her supporters in the western counties of England – but especially in Wales, where Jasper Tudor, Earl of Pembroke was a powerful ally. If their two armies could conjoin, they had high hopes of reinforcement from their northern heartlands. As Margaret and Prince Edward progressed through the West Country, the restored King Edward IV gathered his army and marched out of the capital to decide the fate of the war beyond any further doubt. The king sent messengers to Gloucester instructing the town authorities to bar the gates of the city to Margaret's army, thereby denying her the crucial Severn crossing she needed if she was to reach her Welsh ally. Edward, meanwhile, had left Windsor where he had mustered his army, and by 29 April he was at Cirencester, where he received intelligence that the Lancastrians were soon to leave Bath with the intention of fighting him. Keen to settle the affair, Edward advanced to Malmesbury. Within hours, the Yorkist 'prickers' or scouts ran into Lancastrian foragers who promptly captured them.

Edward immediately realised that the enemy force was close, and learning that Margaret intended to attempt a passage of the Severn at Gloucester, sent urgent messages to his commander there, Sir Richard Beauchamp, to deny her the city at all costs so as to confine her operations to the eastern bank of the river. Although Margaret and Prince Edward had been considerably reinforced in Bristol, especially with artillery, as her army proceeded from Gloucester to Tewkesbury the heavy guns in the rear were overtaken by the Yorkist vanguard and seized, putting the Lancastrians at a huge disadvantage for the coming struggle. It was clear to Margaret that there was no choice but to face Edward in a pitched battle without Jasper's aid, and her exhausted men encamped for the night of Friday 3 May just outside the little town of Tewkesbury.

In 1471 there was no crossing to be had over the Severn at Tewkesbury, the next bridge north of Gloucester being that at Upton-upon-Severn, halfway to Worcester. A canard was rife among the Lancastrian army, perhaps encouraged by Margaret, that Jasper's forces were only hours away, and would soon arrive to reinforce them. Fortified with a somewhat desperate optimism, the Lancastrian soldiers did what they could to prepare artillery positions and defended palisades and trenches throughout the night. Edward's army was approaching from Cheltenham, but in his dash across the country in intense heat his horses and men had become extremely dehydrated and exhausted. This was a concern, and the Yorkist army was somewhat smaller than the Lancastrian – only 5,000 men to the Lancastrians' 7,000. In all other respects, however, the king's army was superior. It had more heavy guns and other artillery than its opponent, and consisted of mainly mounted soldiers who dismounted to fight on foot. Their morale was high, for in King Edward they were commanded by a consummate expert in military matters, battle-tried and recently victorious at Barnet. Richard, Duke of Gloucester and Lord Hastings, who commanded two of Edward's 'battles' or divisions, were also very able commanders who could be depended upon.

On the morning of 4 May, these three 'battles' advanced with trumpets blaring and banners flying aloft. King Edward had the advantage of being able to overlook the Lancastrian encampment, which he observed was flanked by a dense copse from which any Yorkist advance could be ambushed. To counter this threat, the king sent a company of mounted spearmen there, giving them orders to break up any attempts at flanking operations by the enemy. This precaution was to pay off handsomely once the action commenced.

As the Yorkist army advanced, it found its progress severely impaired by a network of sunken lanes, hedges, ditches and embankments – quite apart from the Lancastrian defences prepared overnight. The Duke of Somerset, the chief Lancastrian general, had quickly seen how this landscape could be put to useful effect. At certain points in his line, he deliberately left gaps so that large counter-attacks could be made as the action developed. The Yorkist artillery bombardment soon opened, as Gloucester's archers advanced to loose volleys on their Lancastrian opponents. The Lancastrian artillery responded just before Richard's Yorkist forlorn hope closed with the front line. It was a valiant assault, but because of the difficulties of the terrain no appreciable progress was made. The Yorkists retired in good order, however, and fell back in obedience to a direct command from the teenage Richard of Gloucester, who was already showing a precocious military skill to match that of his brother the king.

Gloucester gambled that a Yorkist retreat in the fog of battle might be misinterpreted as a general rout by the enemy commander – and this proved to be the case. Somerset's men flooded through the gaps deliberately left open in his line, and threaded their way through the sunken lanes with the intention of flanking Edward near to the wooded park mentioned earlier. Gloucester's ruse worked, and as the Lancastrians came on at the charge, he suddenly ordered his men to about-face and engage them hand to hand. The Lancastrians were taken by surprise and fell back in some disorder, but were far from routed. At this point, the 200 mounted spearmen the king had stationed in the woods charged and cut down the fleeing Lancastrians before they could reach their encampment. King Edward immediately supported his brother, and Somerset's Lancastrian 'battle' began to disintegrate. Fleeing through the sunken lanes and ditches, many were ruthlessly butchered or taken prisoners. The furious Somerset had relied on his comrade Lord Wenlock to come to his aid in just this eventuality; he made straight for Wenlock during the retreat and angrily questioned him as to why he had failed in his duty, but before the poor man had time to make any reply his skull was smashed in by a battle axe wielded by the vengeful duke.

This bloody deed summed up the Lancastrians' desperate situation. King Edward now assaulted their main defensive line and with typical courage and skill, carried by force. As we have seen before, the deadliest time in any battle in these wars was the rout afterwards, and Tewkesbury was no exception. The Yorkists were now running amok in the Lancastrian camp, burning and sacking the baggage train, and murdering any found within, whether combatants or camp followers. The panicked Lancastrians fled into a meadow by the Severn where they cast off their armour in a desperate bid to gain the far bank – the place is still called 'bloody meadow'. Over 3,000 lost their lives here, but some men did manage to escape, and regrouped across the river near an old mill. From there they made their way to the town, home to several large churches where they hoped to find sanctuary. Others, including some of the most eminent Lancastrian nobles, went to Tewkesbury Abbey seeking protection; among them was the crestfallen Margaret.

Her young son, Prince Edward, was taken prisoner in a small wood. Sir Richard Crofts brought him to King Edward – an annuity of one hundred pounds had been promised to the man who took the young man alive. The furious king confronted the defeated and frightened lad – really a boy in man's armour – and asked by what right he invaded the realm. The young man made to justify his own claim, but before he could finish his sentence the king smashed his gauntlet across his face. The Duke of Gloucester, Lord Hastings, the Duke of Clarence and a few other knights present took the whimpering prince outside where he was stabbed to death. This was a cruel, bloody deed, but by no means unusual in this savage conflict. The prince's body was laid to rest in a common grave in the abbey grounds with many of his slain soldiers.

It now dawned on the desperate individuals hiding within the abbey that there was no right of sanctuary operative there. In such a case, and with the blood of a prince on his hands already, Edward may have simply stormed in and taken them for execution. The punishment for treacherous rebels was decapitation, then quartering of the body for public display, but the king refrained from this, his bloodlust perhaps already sated. Two days later, however, Edward had Somerset and many other leading rebel prisoners executed. Some time later, Margaret, having heard the grim news of her son's ignoble death, sent a message offering to surrender. She found sanctuary in a small nunnery nearby, but gave herself up to be taken in Edward's chariot, where she was displayed to the baying London mob, and thence to the Tower of London. There she would stay, a broken woman, until she was ransomed by her father, the Duke of Anjou. On the very evening she arrived, her husband Henry, the former king, was murdered nearby, probably by agents of the Duke of Gloucester. A pathetic attempt was made to explain Henry's death as having been due to heart failure when he heard of his son's death. Examination of his skull many years later showed that he died from a blow to the back of the head. So ended the tragic life of a most unfortunate monarch.

After such a crushing victory for the king, it may be imagined that all Lancastrian hopes were dashed, and that the war was finally over. But the cause of the Red Rose of Lancaster still lived on, and in fact King Edward IV was still threatened by large forces, commanded by the Earl of Pembroke in Wales and Thomas Neville, 'the Bastard of Fauconberg', who was marching an army of 16,000 men through Kent with the objective of storming London from Southwark, just as King Sweyn and Duke William had done in centuries past. As on previous occasions, the trained militia of the city was strong enough to repel Fauconberg's attack. Margaret of Anjou was ransomed in 1475 and died seven years later. To all intents and purposes, the Lancastrian cause was lost, and the Wars of the Roses at an end. But after so much drama and bloodshed, and with many bitter blood feuds unresolved, it was only a matter of time until they erupted again in a final spasm of violence.

23

STOKE FIELD, NOTTINGHAMSHIRE
(1487)

Over 100,000 men lost their lives on the major battlefields of the Wars of the Roses, and probably an equal number perished in minor engagements or as a consequence of famine occasioned by the constant disturbances. In proportion, then, these wars were somewhat more costly than the later English Civil Wars of the seventeenth century. Many of those killed were from the highest social strata, noblemen of ancient families established since William the Conqueror's time. The bitter division between the parties did not disappear overnight, and even after the crushing defeat at Tewkesbury there were many Lancastrian sympathisers who hated Edward's rule and waited for glad tidings of his demise.

It is often stated, quite incorrectly, that the Battle of Bosworth Field in Leicestershire on 22 August 1485 was the last battle of the Wars of the Roses. As we will see, there was in fact one more bloody slaughter to be fought before the conflict was finally resolved – Stoke Field. Before we look more closely at that battle, however, we must understand how Henry Tudor had come to the throne of England as King Henry VII.

Henry Tudor, Earl of Richmond, was born in 1457 to Margaret Beaufort, a great-granddaughter of John of Gaunt, the third surviving son of Edward III. Henry's father Edmund died before he was born. As soon as Edward IV regained the throne, Henry was forced into exile in Brittany, where he stayed under the protection of Duke Francis II for fourteen years. King Edward IV died in April 1483, to be succeeded by his young son Edward V. The boy survived for only two months under the 'protection' of his uncle Richard of Gloucester. Edward and his younger brother Richard mysteriously disappeared, and it was widely believed that Gloucester had them both murdered – he immediately succeeded Edward as Richard III, and had every motive, though many still dispute his guilt. By 1483, Margaret Beaufort had long been remarried to Lord Stanley, a Yorkist, but despite this she continued to press her son's rather slender claim to the throne.

After a previous failed expedition, Henry finally enlisted the aid of the French king for another one, and on 7 August 1485 he landed with a force of 2,000 French and Scottish mercenaries at St Anne's Head, where his small fleet anchored in Mill Bay, Pembrokeshire. Wales, and especially south-west Wales, was a stronghold of Lancastrian sympathisers. Henry was also a descendant of the ancient Welsh royalty, and deliberately appealed to Welsh sentiment, marching towards England under the banner of a Red Dragon. By the time he crossed the border into England and reached Newport in Shropshire, his army was 5,000 strong. By 18 August Henry had reached Tamworth in Staffordshire, and on the next day he met Lord Stanley, who privately assured him that he would support him in the forthcoming battle. The army then marched from Atherstone, Warwickshire towards Market Bosworth, a small town just inside Leicestershire. On the 21st, Richard's army was seen encamped outside the town, and the two sides prepared for a battle the following morning.

Richard III supposed that Lord Stanley's loyalty could be taken for granted because he held his son George as a hostage. Richard departed Leicester with the Yorkist army on 17 August, and it is said that as he rode by an old 'cunning woman' tried to bar his way, warning him that if he went on his dead body would return, naked and slung over a horse. The two armies were in sight of one another by 22 August, but neither Richard nor Henry knew for certain which side Lord Stanley, with his crucial 4,000 troops, would choose. To make matters clearer in his mind, Richard sent a messenger to Stanley threatening to kill his son George if he failed to support him. Stanley replied that he had other sons, and the incensed king gave the order to execute George (Lord Strange) but was restrained by his principal commanders. Henry also sent to Stanley to know his intentions, but Stanley's reply was by no means reassuring.

Henry therefore had no choice but to attack Richard's army of about 10,000 with only 5,000 soldiers. Whatever else he may have been, Richard was a very able military commander. He chose to draw up his forces on Ambion Hill, where his artillery on his right flank had a clear view over the Lancastrian position. The Duke of Norfolk anchored the king's right wing with 3,000 spearmen, with the king in the centre with another 3,000 men, and on his left flank the Earl of Northumberland's 3,500 men stood with their backs to the town of Market Bosworth. A marsh also hindered Henry's advance. For his part, Henry was so inexperienced in war that he waited in the rear of his army with a small bodyguard, leaving the fighting to his most able commander, John de Vere, Earl of Oxford.

As Henry's men negotiated their way around the marsh – with great difficulty, for they had been instructed to stay within ten paces of their unit's banners – the king's artillery opened fire, soon followed by deadly volleys of arrows. The Welsh archers responded with volleys of their own, and when the front ranks closed with pikes and halberds Henry's men held off the Duke of Norfolk's attack. Richard could see Henry bringing up the rear, and decided to charge him and kill him before Stanley could enter the fray. The furious king, a famous soldier of immense courage, killed Henry's standard-bearer Sir William Brandon and then knocked Sir John Cheney from his horse with a broken lance. Henry quickly dismounted so that he would be less easily recognised in the melee, taking refuge in a formation of steady Welsh pikemen who managed to repel Richard's horsemen, but at one point Richard was within striking distance.

The Earl of Northumberland, who should have come to Richard's support, seems to have either procrastinated, or to have been unable to form up his wing in time to aid the king. Stanley, however, observing the hapless Henry's plight, quickly committed his 4,000 troops at this key stage of the battle. Richard lost his horse in the marsh, but even though he had only a few brave followers left beside him he stubbornly refused to retreat. He is said to have declaimed, 'God forbid that I should retreat. I will win here as a king, or die as one!' A Lancastrian by the name of Rhys ap Thomas fought his way to Richard, who was promptly surrounded and bludgeoned to death. The blows given were so heavy that his helmet was smashed into his skull. When Richard's body was recently exhumed it was found that the skull had nine massive head wounds, and that the back of the skull had been sliced off by a blow from a halberd. Richard's bannerman continued to hold the royal standard aloft even when both of his legs had been cut from beneath him, but within minutes news of the king's death spread through the Yorkist ranks and they fled the field, leaving about 900 dead. Henry's casualties were quite light for a conflict in this war, maybe less than 500. He was crowned king on the field of battle.

In many histories, the Wars of the Roses are implied to have ended at that point. Sadly, there was one bloody postscript yet to come.

It might be supposed that the Yorkist cause had perished with Richard. But even now, the Yorkists entertained faint hopes that the Earl of Warwick, young son of George, Duke of Clarence and nephew to Edward IV, had somehow escaped capture. In fact, Henry VII took precautions to have him closely confined in the Tower of London. Despite this, it was put about that the young earl was in exile, and the ten-year-old son of an organ builder called Lambert Simnel (some called him John Simnel) was tutored by an Oxford clergyman named Richard Symonds to perfectly impersonate the real earl. If the scheme were to stand any chance of success, Simnel needed to replicate all the complex mannerisms and etiquette of the court, to remember with clarity important life events, both the earl's and those of his relatives. His education in the classics, languages and religion had to be peerless, and to his credit Symonds did a good job, for it was said that had he succeeded Simnel would have been one of the best-educated monarchs in English history. Symonds used harsh methods to achieve this result, however.

The main backer of the plot was the Earl of Lincoln, who obtained 2,000 crack Swiss and German mercenaries for an expedition to overthrow Henry VII. These superb soldiers were commanded by Martin Schwartz, an experienced and brave officer. They landed in Ireland, where another force of about 5,000 Irish 'Kerns' or light infantry, men much like Glyndwr's Welsh militia, were also hired. Lambert Simnel was crowned as 'King Edward VI' in Dublin using a coronet taken from a statue of the Blessed Virgin. Simnel, accompanied by Lincoln, Schwartz and the famous Irish soldier Sir Thomas Fitzgerald, as well as Viscount Lovell, landed in Lancashire where a few local supporters joined them. With an army of over 8,000, many of them seasoned European veterans, the imposter Simnel constituted the most serious threat King Henry had yet faced.

The Earl of Lincoln was the main Yorkist commander, and he marched across the Pennines in June 1487 to reach Masham in the Dales. He hoped to receive support at York, but the city elders refused to back him. This was a serious psychological blow to the rebel army. They were forced to fight their way through the great expanse of Sherwood Forest until they reached Nottingham. When his army reached Southwell, it made for a crossing of the River Trent near Fiskerton. Eventually, they reached the small village of East Stoke in Nottinghamshire, where quite soon they encountered Henry's army arriving from Newark, which he had fortified against the rebels. On 16 June, Henry saw the rebel banners flying atop a ridge called the Rampire. He drew up his own army, of 12,000 men, in three lines just south of the village of East Stoke. Lincoln's men stood with their right flank bisecting the Fosse Way near two windmills. He was quite outnumbered, but having come thus far, and with little hope of gathering further support, he hazarded battle.

The king's army, considerably reinforced by Rhys ap Thomas from Wales, and by the arrival of Lord Scales, arrayed in three 'battles'. Just before battle commenced – and as at Mortimer's Cross – an exhibition of odd lights in the sky unnerved many of the men, but when they deployed forward the king's archers soon took a deadly toll on the Irish 'Kerns', who were wearing little if any armour. Lincoln's men, particularly Schwartz's mercenaries, had handguns, crossbows and artillery pieces, but eventually the Irish, goaded by a hail of arrows, charged down the ridge. A three-hour struggle followed. The Irish fought with great bravery but, being so ill equipped, began to take very heavy casualties. The Earl of Oxford, commanding the king's army as at Bosworth, bore the brunt of the fighting, and as the king's reserves arrived to reinforce them, and Lincoln's force was gradually whittled down, the rebel army was forced back upon the river. Many of the Irish now fled down a ravine still called 'the Bloody Gutter', where they were easily targeted by archers. With their backs to the river, they were doomed. Schwartz and his mercenaries refused to yield and were overwhelmed by arrows until their bodies 'looked like hedgehogs'. Fitzgerald, the Earl of Lincoln, Sir Thomas Broughton and Lord Kildare all died fighting bravely with Schwartz – only Lovell escaped. It is thought that a body found in a secret passage at his family home some hundreds of years later may well be his.

The Yorkist army lost over 4,000 dead, and the king's army nearly 2,000 – a much higher price than at Bosworth. The boy

Simnel was found cowering in the rebel baggage train with his tutor Symonds. Henry was gracious enough to spare the boy, and instead put him to work in the royal kitchens as a scullion. He later became the king's falconer. Symonds too escaped execution, though he never regained his liberty. Fiskerton Ferry, the only means of escape for the Yorkists, was the scene of a gory massacre that made the Trent run red for some time afterwards. Mercifully, though, this was the last blood to flow in the conflict. After thirty-two years, the terrible civil wars were over.

With the end of the Wars of the Roses, we must conclude the third part of this military history. We leave just before the dawning of the modern era, when war was still fought in a fashion familiar from the conflicts which had gone before. But when we resume, in part four, we will emerge into a new era, in which the longbow, the lance and body armour have been superseded by the pike, the musket and heavy artillery, as well as new innovations in the mass deployment of cavalry, the precursor to modern warfare.

PART FOUR

24

'WHERE ENGLAND'S SORROWS BEGAN': POWICK BRIDGE, WORCESTERSHIRE (1642)

The transition from the old medieval order to the pre-modern age was abrupt, startling even, and effected changes in consciousness – particularly the religious consciousness – which were to fuel yet another phase of bloody civil wars in England. Even before Henry Tudor came to the throne in 1485, religious fundamentalists called Lollards had demanded a simpler faith, with a greater emphasis on the primacy of the scriptures and a disdain for the worldliness of the clergy. The Protestant movement commenced in 1517, and by 1536 King Henry VIII had commenced a campaign to dismantle the monasteries and friaries of England, the so-called Dissolution of the Monasteries. By 1539, the Acts of Suppression had effectively destroyed the ancient system, which was often the only form of social security and healthcare available to the poorest in society. In an orgy of iconoclasm, church art was destroyed and books were burned. There was fierce resistance in the north of England in particular, but Henry was resolute. One of his motives for seizing the assets of the monasteries was financial; he desperately needed funds to build new fortifications against a possible French invasion.

By the time Henry's daughter Elizabeth I came to the throne in 1558, the breach with Rome was complete. A growing portion of the populace, benefiting from increases in literacy, became radicalised, obsessed even, by new and revolutionary ideas. Barry Reay summarises this religious and social transformation thus:

There were many factors at work in England's slide into civil war during those bewildering months from the meeting of the Long Parliament in November 1640 to the raising of the royal standard at Nottingham in August 1642. The intrusion of events in Scotland and Ireland, fear of popery, economic crisis, social unrest, class conflict, the continual tension between Court, Parliament, City, and Country, individual personality, indeed sheer blunder and chance, all played a role in the emerging conflict. But it was the religious factor – what Sir Benjamin Rudyerd described as 'our primum quaerite' – that was perhaps uppermost in those months ... for it was religion which in a real sense stimulated and fired revolution. Discontent with the counter-reforming policies of Archbishop Laud during the 1630s was among the precipitants which 'brought the collapse of governmental institutions from the realm of possibility to that of probability' ... 'For many contemporary writers,' Robin Clifton has observed, 'the essence of the conflict' between Parliament and King 'was in fact a collision between true religion and popery'.[25]

All these powerful forces were in play in the emerging modern consciousness, and the protestant or 'puritan' extremists were in the grip of extreme resentments, which they projected onto Catholics, the nobility, women and the clergy. There was also an element of social class struggle involved, and a split between north and south, and country and town. But these divisions were compounded in 1625 by the accession of Charles I, a ruler

---

25. Reay, B., 'Radicalism and Religion in the English Revolution', in *Radical Religion in the English Revolution*, eds J. F. MacGregor & B. Reay (Oxford, 1984)

stubbornly determined to resist any of the dynamic forces newly unleashed. He was by no means a bad man, but he was obdurate, slightly arrogant, and had an unfortunate personality. He was a small, diffident man, sensitive and socially gauche, with a lifelong stammer. He married a Roman Catholic at a time when this was bound to be perceived as virtual treason by a large number of his subjects. Like his father, James I, he believed in the Divine Right of Kings – a doctrine bound to put him on a collision course with his more radical protestant subjects in an age when ideas of democracy and the equality of persons before God were uppermost in their minds.

By 1642, war between king and parliament was inevitable. On 22 August, Charles raised his standard on Standard Hill, Nottingham. In an unfortunate sign of things to come, the heavy banner collapsed in the wind and landed in the mud. The king, finding few recruits to his cause in the radical city of Nottingham, soon left to raise his army elsewhere. So began a horrific series of civil wars that would see the king's reign end on the scaffold on 30 January 1649.

In the 150 years since the Wars of the Roses had ended, many military innovations had arisen. Heavy armour, the distinguishing hallmark of the elite nobility and their retainers for hundreds of years, had been rendered obsolete. Pikemen still wore helmets, and some wore breastplates, but the new weapons of the infantry were so heavy and cumbersome that additional, ineffective armour no longer justified the encumbrance or financial outlay. Artillery had developed rapidly; there were both heavy, wheeled guns and lighter pieces called 'sakers' firing grapeshot, which fragmented to deadly effect. During the Thirty Years War (1618–48), the Swedish commander Gustavus Adolphus had introduced revolutionary new mass-cavalry tactics. The Royalist general Prince Rupert introduced similar cavalry tactics into England. Each cavalier was, in theory, armed with a pistol. The troopers would then form a line, or 'caracole', and advance at a brisk trot to the enemy line, discharge their pistols, and then retire. A second line would repeat the process before the first line wheeled around and charged through any gaps in the enemy ranks in closely bunched groups. Fleeing infantry would then be cut down by the sword, and the enemy baggage train ransacked.

The English Royalists, or Cavaliers, were brave but also infamously ill disciplined, and a great risk was that, in the heat of the pursuit, they would detach themselves from the main action at a crucial moment – as happened at the first major battle at Edgehill in 1642. The bloodthirsty Prince Rupert of the Rhine favoured a policy of charging the enemy with drawn swords rather than pistols, but the Roundheads, as the Parliamentarian troops were known (for their close-cropped haircuts), retained the 'Dutch' method of discharging pistols at the trot. The infantry would advance to the beating of drums in dense ranks armed with pikes up to 16 feet in length. Behind a screen of musketeers, these blocs of pikemen would then engage the enemy at 'push-of-pike', aiming to break their cohesion. Operating together, the men would lower their pikes in unison, a sure deterrent to enemy cavalry, which could not breach the formation so long as it held firm. Morale was the key to victory; a well-disciplined and trained unit showed its steadiness and experience by keeping their pikes perfectly shouldered en masse, without any sign of wavering. When the war commenced, however, very few units had yet attained anything like such discipline or proficiency, and both sides had much to learn about the new military methods.

The first engagement of the war, the preliminary cavalry skirmish at Powick Bridge, perfectly demonstrates just how callow and unprofessional the two armies were at the outset of hostilities. Robert Graves made the interesting observation that support for the parliamentary cause was strongest 'in those areas where Celtic blood ran thinnest'; that is, in the south-east, London, Essex and East Anglia and the south-east Midlands.[26] By contrast, support for the king was strongest in the 'Old

---

26. Graves, R., *The White Goddess: An Historical Grammar of Poetic Myth* (Faber & Faber, London, 1948)

North', Wales, the western Midlands and the south-west – those areas least affected by modernising and radical ideas from the Continent. The Lords in Parliament, and about one-third of the Commons, supported the king, as did the bishops and all the university colleges bar Wadham. The Church, both Anglican and Roman Catholic, and the nobility and gentry of the countryside, along with their feudal retainers, also sided with the monarchy on the whole. But the Royal Navy went over to Parliament, and the crucial financial support of the City of London was also denied to Charles. More important, however, was the king's lack of ports, through which aid from friendly monarchs overseas might otherwise have reached him. Therefore, the main strategic aim of the Royalists was to intimidate or capture London early on.

The king managed to raise a small army of 4,000 infantry, and about half that number of cavalry, in these more sympathetic regions. It was assumed by the Parliamentarian commanders that, having lost control of the capital to their forces, Charles would eventually be forced to come to terms. But as we have seen, the king was stubborn, and the hot-headed Prince Rupert, his main cavalry commander, was contemptuous of the Parliamentarian militia and itching to see combat action as soon as possible. On 13 September, the prince was granted his wish.

A consignment of silver plate in a convoy of wagons had left Oxford bound for Shrewsbury where it was to be delivered personally to the king by Sir John Byron. Byron reached Worcester with a small force of cavalry, and the amateurish city garrison let him through; the gates were unlocked anyway, and in a state of disrepair. Seeing these dilapidated defences, Byron grew anxious that he might be overtaken by Robert Devereux, Earl of Essex, the commander of the Parliamentarian army, who was in close pursuit. Byron felt that he could not risk leaving Worcester for Shrewsbury unless he was considerably reinforced by cavalry, and his hunch soon proved correct.

Parliamentarian scouts under the command of Colonel Nathaniel Fiennes approached the Sidbury Gate on the south side of the city. It was open and unguarded, but the Roundhead troopers didn't realise that; instead, they smashed it with an axe and fired shots. The garrison belatedly turned out and chased off the outriders. Meanwhile, a messenger had been dispatched to the king requesting aid, and on 22 September Prince Rupert, with the cream of the Cavalier cavalry, many distinguished nobles among them, headed off to reinforce Byron. The next day, they set out from Bewdley for Worcester by way of Astley, Shrawley and Hallow, arriving in St John's, on the west bank of the Severn, about midday.

Meanwhile, Fiennes had withdrawn with his cavalry to Powick, a village about 3 miles south-west of Worcester with a bridge over the Teme so narrow that only two horsemen could cross abreast of one another. From Powick Fiennes had a clear view over the city, so as soon as the Royalist wagon train left he could immediately intercept it en route to Shrewsbury. He confidently expected his comrade Essex to appear with the main army and invest the city within hours, and was completely unaware of Prince Rupert's arrival to begin with. A large number of citizens had walked out to Powick to gawp at the odd phenomenon of armed soldiers, but none of them, including the Puritan divine Richard Baxter, knew of Rupert's whereabouts. Suddenly, Baxter tells us, a breathless messenger arrived to report that Byron's treasure train was on its way out of the city.

The Roundhead troopers reached the narrow bridge over the Teme and slowly filed across. Fiennes commanded about 1,000 men, so this took some time. They were soon shocked, however, to come across the Royalist force resting in their path. Among them were Prince Rupert, his brother Maurice, Royalist commander Lord Digby, Lord Wilmot and Sir Lewis Dyve – some of the bravest and most dashing Royalists – and 700 of their men. Rupert had neglected to post pickets. Fortunately for him, the enemy soldiers were simply so astonished that they froze. Rupert did not. He leaped into his saddle, drew his sword, and bellowed 'Charge!' at the top of his voice. As one man, the Royalists all followed him, and within moments the Roundhead cavalry were chased down the narrow country lane – and back to the bridge.

The result was absolute chaos for Fiennes and his men. As they struggled to turn around in the narrow lane, then found themselves blocked at the even narrower bridge. Panic spread from the men to their mounts. Many soldiers were thrown over the bridge into the river. Ahead of them Rupert's brave band of comrades, most of them wounded by swords, had hacked their way into the Roundhead force, killing forty men and wounding over a hundred. Three brave Parliamentarian officers, Colonel Edwin Sandys, Major Alexander Douglas and Captain Edward Wingate, tried to hold the narrow lane – Sandys and Douglas both died in the attempt. But by now the panic had infected the whole Parliamentarian force, and in a desperate rout those who could rode hell-for-leather through Upton-upon-Severn, and thence as far as Pershore. Here they met the Earl of Essex and the main Parliamentarian army, and their evident panic quite unnerved their comrades.

In itself, this was a minor skirmish – amateurish, almost comical at times. But it was also deeply tragic, for it was but the prelude to much bloodier times ahead. Essex arrived in Worcester the next day, but by then Rupert and his men, along with the king's silver plate, had departed for Shrewsbury. When news reached the king of the main Parliamentarian army's proximity to Worcester, his commanders urged him to depart with all speed – for with good fortune he would gain two days' march on his enemies in the inevitable race for London. As soon as he did so, Essex had no choice but to interpose his army between the king and the capital, and on 23 October 1642, at Edgehill in Warwickshire, the two main armies confronted each other for the first time.

There was one final, rather strange legacy of the battle. It so happened that when the civil war ended, almost exactly nine years later at the Battle of Worcester in 1651, the action largely took place around Powick Bridge. As Parliamentarian preacher Hugh Peter declaimed to his victorious comrades then, 'Go tell them you were at Worcester ... where England's sorrows began, and are now happily ended.'

25

ROUNDWAY DOWN, WILTSHIRE (1643)

In October 1642, so far from being happily ended, England's sorrows were about to begin in deadly earnest. On 22 October 1642, Royalist scouts encountered their Parliamentarian adversaries outside Kineton, a small village in Warwickshire. The Roundhead garrison of Banbury had appealed for aid to the Earl of Essex as soon as the king's outriders approached, and despite being unprepared he immediately marched towards what he presumed to be the king's main force. He was quite correct, for the king was nearby with his entire army.

Anxious for a decision in a main battle, Charles had selected a strong defensive position on a 600-foot-high V-shaped ridge. This was Edgehill, dominating the road to London along which Essex and his men must retreat if they were defeated. Essex therefore had no choice but to accept battle. Charles had between 11,000 and 13,000 men in his army by now, and the gallant show by Prince Rupert at Powick Bridge had inspired a certain hubris among them. The Royalist cavalry were, at this stage of the war, far superior, by virtue of their innate skills in horsemanship and greater funds and equipment. The king's artillery, too, was better trained and more numerous. But in the most crucial arm of all – the infantry – the Parliamentarians had the edge in the shape of the London trained bands, militia who regularly drilled together, under experienced officers who had served in the Continental wars. These men were something like soldiers, even though they had yet to experience battle. The king's infantry were, by contrast, hirelings, with only desultory training if any, and no religious or 'ideological' underpinning to their service. Many of the Roundheads, however, were religious fanatics who saw their struggle in eschatological terms, and fondly expected that the king's overthrow would see Christ Jesus Himself return to rule in glory.

Although Essex had over 18,000 men in the immediate area, he could only concentrate about 12,000 or at most 13,000 on the battlefield, and so both sides were evenly matched on the day. Prince Rupert, with his famous cavalry, was placed on the king's right flank, with another large wing of cavalry, lifeguards and dragoons under Lord Wilmot on his left. The king was in the centre, and initially his infantry was under the command of Lord Lindsey, but following a dispute over infantry tactics Lindsey resigned at the last minute, to be replaced by Lieutenant-General Ruthven, whose 'Swedish' formation was finally adopted. These disputes took up a considerable time, and it was after midday when the king finally rode along his line encouraging the troops. No shots had been fired in anger thus far, but the sight of the king, whom many Roundheads equated with the Antichrist, infuriated the Parliamentarian gunners so much that they opened up a barrage. The king's gunners immediately responded, and the first great battle of the First English Civil War was underway.

Opposing Rupert's Cavaliers, Essex positioned his own cavalry under Sir James Ramsey. On his other wing, opposing Lord Wilmot, was Lord Fielding's brigade of cavalry and dragoons, with supporting musketeers and a number of heavy guns in defensive positions. Renowned Scottish soldier Sir William Balfour and Sir Philip Stapleton were positioned in a wood just behind the Parliamentarian frontline as a cavalry reserve. This precaution was to save the day for Essex later on. The Royalist army had been moving down from the ridge for about two hours when suddenly, Rupert impetuously charged in his usual manner. Wilmot's cavalry on the other wing followed suit, and both flanks of the Roundhead army collapsed, with the Cavaliers in gleeful pursuit as they made for the village of Kineton. But Rupert's men strayed so far from the main battlefield that Sir William Balfour's cavalry reserve opposite the king's centre was able to charge. Supported by the infantry, he began to turn the king's left flank. In the sudden confusion, the young Prince of Wales and his brother the Duke of York were forced to hide behind a hedgerow.

The king himself was now in very serious danger. Balfour's men had overrun the Royalist artillery, killing the gunners and cutting their traces. The king's own standard was captured by an ensign called Arthur Young, and his standard-bearer, Sir Edmund Verney, was killed. The Earl of Lindsey was seriously injured, and he later died of his wounds. By now some of Wilmot's cavalry were returning to the battlefield. A Royalist cavalryman, Lieutenant-Colonel Welch, managed to recapture the royal standard as it was being taken to the rear by Roundhead troopers. Welch also captured two cannon. This heroic exploit appears to have been attributed at a later date to a Captain John Smith, due to the fact that Welch was involved in various scandals implicating royal personages, and was an Irishman; Captain Smith was English. Whoever recaptured the standard, some semblance of order was restored in the Royalist centre. Balfour's timely assault had almost broken the Royalist line, but it was too late in the day to exploit the advantage. Both sides withdrew for the night, which was bitterly cold. Each had lost about 1,500 men killed, and a great many more wounded.

Neither side had a heart to resume the battle in the morning. The king offered Essex a royal pardon if he would accept terms, but the offer was rejected with contempt after so much bloodshed. The Roundheads had acquitted themselves manfully, and were in no mood to compromise now. Essex withdrew towards Warwick, leaving a large part of his artillery behind him. Prince Rupert, whose dread reputation and cruelty were well known, raided into Kineton village and slaughtered the Parliamentarian wounded who had been left there. Among the Roundheads, Rupert was suspected of being a warlock. It was rumoured that he was invulnerable to musketry, and that his dog, called 'Boy', which rode into action alongside his horse, was his 'familiar spirit'. Rupert did all he could to enhance his notoriety, and his men followed his example. Within weeks, strange stories circulated that ghostly armies were assembling to re-fight the battle by night. These spectral armies were seen by many reliable witnesses, and are still occasionally reported nowadays.

The two armies now made for London, and Rupert's advance troops got as far as Brentford. But the Parliamentarian army was now considerably reinforced by the London trained bands, and in November 1642, at Turnham Green outside London, Essex confronted the king's army with 25,000 men. The king's army was only half that size, and after a desultory exchange of artillery the king withdrew to Oxford, his provisional capital. The war had now spread all across England, and small-scale skirmishes, sieges of castles and large country houses, ambushes of enemy supply trains and consignments of monies took place everywhere. Prince Rupert took care to be at the forefront of many of these actions, and, as we have seen, became a hate figure for the Roundheads.

By the 'Royalist Summer' of 1643, the tide of the war had begun to turn in the king's favour. Parliament's hero John Hampden was killed in a sharp skirmish with Rupert at Chalgrove Field in Oxfordshire in June of that year. Sir William Waller was besieging Lord Hopton at Devizes in Wiltshire, but Prince Maurice, Rupert's brother, managed to escape the Roundhead cordon to ride for help, leaving the wounded Lord Hopton, whose 3,000 men were out of ammunition, to hold off Waller, whose army was somewhat larger. Prince Maurice managed to reach Lord Wilmot, the Lieutenant-General of Cavalry for the king, and with almost 2,000 cavalry they set out to relieve the blinded Hopton. On the morning of 13 July 1643, Wilmot's force charged the Parliamentarian cavalry, or 'Lobsters', under Sir Arthur Hazelrig. These 'Lobsters', armoured cavalrymen, were swiftly overwhelmed and driven down the steep hill overlooking the village of Roundway. Hopton, meanwhile, hearing the cannon fire from Wilmot's two 'gallopers' (light guns much like an earlier form of horse-artillery), had emerged with his Cornish regiments from Devizes to support Wilmot's attack. Many of the Parliamentarian cavalry had perished when they had been forced off a precipice called 'the bloody ditch' on Beacon Hill. The Roundhead infantry panicked, and ran straight into the Cornish regiments. Waller's men lost 600 men killed in a sharp action. About 1,500 more Parliamentarians were taken prisoner, and Waller lost all his guns, horses and baggage.

The victory marked a high point for the Royalists, and the Roundheads were simply stunned. One captured officer remarked that the 'hand of God Almighty' was responsible for the defeat – which tells us much about the low morale of the Roundheads afterwards. The vital port of Bristol was now open to the king, and on 26 July it fell to Prince Rupert. Virtually the whole south-west of England was now in Royalist control, and through Bristol precious arms, munitions and supplies could reach the king. There was briefly a plan to attempt to capture London, but Charles was not able to concentrate against the city while strong enemy garrisons remained in his rear. Deciding instead to reduce them one by one, he first attempted to besiege Gloucester, which was a hotbed of Roundhead resistance and prevented easy communications with South Wales and Ireland.

The small battle at Roundway Down – or, as the Royalists mockingly called it, 'Run-away Down' – was the high point of the king's fortunes. Now, he had only to take Gloucester, held by Colonel Massey, to consolidate the gains already made during the 'Royalist Summer'. The Earl of Essex knew that he must prevent the loss of Gloucester at all costs, and his army prepared to leave London.

26

THE PROGRESS OF THE WAR
(1643–1644)

The war had so far developed 'not necessarily to the Parliamentarian advantage'. Essex marched an army of over 20,000 men, mostly from the London trained bands, westwards to rescue Massey's beleaguered garrison at Gloucester. Rupert's scouts encountered the Roundhead vanguard outside Newbury in Berkshire. The prince seized the town, and Essex had no choice but to offer battle. In a bold move, he launched a dawn attack preceded by a devastating and accurate artillery barrage, from high ground which the Royalists had been too exhausted to occupy on the previous evening. The Royalist infantry cowered in hedgerows and ditches until Lord Byron led them in a frontal assault on the hill. A great many Royalist noblemen and men of high rank were killed. Over 3,000 of the king's men fell in the desperate assault, but by the evening, with his guns completely out of ammunition, Charles had no choice but to break off the attack and retire once again to Oxford.

Essex limped back to London, having lost 3,000 dead and many more wounded. But although the battle may be called a tactical draw, in strategic terms it was a reverse for the king, although his cavalry took Reading in Berkshire. It marked, too, a considerable psychological turning point. The Parliamentarian side was split, as Charles well knew, between Reformist Presbyterians – who were relatively moderate – and 'Independents', Seekers, Levellers, Baptists, Fifth Monarchists, Quakers, Ranters, 'Muggletonians' and a host of other so-called 'fanaticks'. These latter were extremists who saw any compromise with the king as a compromise with the Antichrist. The moderates were more willing to approach the king for a peace treaty, but they did not realise the strength of feeling among the rank and file of the army, who increasingly saw all conciliation as treachery and apostasy. London was the epicentre of these radical ideas, and as long as it held out no negotiated peace was possible.

At the end of March 1644 came news that lifted Parliamentarian spirits and gave hope for a successful campaigning season during the forthcoming summer. At Cheriton in Hampshire, Sir William Waller decisively defeated Lord Hopton's Cavaliers, and suddenly Roundhead hopes were raised. The king's army, already quite small, was depleted by this defeat, and Essex captured Abingdon when the king recalled the garrison to supplement his main field force. Charles found that his refuge and temporary capital at Oxford had become a potential trap. He decided, therefore, to leave Oxford with the 8,000 men under his direct command. This he was unable to do, because he was blockaded at Banbury. If he was to escape, he needed Prince Rupert to create a diversionary attack from Shrewsbury, either in the direction of York, to prevent a juncture of the northern Roundhead forces with the Scots Covenanters (with whom Parliament had concluded an alliance) or, failing that, to march to Worcester and thence to Oxford. But the order was not worded explicitly enough. Charles intended Rupert to do one or the other of these things, but instead he tried, and failed, to do both, setting out over the Pennines to York, which he intended to take before marching south to relieve the king. The misfortunes which stemmed from this unclear order so disturbed Rupert that he kept the order on his person ever afterwards as a defence for his decision.

The king attempted to take his main force to Daventry, expecting Rupert to be advancing towards him, and left a smaller force to guard the bridge over the River Cherwell at Cropredy in Oxfordshire. Waller's combined cavalry, infantry and eleven guns attempted to take the bridge. Initially the assault was successful, but a counter-attack by Royalist cavalry under Lord Cleveland captured the Parliamentary guns and broke their line. Waller was forced to flee, leaving all his baggage and guns behind along with many dead and wounded. This timely victory, small though it was, pleased the king greatly. He had just become the father of a little daughter he had yet to see, and now that Oxford was a redoubt again, and not a trap, he had fond hopes of being reunited with his family. Rupert was marching towards York with an army of nearly 20,000, and on 1 July the city was finally relieved. But an army of a similar, if not greater, size consisting of Roundheads and Scots 'Covenanters' or Presbyterians was approaching the city, where the decisive battle of the war now took place at Marston Moor, on 2 July 1644.

To be fair to Rupert, his skilful march over the Pennines and his evasion of the allied forces on the approach to York was a masterpiece, but his behaviour on arriving there immediately unravelled the advantages gained. The allied armies combined comprised a total of 24,000 men, and if he were to take them on with only 17,000 effective soldiers he would almost certainly be defeated. He sent a peremptory, even arrogant demand to the commander of the York garrison, William Cavendish, Marquess of Newcastle, to send his available infantry to him at Marston Moor. The sophisticated Cavendish was a favoured courtier, and he resented Rupert's tone. It was therefore late in the day when he reluctantly reinforced Rupert, who was determined to force a decision at Marston Moor. Lord Fairfax, the Parliamentarian commander, with his son Sir Thomas Fairfax and David Leslie, a famous cavalry officer who had served in the Thirty Years War under the Swedish Gustavus Adolphus, now recalled their forces to prevent Rupert's cavalry from exploiting any gaps. Another, equally famous cavalryman, Oliver Cromwell, was also to make his name in the battle, with 3,000 of his 'Ironsides' of the Eastern Association under his command, as the two cavalrymen prepared for the ultimate showdown. John Drinkwater wrote:

> And now the marshall'd armies who ride for Charles the King,
> Shall tighten rein and think of death as of a present thing
> When down the lanes of battle the armoured Ironsides ring ...[27]

Sporadic fighting and gunfire broke out in the early afternoon. Forty allied guns bombarded the Royalists, who were still awaiting reinforcements from York. When they got there, Newcastle entreated Rupert to delay the battle until yet more reinforcements arrived. But Rupert's rash temperament and his contempt for the commanders of the garrison made a battle inevitable. It was therefore quite late on in the day when the main action commenced. The Parliamentarian infantry pushed back the Royalist infantry on Rupert's right flank in pouring rain. Cromwell, with David Leslie in support, exploited the breakthrough on the allied left flank, but Rupert charged in his usual style, with his faithful hound 'Boy' running alongside him. The cream of the Cavaliers smashed into Cromwell's 'Ironsides' and the wounded Cromwell was sorely beset from all angles, but Leslie's experienced and tough Scots regiments extricated him. 'Boy' was killed in the savage melee, and Rupert was devastated. He was forced to hide in a cornfield during the Royalist retreat.

By late evening, the entire allied force had begun to advance. Despite a desperate resistance, the Royalist army was pushed back. The elite 'Whitecoats', recruited by the Marquess of Newcastle, had sworn to dye their uniforms red with the blood of the Roundheads. They retired to an enclosed copse called White Sike Close, where they acted as a rearguard for the fleeing Royalist army. They refused all offers of quarter, and only

---

27. Drinkwater, J., 'The Gathering of the Ironsides', *Cromwell and Other Poems* (1913)

thirty of the 1,500 men survived the battle. In all, over 4,000 of the king's men lost their lives to allied losses of 500. It was a strategic disaster. York was lost, and with it the entire north of England and all the ports of the east coast. To compound this, on his march to York, Rupert had committed many atrocities and burned many towns, killing thousands in Lancashire. The broken prince, sobbing for his lost canine companion, no longer found sympathy among the common people of England, who began to see the formerly gallant Cavaliers as arrogant, brutal, plundering saboteurs.

Yet, for all that, the king was still undefeated, and a solid bloc in the west, the south-west and the western Midlands remained stubbornly loyal. A typical example came at the siege of Dudley Castle, a Royalist stronghold. The Midlands was almost equally divided between the King and Parliament, but, on the whole the area we now call the 'Black Country' was Royalist, whereas nearby Birmingham was for Parliament. Colonel Thomas Leveson, a local Catholic, was such a thorn in the side of the Parliamentary forces that he was sentenced to 'perpetual banishment' after the war. But it should not be supposed that there were neat territories dominated by one or the other of the belligerents. A county like Worcestershire, which as its city motto proudly states was 'Faithful in War and Peace', was actually in a ferment about the continual depredations of both armies. A new movement calling themselves 'Clubmen' emerged, resolved to band together against plundering soldiers of either side, on a principle based around mutual aid. Their motto was, 'If you offer plunder to take our cattel, be assured we will give you battel.' In March 1646, the people of Worcestershire, at the epicentre of the wars from beginning to end, lamented that the local folk had been 'exposed to utter ruin by the outrages and violence of the soldier(s)' and that they had initiated 'a mutual league for each other's defence … against all murders, rapines, robberies or violence which shall be offered against any soldier or oppressor whatsoever'. In short, the local population in the Midlands, so desperate as to be immune to the blandishments of either side, were protecting themselves against both armies, and any defeated soldier was unlikely to find succour among the hard-pressed country folk.

To restore the situation, Charles decided to attack Plymouth, the vital south-western port that was the sole Parliamentarian outpost in the region. Attempting to lift the siege, Essex bought 10,000 men to confront the king at Lostwithiel in Cornwall. Surrounded on all sides, Essex and Sir William Balfour managed to break out of the Royalist encirclement. Essex himself was forced to escape in a fishing boat. The Roundhead infantry were not so fortunate, and finally agreed to surrender to the king on 2 September, two months after Marston Moor. The king could not feed so many prisoners – nearly 7,000 – and so he ordered them to lay down their arms and march to Portsmouth. This was easier said than done. The men were already starving, many were wounded and sick, and they had no means of defending themselves. Nearly 2,000 of them were harried to death by Royalist sympathisers.

Lostwithiel was an indisputable victory for the king, but in strategic terms he had merely consolidated his hold over his own natural territory. It made him complacent at a time when he really should have been fearful for the future. This insouciance about strategic matters soon led to a fatal error. At the end of October 1644, Charles attempted to relieve several important Royalist garrisons before winter set in. Donnington Castle outside Newbury in Berkshire, the scene of two battles in the First Civil War, was under the command of Colonel Boys, who had refused all offers of surrender. The Committee of Both Kingdoms, as the allied command now called itself, was aware of Royalist movements towards Newbury, and it was decided to attempt a night march across country to surprise the king's army of 9,000 men by a dawn attack from Clay Hill overlooking the king's positions, particularly Shaw House and Donnington Castle. The Roundhead movements, however, were observed by Royalist pickets, and the king ordered Prince Maurice to defend the vital village of Speen.

The main battle did not commence until dark, as at Marston Moor, and was a confused affair. For some reason Cromwell seemed reluctant to commit his men, perhaps because it was already too dark to see 'field signs' distinguishing the combatants. Despite being outnumbered two to one, the king's men managed to escape the allied trap during the night. Both sides lost 1,500 men killed in yet another narrow escape for the king. Charles went to Bath, where Rupert was based with his cavalry, and a week later the Royalist garrisons were relieved by him. The Royalist army, now substantially weaker than it had been, retired to Oxford to await the king's command.

It was felt by many radicals that lacklustre or potentially treacherous commanders had deliberately let the king escape. In January 1645, the Committee of Both Kingdoms established a New Model Army, commanded by Sir Thomas Fairfax as its captain-general. From now on, the psychology of the combatants was altered. It was to be nothing less than total war. In the increasingly radicalised ranks of the Roundhead army, there were many who were no longer content to depose the king. They now wanted his head.

27

'THE WORLD TURNED UPSIDE DOWN' (1645–1649)

Out of a total population of 5 million, it is estimated that almost 200,000 people died during the English Civil Wars, about half of them civilians. The attendant miseries may be imagined: famine, looting, rapine, destruction of ancient communities, intra-community hatred, the unwanted billeting of troops, disease and despair. It was clear to both sides that a decision must come soon. The amateurish skirmishes like Powick Bridge were now a thing of the past, and just as the Cavaliers had degenerated into brutality, so too fanatical elements within the New Model Army were being radicalised by mountebank preachers who were often what we would call non-commissioned officers. Such men were determined to overthrow not only the established order, symbolised by the king, but also the established Church of England. 'The years 1640 to 1660 witnessed the most complete and drastic revolution the Church of England has ever undergone. Its whole structure was ruthlessly demolished.[28]

---

28. Shaw, W., *History of the English Church During the Civil Wars & under the Commonwealth* (1900)

Reay comments on Christopher Hill's demonstration in *The World Turned Upside Down* that 'the decade of the 1640s was a time of immense overturning. Well-established, if not always well-respected institutions collapsed like the proverbial house of cards.' He points out that by 1641 the Star Chamber, Court of High Commission, the Councils of Wales and the North had all been abolished. 'Episcopacy and Church Courts followed in 1646, the House of Lords three years later.' In 1641 the Earl of Strafford was executed, and the Archbishop of Canterbury was next in 1645. Of course, in 1649 it was the king's turn. 'New bodies, the county committees,' he writes, 'had the power to haul errant ministers and politically suspect land-lords before them, and to deprive them respectively of their parishes and their lands. Ordinary parishioners – husbandmen, artisans, even labourers and women – could testify before such committees to the competence and political reliability of those who had hitherto been their social superiors, men who in their own eyes at least, had been beyond reproach.'

In short, revolutionary forces had been unleashed, and the king's life, though he little suspected it, was in grave danger.

By spring of 1645, Rupert was in action again. He captured Leicester, but while he was preoccupied, Fairfax and his New Model Army of 21,000 well-trained and highly disciplined soldiers, many of whom saw their duty in terms of an eschatological destiny, laid siege to the king in Oxford. Charles decided to march towards Rupert's forces. Near the village of Naseby in Northamptonshire, the Royalist army took up a strong position on a ridge called Dust Hill between Little Oxenden and Great Farndon. On the morning of 14 June, Royalist scouts were sent out to look for Fairfax and his army but a dense mist meant that they failed to see their scarlet ranks only 3 miles away. Rupert was certain that Fairfax was nearby, and went out to scout for himself. He soon encountered troopers from the New Model cavalry, and immediately ordered his army to deploy forward into their battle formations. Once again, Rupert's aggressive dash and bravado were inverse to his actual military strength. This was partly the king's fault, because he was determined to fight even though he was outnumbered by almost two to one. Rupert wanted to retire westwards so as to be reinforced by Goring's regiments of cavalry and extra artillery, but the king refused. Consequently, against 14,000 men of the New Model, Charles could only muster 7,500 soldiers.

Meanwhile, the Parliamentarian army took up positions on a ridge opposite the king. Skippon's infantry massed on Red Hill Ridge, just behind where the monument to the battle now stands, about a mile north of Naseby. Cromwell's 'Ironsides' were on the right flank, and on the left flank Cromwell's son-in-law, Henry Ireton, commanded another large body of horse. Cromwell deliberately sent a company of dragoons to enfilade any advance by Rupert along the line of a hedgerow on Ireton's flank. Like Edward IV at Tewkesbury, this eye for detail reaped handsome dividends in the action itself. The two princes, Rupert and Maurice, immediately fell into just the trap Cromwell had prepared. Fairfax lured Rupert forward by seeming to retire, so the prince made a rash charge. Sir Jacob Astley, commanding the Royalist infantry, moved forward in the centre, and on the king's left flank about 1,500 Northern Horse, men rendered homeless when Charles lost the north country, faced Cromwell's cavalry.

Incredibly, the battle developed exactly as at Edgehill in 1642. Rupert's Cavaliers, 2,500 strong, overran Ireton's cavalry, but careered on towards Naseby, where they were drawn into a firefight with musketeers and dragoons around the Parliamentarian baggage train. In the centre, too, Astley had initial success, and Skippon himself was wounded. Ireton charged forwards to assist Skippon with his own troop and some of the dragoons who had been sent to guard the Sulby hedgerow. The Royalist infantry, although small in number, were excellent veterans who stood to repel Ireton's charge. Their pikemen threw Ireton himself from his horse, who was badly wounded and captured. Hand-to-hand combat in the centre was savage, and the

Royalists went into the fray with swords and the butts of their muskets. Many of Skippon's men fled towards Northampton, but others regrouped as the wounded Skippon tried to rally them. There were now signs of movement on the king's left flank as Langdale's cavalry came on at the trot. The ground was broken up by a rabbit warren, and so Langdale's horse, who were in every way inferior to the 'Ironsides', were quickly put to flight. With most of Rupert's cavalry still off the field, Charles saw that he was in great danger. He bravely ordered his own reserve and lifeguards to reinforce Astley's hard-pressed left flank, but the Earl of Carnwarth quickly grabbed the king's bridle, shouting, 'Will you go upon your death?'

As soon as the Royalist infantry saw the king retreating, their morale collapsed. By the time Rupert returned, the situation was irretrievable and so he too retreated towards Leicester. Astley's men had no choice but to surrender, with one notable exception. Rupert's elite 'Bluecoats' refused all offers to surrender, and fought on until they were annihilated. Cromwell's men showed no mercy, and when they encountered Welsh camp followers they mistook their Welsh for Irish Gaelic, and all 200 were cruelly put to the sword.

At last, the king had been decisively defeated in open battle. His entire army was lost, except for 4,000 scattered cavalry. A thousand Royalists died and 5,000 were taken prisoner, along with almost as many on the Parliamentarian side. The Royalists also lost all the king's artillery, his baggage, £100,000 in treasures and, most damning of all, his private papers, among them correspondence which proved beyond all doubt that Charles was intriguing to bring an Irish Catholic army into England. To the radicals this was proof of his treason, and they demanded summary jurisdiction as soon as he was in their hands.

James Campbell, Marquess of Montrose raised the Highland clans and 2,000 Irish Catholic soldiers and in a lightning campaign in 1646 almost won Scotland for the king. Charles still had many stubborn garrisons holding out, too. But when the West

Country fell to Fairfax, and Bristol on 10 September 1645, Rupert fled England in disgrace. In May 1646, Charles gave himself up to the Scottish Covenanters, who immediately sold him to the English Parliament. But even now, Charles was obstinate, and treated his captors with barely concealed contempt. Charles had one last hope. The coalition between the Presbyterians and the Independents was fragile, and may not hold.

But the influential Cromwell became increasingly frustrated with the king, and on 5 June 1647 Cornet Joyce arrived to take the king into custody. When the king asked to see his authority for such a request, Joyce asked him to look out of his window. Charles peered out, and seeing a troop of 'Ironsides' standing to with swords drawn and pistols loaded he declaimed, 'It is as fair a commission, and as well-written, as I have seen in my life.' In August, the king was taken to London with an armed escort. He was lodged under armed guard at Hampton Court, but in November he escaped to Carisbrooke Castle in the Isle of Wight. Unfortunately for him, he was detained again by Colonel Robert Hammond, and confined in a room with barred windows. All attempts at escape were foiled.

In 1648, the Duke of Hamilton, encouraged by letters Charles had smuggled out, attempted an invasion of England from Scotland, but he was easily beaten at Preston by Cromwell, who was now the most influential army commander. This desperate last effort condemned Charles to the scaffold, because the army was now effectively in control. They resolved that 'it was their duty, if ever the Lord brought them back in peace, to call Charles Stuart, that man of blood, to account for all the blood he has shed and the mischief he has done'. Cromwell was explicit: 'We will cut off his head with the crown upon it!'

Royalist risings took place sporadically in Wales, the north of England, Kent and Essex, and there was a mutiny in the fleet. Cromwell's generals mercilessly crushed them all, and following 'Pride's Purge' of Parliament on 6 December 1648, when 101 members likely to temporise or prove lenient towards the king were escorted out under armed guard, the king's situation was hopeless. A show trial was arranged in Westminster Hall. The king offered no defence, and refused to recognise the authority of his judges. Troops were ordered to open fire on any demonstrators. Fifty-nine of the sixty-eight MPs sitting at the trial, the so-called 'Regicides', signed the king's death warrant.

Tuesday 30 January 1649 was a bitterly cold day. Charles wore two shirts so the crowd would not think he was shivering from fear as he was escorted to the scaffold in Whitehall by William Juxon, Bishop of London. Large crowds were in attendance. Charles stood before them, saying, 'I go from a corruptible to an incorruptible crown, where no disturbance can be, no disturbance in the world.' At a given signal, the king was beheaded, and ghoulish onlookers came forward to dip their scarves and handkerchiefs in the king's blood. The world had indeed been turned upside down – but the Stuart cause was far from lost. The king's handsome young son, also called Charles, survived him.

28

WORCESTER, WORCESTERSHIRE (1651)

The Battle of Worcester, fought on 3 September 1651, is far from forgotten. I have been to two spectacular re-enactments myself, and the events of that fateful day are so well known that they scarcely require repeating – and yet many forget that the civil wars did not end at Naseby. Worcester *is* often overlooked, even though it was in a sense the climactic battle of the wars, and so I feel the Third English Civil War (the Second Civil War being the campaign culminating in the Battle of Preston in 1648) deserves to be remembered on that account alone. But this is a personal account, and of all the battles in this book this is the one with the most intimate connections to me, and its location the one with which I am most familiar.

Once the momentous execution of their anointed king had taken place in 1649, the revolutionary forces were given free rein. In May 1649, Levellers in Burford mutinied upon hearing rumours they were being sent to put down rebellion in Ireland. Instead, they planned to take Oxford, seize the armoury and food depot there, and proceed to London, where their leader 'Free-born John' Lilburne was a prisoner in the Tower of London. Cromwell surrounded the town of Burford in Oxfordshire by night in May 1649, and stormed in, taking the Levellers' pickets unawares.

Most escaped, but 400 were taken as prisoners and herded into the nearby church, which still bears graffiti pertaining to their uncomfortable stay. In the morning the prisoners were gathered to witness the summary execution of a random sample of their comrades in the churchyard.

The Levellers rose again in September, and there were further sporadic, communitarian-inspired uprisings, especially among the miners of Derbyshire. These were not signs of a consensual or convivial atmosphere in the 'New Jerusalem' of the 'Commonwealth' or republic which England had become, and on 23 June 1650 the eldest son of King Charles I, Charles Stuart, known as 'the Black Boy' (his mother had Italian ancestry which emerged in his swarthy complexion and raven-black curls), landed in Scotland, at precisely the moment when Cromwell's English army was preparing to invade – the moment, in short, when Scottish Nationalist and Royalist sympathies were most likely to cohere.

On 3 September 1650, exactly one year before the Battle of Worcester exactly eight years before his own death, Cromwell smashed the Scots army under David Leslie at the Battle of Dunbar. But Cromwell's health was extremely compromised, and so Charles slipped over the border with an army of 16,000 Scots at the end of July, in hopes of gathering support in the formerly Royalist northern region of England. Cromwell dispatched Major-General John Lambert, a reliable cavalry commander, to shadow and harass Charles and his army as they progressed south. By the time the Scots reached Lancashire, another Roundhead cavalry force intercepted Charles on his line of march towards Worcester, a reliable Royalist stronghold, 'Faithful in War and Peace' as the city motto avers to this day.

The bedraggled Royal army limped into Worcester, not as a threatening invader, but rather as an exhausted and diminished quarry, finally brought to bay in a once friendly refuge. A stand had to be made, and if, as seemed likely, Charles was heavily defeated, there were several escape routes – to Wales and Ireland, towards

Scotland, or, as eventually proved necessary, a flight to the south coast or London, where the anonymity afforded by one of the most populous cities in Europe might prove useful. And yet, Charles had inherited from his father an almost maniacal optimism in the face of adversity, which seems to have been a genetically inherited trait with the Stuarts. Hardly any support had been forthcoming from the northern gentry of England, mainly because, as Richard Baxter remarked succinctly, 'they (the Scots) were perceived as (more) flying than marching into England ... and few men will put themselves into a flying army which is pursued by a conquering enemy'. The Scots were anyway desperate to get home, and their commanders, such as the Duke of Hamilton, although brave, were hopelessly out of touch with strategic realities.

But the young Charles Stuart was quite another matter. He was fanatically brave, desperate to avenge the death of his father, and at Worcester he was in a Royalist stronghold with strong natural defences. He knew that no further military opportunity was likely to arise for a very long time, and he was determined that this should be his day. He arrived at Worcester via Newport and Wolverhampton on 22 August. Cromwell was at Nottingham, and after gathering an army of 28,000 he set out for Worcester. General Lambert, who had been sent to harry the Scots, retired before Charles but was careful to secure the bridge over the Severn at Upton-upon-Severn, a potential escape route if Charles was defeated. Sir Edward Massey, a Parliamentarian defector and probably the only truly competent Royalist general, was suddenly surprised while he was at Hanley Castle, 2 miles north of Upton. In a desperate, even heroic attempt to redeem the matter, he was killed trying to detonate pre-laid mines beneath the bridge. Charles established himself at 'Fort Royal' in the city and converted the adjacent buildings into the 'Commandery'. Worcester stood at the confluence of two rivers, the Teme and Severn, which protected him from General Lambert's forces to the south-west. The heavy cannon of Fort Royal defended the Sidbury Gate, the East Gate, and the city walls overlooked

Cromwell's forces to the south-east. The Scots cavalry under Leslie were billeted in the north of the city as a reserve to repel any Parliamentarian breakthrough in the area called Pitchcroft near the modern racecourse.

Cromwell decided to mount a three-pronged attack. General Fleetwood's garrison from Banbury had joined the Roundhead forces at Upton-upon-Severn. Fleetwood was commanded to take charge of the attack from the south-west, exactly where the earlier Battle of Powick Bridge had been fought nine years before. Cromwell had twenty large boats floated upstream, and a bridge of boats was built in a bold move which completely hoodwinked the Scots infantry guarding the junction of the two rivers. Lambert sent a troop of cavalry across a ford below Powick Bridge, and they chased off the Scots musketeers. Charles, watching the battle develop from the top of Worcester Cathedral tower, was horrified to see Cromwell's regiments crossing the improvised bridge.

The Scots were demoralised, far from home, and keenly aware that the day of the battle was the anniversary of Cromwell's crushing victory over Leslie at Dunbar the year before. They immediately collapsed as soon as the main Roundhead force advanced on Powick Bridge. In panic, both the Royalist cavalry and infantry, many trying desperately to surrender, ran through the western suburb of St John's with Lambert's musketeers firing volleys into their dense ranks. St John's church in Bedwardine still bears the marks of musket balls, and because it had been a rallying point it was plundered and set ablaze by the advancing Roundheads, many of whom had by now abandoned all respect for 'outward show' of the sacred. Charles raced from the cathedral to the retreating troops, beseeching them to form ranks and return to the fight, but all in vain. It seemed that Cromwell's 'fortunate day', as he called 3 September, was smiling on him again.

A strange tale is still told in Worcester that Cromwell made an infernal pact to win the day. While Cromwell was supervising the positioning of his siege artillery at Perry Wood to the south-east of the city, a summons arrived to the Lord Protector to meet a mysterious messenger. Accompanied by a Colonel Lindsay, Cromwell rode to an isolated glade where, to Lindsay's horror, the Devil himself was awaiting Cromwell. The Adversary offered Cromwell a stunning victory, in exchange for his soul, which would be his for the taking seven years exactly from that day. Cromwell demurred and stated that a term of twenty-one years was the usual arrangement, but apparently his haggling was unsuccessful. Cromwell died exactly seven years to the day after the battle was won, and Lindsay, a formerly loyal soldier, was so horrified that he fled the field and refused to fight for Cromwell again. But in truth, Cromwell needed no diabolical assistance. Charles was stubbornly brave, but his Scots army had no heart for the fight.

Charles was not content to flee without making one last desperate effort. Cromwell had crossed the Severn to confer with Fleetwood and Lambert at a house just outside Powick (now an Indian restaurant called Cromwell's). Charles was astute enough to realise that the Roundhead forces outside Fort Royal were now under his guns, leaderless and without instructions. He immediately decided to attack, leading his men from the front in a gallant charge. Charles charged out of the east gate and drove back the Roundhead besiegers. He had ordered Leslie's cavalry reserve to join the attack, and had this order been obeyed Charles would almost certainly have prevailed. Unfortunately, the Roundheads quickly rallied and the valiant Charles was one of the last to squeeze in through the closing city gate, and only then by having discarded his cumbersome armour. By now the whole city was in absolute chaos. The Royalists were now confined to the northern half of the city, and in the vicious street fighting they suddenly began to rally. Cromwell admitted as much: 'It was as stiff a contest as I have ever seen.'

Charles fell back through the narrow streets towards the Commandery, where the Duke of Hamilton was preparing to organise one last desperate attack. By now Cromwell had divined the danger on his right flank, and swiftly returned to take charge there. After five hours of savage fighting, and with over 50,000 men engaged in hand-to-hand combat in the ancient medieval streets, Leslie's cavalry fled the city through the north gate. Many were hunted down before they made it home to Scotland. At Bewdley, 13 miles away, 300 were slaughtered when their horses were blown. Richard Baxter 'of Kidderminster' declared,

> Kidderminster being but 11 miles from Worcester, the flying (Scots) army passed through the town, and some by it; I was newly gone to bed when the noise of the flying horse acquainted us of the (Royalist) overthrow; and a piece of Cromwell's horse guarding Bewdley Bridge had tidings of it ... 30 troopers cried out 'stand!' and fired at them, and they either hasted away, or cried Quarter ...[29]

The streets of Worcester were littered with dead horses and dying soldiers. Charles nearly ran into a company of Roundhead musketeers, but a baker's wagon was commandeered and so obstructed them that he managed to escape through a nearby house with Roundhead officers in hot pursuit. It was to be the first of many other such thrilling escapes in the weeks ahead. The Duke of Hamilton was not so lucky, and later died of his wounds. Some 7,000 Royalists were taken prisoner and were herded into the cathedral. For Cromwell this crushing victory was his 'crowning glory' – even if he had sold his soul to achieve it.

Many of the Scots prisoners faced the terrible fate of transportation to the West Indies, but Charles was not among them. With about sixty close companions, he made his way north on the heels of the Scots cavalry, many of whom were murdered by the angry English communities they rode through on the way home. Charles drew off from the main party at Whittington Heath outside Stourbridge, and his group pretended to be in the company

---

29. Baxter, R., *Reliquae Baxterianae* (1696)

of foreigners visiting a wine fair by speaking French. They moved on through Wordsley to Whiteladies House near Brewood in Staffordshire. Charles, by now disguised as a country labourer, and with his formerly long hair close cropped, doubled back to confuse the pursuing Roundheads. At one point he was forced to hide in an oak tree in Boscobel, where he remained until dusk.

Eventually Charles was taken to Moseley Hall, just outside Wolverhampton. Colonel John Lane, a staunch Royalist and an MP following the Restoration, was the owner of the house, and an ancestor of mine. My paternal grandmother would often recount that after the Restoration the family were rewarded with a payment from the Crown of £1,500 per annum 'in perpetuity' for their loyal service in this desperate time (inevitably, this was later rescinded, much to her chagrin). The colonel's sister, Jane Lane, took Charles to Rowley Regis disguised as her groom. She had an exemption from the military authorities to visit her pregnant cousin in Bristol. When her horse threw a shoe at Rowley Regis, a farrier struck up a conversation with Charles about the late battle nearby. The man said that the whole Scots army had been routed, but that the villain Charles Stuart had escaped. Charles replied that there must be many English Royalist 'villains' at large too, and thought the man gave him a knowing look. But by a miracle, this was not reported, despite the reward. Charles was so disturbed, however, that he asked for the royal standard, which he had rescued, to be concealed.

After many weeks of anxious wanderings, Charles escaped across the sea to France from Shoreham aboard a ship named *The Surprise*. Jane Lane was soon under suspicion, and was forced to follow the putative king into exile in France a few weeks later. For the time being, the Stuart cause was lost. But centuries of tradition, combined with growing disenchantment with the new order, ensured that one day Charles Stuart would return as king in more than name.

SEDGEMOOR, SOMERSET (1685)

On 3 September 1658, Cromwell died. John Evelyn, a diarist of the time, remarked that it was 'the joyfullest funeral I ever saw, for none cried but the dogs, which the soldiers hooted away with a barbarous noise, drinking and smoking tobacco in the streets as they went'. Cromwell's son Richard became the new Lord Protector, but his heart was not in it; after only eight months he resigned. On 2 January 1660, George Monck, Duke of Albemarle led his troops over the border into England from Scotland and proceeded to London, arriving on 3 February. An approach was made to Charles suggesting that the monarchy could be restored if he would agree to a general amnesty for all former combatants excepting the regicides, for whom Charles would countenance no pardon.

Charles was proclaimed king on 8 May 1660. Some would never resign themselves to the rule of the supposed Antichrist; Thomas Venner, a London cooper and former soldier, donned his armour and led a small, doomed uprising among the London radicals in 1661, but after so much misery, bloodshed and ill will for such a protracted period, there was a general desire for peace, and, more than that, for joy, gaiety, laughter – and sex. Charles had learned bad habits in his exile, much of it spent in Continental brothels. Upon his return he was notoriously libertine, and was called by wits 'the father of his people' because of the large number of his illegitimate children.

Unfortunately, however, Charles had no legitimate heirs. This meant that he was likely to be succeeded by his brother James, Duke of York, whose conversion to Roman Catholicism could not be borne by those with Parliamentarian sympathies, now known as Whigs. They supported the claim of an illegitimate son of Charles, also called James (Scott), Duke of Monmouth. Monmouth's bona fides were disputed by some, but he was, at least, a Protestant. The opposing Tories, who supported the Duke of York, were named in honour of mythical sea pirates from Ireland. The Whigs were originally border brigands from Scotland.

Shortly after Charles II died in February 1685, Monmouth made a surprise landing at Lyme Bay in Dorset and marched to Taunton in Somerset, where he proclaimed himself king. He intended to march on Bristol and seize the armoury and food depot there with an army of 4,000 men, for the most part country labourers caught up in the excitement. They were brave, but hopelessly ill equipped and trained. Lord Grey led a detachment of 800 cavalry and four cannons with Dutch gunners. The novelist Daniel Defoe enlisted with Monmouth's army, and was later heavily fined, but unlike many prisoners, and thankfully for English literature, he was at least spared execution by Lord Chief Justice Jeffreys at the so-called Bloody Assizes in the aftermath of the rebellion. Monmouth's force were slowly penned in until they retired to the town of Bridgwater in Somerset.

The king's army was led by Louis de Duras, Lord Feversham, originally from France, but his second-in-command was Colonel John Churchill, one of the greatest military commanders in history and an ancestor of Sir Winston Churchill. Although the royal army was small – just 3,500 men in total – it was vastly superior to the rebel army in quality. Two regiments, recently returned from Tangier under Percy Kirke, were ruthless and experienced cavalry who hunted down the rebel fugitives after the battle, known as 'Kirke's Lambs'. The king's army included well-trained and professional cavalry regiments, and seventeen cannon. Nevertheless, Feversham's progress was slow, mainly because of the problem of hauling the heavy guns in the treacherous terrain of the Somerset 'rhynes' or drainage ditches.

With the king's army encamped behind the Bussex Rhyne near the village of Westonzoyland in the Somerset Levels, Monmouth decided to make a surprise attack after dark and led his army out of Bridgwater just after dusk on 6 July 1685. They were guided toward the king's forces by a local man, Richard Godfrey, who knew the rhynes like the back of his hand. Lord Grey's rebel cavalry were at the front, but in the dark, and with the necessity of absolute silence, it was almost impossible to cross the rhynes undetected. Just as the rebels crossed Langmoor Rhyne, they were surprised by Feversham's pickets and a shot was fired. A messenger rode immediately to alert Feversham and his cavalry quickly responded. The night was damp and foggy, and so the king's cavalry around Chedzoy village, and General Oglethorpe at nearby Bawdrip, had great difficulty finding Monmouth's army. Lord Grey, however, decided to lead his cavalry forward in the pitch darkness, so as to outflank the royal cavalry. The ill-equipped infantry, many of them unarmed save for pitchforks, also engaged the king's men behind the Bussex Rhyne. The rhyne was 17 feet wide, so it was necessary for the armies to line up on either side of it and fire their weapons.

The Dutch gunners in the rebel army kept the king's guards and Dumbarton's Brigade pinned down until they unfortunately ran out of ammunition. They had left a reserve supply at Peasey Farm a few miles away, but as soon as the cannon fire ceased the royal cavalry attacked. Lord Grey's rebel cavalry had ridden off the battlefield and was lost until dawn. The Bishop of Winchester was persuaded to lend the king's artillery his stable of horses, and they hauled six cannon forward to support the royal cavalry. The rebel peasant army fought on bravely through the night, but as soon as day broke they retreated. Monmouth, Lord Grey and many senior rebels rode into the nearby Polden Hills, but the majority of the rebel army were ruthlessly hunted across the Somerset Levels back to Bridgwater. Many made a stand, but 'Kirke's Lambs' surrounded them, killing many hundreds. About 500 men were taken prisoner and herded into the parish church at Westonzoyland. In the Bloody Assizes, Judge Jeffreys had many more executed; their bodies were displayed on gibbets along the local roads.

In all, 1,300 rebels were killed, and many suffered the grim fate of transportation to the colonies. Few returned to see their homes again. The king's army lost just 200 men, and the victory was overwhelming. Monmouth had no choice but to disguise himself as a peasant, and he made good progress until he was eventually captured near Ringwood in Hampshire, only a short distance from the coast. Monmouth's fate was an awful one, for his uncle, King James II, was determined to make an example of him. He was condemned to execution by beheading at the Tower of London. He bore his fate with remarkable stoicism, and paid the axeman 6 golden guineas to make a clean job of his execution, with another 6 guineas to follow afterwards. Unfortunately, the king's agents knew of the arrangement and paid the executioner a larger sum to botch the beheading. Monmouth had promised that if the man did not strike a clean blow the first time he would 'look him in the face'. The axe had been deliberately blunted, and when the first blow failed, Monmouth was as good as his word, and even extended a hand to feel the blade. It took five blows of the axe until the poor man was eventually decapitated.

Monmouth did not die entirely in vain. The ruthless cruelty of Judge George Jeffreys was widely resented, especially in the West Country. For many generations no royal personage was safe to visit the region. Whig opinion was galvanised, and eventually, at the Battle of the Boyne in Ireland in 1690, King James II was heavily defeated by the Protestant William of Orange following the so-called Glorious Revolution. James fled to France, but his seeming cowardice at the battle ensured that he was not remembered affectionately by the Irish, who called him 'James the Shit'. At last, the long and bloody civil wars were at an end.

Afterword

'THE BATTLE OF EVERMORE'?

Sedgemoor was actually not the last battle fought on English soil, and certainly not the last fought on British soil. In November 1715, an army of Scots Highlanders 2,000 strong crossed the border into England and reached as far as Preston in Lancashire where they were reinforced by 500 or so English Jacobite sympathisers (supporters of the Stuart claim to the throne). A government force of about 3,000 men was dispatched from Manchester and quickly surrounded the town. The Jacobites retired behind barricades and the government soldiers were forced to burn houses containing snipers, losing about 300 men over a period of three days in the process. About thirty rebels also lost their lives. The Scots stubbornly refused to surrender at first, but as the regular army tightened its grip they were eventually forced to gather in the centre of the town where they laid down their arms. The ringleaders were sentenced to death, but the 1,500 taken prisoner were condemned to transportation. This first Jacobite rising was not to be the last, however.

In 1745, Charles Edward Stuart, known as 'the Young Pretender' or 'Bonnie Prince Charlie', secured French backing for a landing in Scotland. The Scots Highland clans rallied to him, and in September 1745 his small army cut a government force to pieces at the Battle of Prestonpans. With 6,000 troops Charles invaded England near Carlisle, and eventually reached Swarkestone Bridge on the River Trent just south of Derby. A government spy gave the Jacobites the false information that a large Hanoverian (that is, government) army was moving towards them. The Scots were desperately short of food, and otherwise unprepared for battle, and so retreated back into Scotland. At Falkirk Muir in January 1746, a chaotic battle was fought in a blinding snowstorm. About 9,000 Jacobite clansmen put a government force of a similar size to flight, but casualties on both sides were relatively light – less than 100 dead on both sides, with about 200 government soldiers wounded. The government artillery was lost, but the infantry and dragoons escaped to fight another day.

Prince William, Duke of Cumberland, youngest son of King George II, confronted Charles at Culloden Moor near Inverness on 16 April 1746. The two armies were of roughly similar size, about 8,000 on each side, but Cumberland had drilled his men to receive the wild clansmen's famed 'Highland Charge' by thrusting with their bayonets to their right, rather than at the men immediately in front. The ferocity and velocity of the charge, and the devastating blows from the claymore – a huge sword which could literally cut a man in half – was a stern test even for the most disciplined professional soldiers. But by thrusting to the right with their bayonets the government soldiers nullified the targe, the small defensive shield the Scots carried.

Charles took personal command and lined the clansmen up opposite the government cannon, enticing Cumberland to attack. Instead, for almost forty minutes, the Jacobite army simply stood still in dense ranks as they were blasted to pieces by Cumberland's guns and mortars. Eventually, the highlanders attacked, and managed to break through the first rank of Cumberland's force on one flank. But by the time this was achieved, the momentum behind the charge was spent and they were forced to retreat, losing 2,000 dead. Cumberland's army lost 300–400 men, and the pursuit was merciless. Many atrocities were committed, and the rebel areas suffered punitive reprisals from which they never recovered. After many adventures, 'Bonnie Prince Charlie' escaped to France.

Even this 'last battle on British soil' was not quite the end of armed conflict in Britain, though it was the last serious 'battle' in the proper sense of that term. On 1 June 1831, Welsh coalminers and other workers in the area around Merthyr Tydfil besieged local dignitaries in the Castle Inn led by one Lewis Lewis. Up to 10,000 men, and some women, marched under a red flag into the town (the Red Flag was later to be adopted as the banner of International Socialism). Many chanted 'Down with the king!' or 'Bread and cheese!' and proceeded to loot businesses and burn debtors' records. To restore order, several regiments of regular troops, mainly Scots along with some local yeomanry, were ordered to clear the town of insurgents, but the local miners were armed, and many had military training and plenty of explosives to hand. The government troops were driven off. For five days the insurgents held the town, until finally the army dispersed the demonstrations, killing a few dozen people. Lewis Lewis and another man, Richard Lewis, were tried and sentenced to death by hanging. The latter, known locally as 'Dic Penderyn', was actually innocent of his supposed crime of stabbing a soldier; another man confessed to the offence on his deathbed many years afterwards. Unfortunately, Richard Lewis had already been hanged.

On 31 May 1838, John Tom, a Cornishman who had taken the name of 'Sir William Courtenay', led one of the strangest rebellions in British history. Tom was mentally ill and suffered delusions of grandeur. He had previously attempted to stand as an MP. At this time there was widespread rural poverty, and much resentment at the harsh new 'Poor Law' in Kent, where 'Sir William', who had abandoned his wife and then changed his identity, was then residing. Somehow, Tom obtained a good-quality white horse, and dressed himself in exotic costume. He also armed himself with a sword and several pistols. The local farm labourers, many of them on the verge of starvation, and sorely aggrieved on other counts, proved receptive to Sir William's millenarian speeches, and a group of about forty processed in the area around Hernhill in Kent, with Tom leading the way on his fine horse. Another follower held a loaf of bread impaled on a pole aloft as they marched, and anxious local gentry became alarmed when they heard chants of 'bread or blood!'

Thus far, this rather comical scene gave no real cause for concern to the authorities, but when a local magistrate issued a warrant for Tom's arrest, constables were sent out to arrest him and disperse the demonstrators. Only one demonstrator besides Sir William had a pistol; the rest were armed with staves, billhooks and stones. The best account of the ensuing Battle of Bossenden Wood, or Blean Wood, as it is also known, is to be found in E. P. Thompson's classic *The Making of the English Working Class* (1963), which contains accounts of many other such obscure confrontations of the period. A constable was sent to Bossenden Farm where Sir William and his troop of about forty followers were gathered. When the constable was shot and killed by Sir William, the anxious local farmers and gentry sent to Canterbury for help from the regular army. A detachment of 100 men and three officers of the 45th Regiment of Foot (which, ironically, was to become involved in another similar incident the following year) were dispatched to surround and disarm the 'rebels' in a small copse near the farm. When they entered the wood with fixed bayonets, there was serious resistance, and many soldiers were injured. One officer, Lieutenant Bennett, was shot by Sir William and killed. The soldiers returned fire, and Sir William was shot dead, before the 45th finally stormed the wood and killed eight of his followers, who resisted for some time, quite convinced of the justice of their cause.

The following year, 1839, saw the last armed uprising against the British government, the Newport Rising. John Frost, a Chartist radical, reprised the attack on Merthyr eight years previously, and under quite similar circumstances. On 4 November, radicals and coalminers assembled by night with the intention of storming the Westgate Hotel in Newport, Monmouthshire, where some of their comrades were being held prisoner. A large mob, perhaps as many as 10,000 men, some of them equipped with pistols but the majority with edged weapons, surrounded the hotel and at one point managed to break in. The 45th (Nottinghamshire) Regiment of Foot – the same that had stormed Bossenden Wood the year before – defended the building and repulsed the Chartists, killing at least twenty-two (some may have died secretly of their wounds subsequently). About 500 special constables, and reinforcements of regular troops, managed to quickly restore order, and they pursued the fleeing miners, who threw away their incriminating weapons. Many were sentenced to transportation. Despite this last 'armed conflict', the South Wales coalfield remained a centre of radicalism until the demise of the coal industry in the late twentieth century.

In November 1910, miners clashed with the constabulary at Tonypandy, and one miner was killed and many more seriously injured. Bitter labour disputes often ended in serious violence, even as late as 1984, during the so-called Battle of Orgreave, which authorities referred to as a riot. About 5,000 unarmed pickets were overwhelmed by 6,000 riot police, police 'cavalry' equipped with heavy batons, and fierce dogs. The fighting was some of the most serious in any industrial dispute for many years, but thankfully there were no fatalities on that hot summer's day, though miners were killed elsewhere in the dispute.

The following year, on 1 June 1985, the Battle of the Beanfield took place when an injunction by the High Court prohibited the assembly at Stonehenge, Wiltshire, of 'hippie' travellers intent on celebrating the Stonehenge Free Festival, which had been an annual event for some years previously. The Peace Convoy, a hard core of roughly 600 unarmed travellers, many of them women and children, were effectively ambushed by 1,300 riot police, and many of them sought refuge in a field to escape heavy-handed and brutal police tactics in which their mobile homes were wrecked and many were severely injured. Police claims that they were provoked into brutality appeared spurious, since the entire episode was filmed by a TV journalist who said it was some of the most appalling state violence he had witnessed in his career.

But for all the drama involved in these sporadic outbreaks of violence in a supposedly peaceful democracy, they cannot be called 'battles' in the same sense as the events described in the main body of this book. For about 300 years, mercifully, this island has been spared any large-scale military confrontations, though British armed forces have been in almost continuous action overseas. So what, if anything, has been the legacy of all this contention and bloodshed and misery? What mark has it left on the British peoples?

When I was a boy, I would read a book which belonged to my father, *The Miracle of Man*, which contained a complex analysis of the rise of the Nazi regime in Germany and the subsequent Second World War, published within years of the allied victory in 1945. A central argument, which seemed plausible to my young mind, was that the 'German National Character' (I paraphrase somewhat), had been profoundly influenced, in fact warped, by the terrible Thirty Years War (1618–1648), in which one-third of the entire German population was lost through slaughter or famine, and many more displaced. The suggestion was that, somehow, the trauma of this war had been epigenetic – that is, passed on through generations – and had brutalised the German people, inclining them to a defensive solidarity expressed in aggressive militarism. If we accept this premise is correct, however, it cannot apply exclusively to the German people. If it is in some sense true, as I do believe, then how much more true must it be for the British peoples after so many centuries of almost continuous conflict on a small island? We like to pretend that we are a peace-loving, orderly and reasonable folk, not given to intemperate behaviours, but it seems to me that war has left an indelible mark on our national culture, and a barely concealed bellicosity.

I remember the extraordinary speed with which the nation seemed to immediately unite behind the Falklands Task Force following the Argentinian invasion of the British Falkland Islands in 1982. It was, as George Orwell observed in *The Lion & the Unicorn* (1941) about the invasion crisis of 1940, like 'a herd of cattle turning to face a wolf'. This ability to act in concert when threatened by an aggressor has been very useful on occasion, such as in the summer of 1940, but I fear that there is a less attractive side to British militarism, and that it behoves us to face honestly both the limitations of our military capabilities (essentially, that our forces are now auxiliaries of the United States military), and also the way in which our national psyche has been just as warped, in its way, as that of the German and Japanese peoples – who have at least acknowledged as much following bitter defeats. But Britain was not defeated in 1945, and technically was one of the 'victors'.

This, I believe, is a critical problem, because it has produced a sort of cognitive dissonance that perpetuates outmoded and irrational attitudes about war which would be unacceptable in countries with more recent experience of the horrors it truly entails. This martial eagerness, ironically among generations who have never really had much direct experience of armed conflict, is a very dangerous habit of mind, especially as nationalism and xenophobia are becoming politically more prominent. In short, the thought very often begets the deed; those who think war a noble and glorious affair become too ready to glamorise and celebrate something which should really be abhorred. What, then, is to be the future of war? Is it possible that other nations may also share the blessing of three centuries without any major battles on their territory – or, even better still, that war could be eradicated on a worldwide basis?

I hope and pray that may come to pass, but to achieve that end a worldwide change in consciousness will be necessary – no one nation can do it alone. But Britain may find, after so many centuries of war, that it is uniquely qualified to lead the way. The resurgence of belligerence in the UK ever since the Falklands War in 1982, but especially since the EU Referendum in 2016, is remarkable. The famous British sense of humour has increasingly been replaced by mean-mindedness, spite and hatred. Attacks on foreigners spiked immediately following the referendum and more low-level nastiness has become routine. It would be wrong to describe this as 'British' nationalism, for it is predominantly an English phenomenon. The psychological process involved is extremely complex, and for those wishing to delve more deeply into the issues I suggest they peruse Wilhelm Reich's *The Mass Psychology of Fascism* (1933), which explicates the matter in more detail. In essence, however, the rise of authoritarian and fascist attitudes in Germany coincided with two major political and economic calamities: the defeat of the mighty German army in 1918, symbol of the relatively new nation's unity and virility; and the great inflation and economic slump which ruined the middle class in the 1920s.

I suggest that similar psychological forces are in play in England today. The 'victory' of 1945 was in fact the swansong of the British Empire, the end of Britain's status as the pre-eminent world power. In 1956, this was cruelly confirmed when the USA threatened the UK and France with economic ruin unless they withdrew their forces from the Suez Canal zone. This emasculation was temporarily masked by the Falklands expedition of 1982, which seemed to suggest to the world that Britain was still capable of independent military operations, even at remote distances. In reality, the USA furnished the campaign with vital equipment and intelligence, for it was clear that an electoral victory for Mrs Thatcher was the prerequisite for the deployment of cruise missiles containing nuclear warheads to the UK (the British Labour Party was then opposed to this plan).

But with the end of the Cold War, the UK began to demilitarise significantly. The armed forces have found it extremely difficult to meet the demands – even as virtual auxiliaries of the US – of various campaigns in Bosnia, Iraq and Afghanistan. But all this has had dangerous consequences, for the UK now is in a similar position to Germany in the early 1930s. There is a sentimental nostalgia for the days of empire and military glory, and a subconscious desire for war. Although the economy survived the 2008 financial crash – the consequences of which have been principally borne by the working class, the poor, women, the elderly and the infirm – another similar disaster, possibly imminent,[30] would certainly ruin the middle class. The institutions once so well beloved, which have bound the UK together for so many centuries, all now seem under threat: the royal family, Parliament, the Church of England and more recently the BBC and NHS. The schism with the EU may be the start of a similar break-up of the UK itself. Scotland and Northern Ireland both voted to remain in the EU, and the Welsh would have done so had it not been for English settlers there who voted to leave. The ancient hatreds between Celt and Teuton examined earlier in this work could well be rekindled by nationalists.

We have seen how, time and time again, our island has become a war zone throughout the centuries. It was no accident that warfare on this island virtually ceased just when British imperial expansionism began to gather pace. Our military was still active, just overseas. Now, there is nowhere for it to fight unless the USA requests British support, which has almost always been forthcoming (Vietnam being a notable exception). Therefore, the combination of a virtually redundant, demoralised military and the lack of any operational focus is quite volatile. Should a radical coalition or left-leaning government be elected, with a programme which could be construed as threatening the defence interests of the UK, I personally believe a right-wing coup would be a distinct possibility. Of course, this would be dangerous, and the country may divide again as it did in 1642. Could it really be that warfare, after an absence of almost 300 years, will once more rage in our green and pleasant land?

It is, of course, possible – and it was prophesied to me as a child that I would live to see it. Yet, I will strive to do all in my

---

30. This was written at Advent 2019, just before the Covid-19 pandemic.

power to prevent it – and I hope that this book may contribute to maintaining the precarious peace in this island, and all over the world. British militarism and English nationalism are just as abhorrent as their German, Italian and Japanese counterparts in the twentieth century. We would be very great fools to unleash the dogs of war, but unfortunately there are times when we simply choose to believe inconsistent and irrational stories which comfort and soothe us even though they are astonishing falsehoods. The British are not alone in this. The Ancient Greeks propounded liberty and democracy while simultaneously enslaving a large proportion of their population. The Church seems content to accept a 'doctrine of ruthless Laissez-faire' economics[31] as logically consistent with the teachings of Jesus Christ. The USA promulgates 'Freedom and Democracy' while seemingly oblivious to its own virtual genocide of the Native American population (as Hermann Goering remarked at the Nuremberg Trials). 'God', of course, is often invoked to support the warring nations. As Sir John Squire wrote during the First World War:

> To God the embattled nations sing and shout,
> '*Gott strafe England*' and 'God Save the King.'
> God this, God that and God the other thing.
> 'Good God', said God, 'I've got my work cut out.'[32]

But if, as I believe, we are living through an evolutionary process which will transform our mass consciousness, when we come to see our history as a dramatic record of a development in time beginning with Abraham and ending in the Second Coming, then perhaps the prophecy of Micah will be realised at last, and the swords will be beaten into ploughshares and the spears into pruning hooks – and all battlefields will be lost and forgotten, obliterated from our minds forever.

31. Barfield, O., *Saving the Appearances: A Study in Idolatry* (1957)
32. Squire, J. C., 'Epigrams' (1916)

MAPS

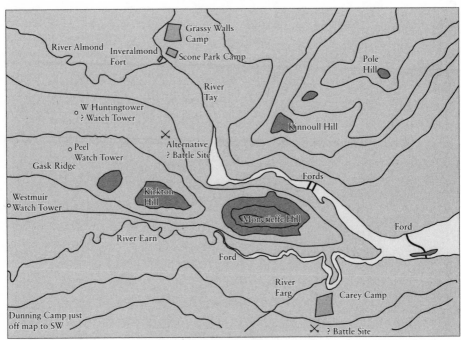

Above: A possible interpretation of the arrangement at the site of the Battle of Mons Graupius, AD 83–84. (From Simon Forder's *The Romans in Scotland and the Battle of Mons Graupius,* Amberley, 2019)

Right: England in 878, showing the extent of the Danelaw. (Courtesy of Hel-Hama under Creative Commons 3.0)

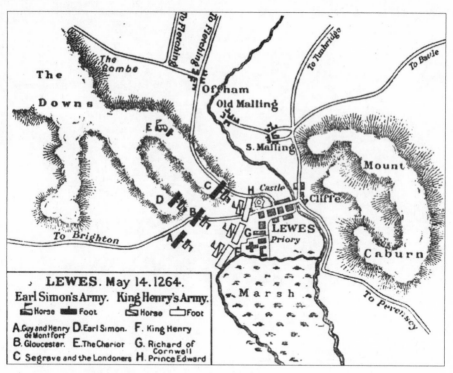

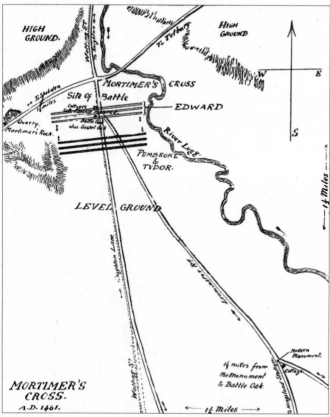

Above: The Battle of Lewes, 1264.

Left: The Battle of Mortimer's Cross, 1461.

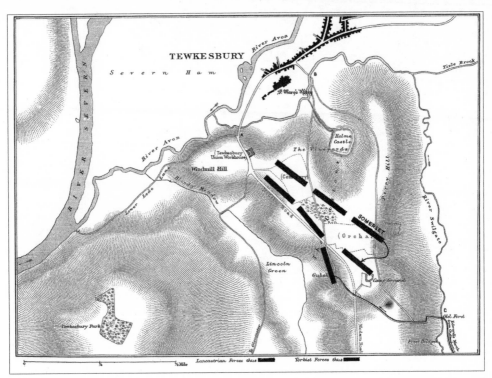

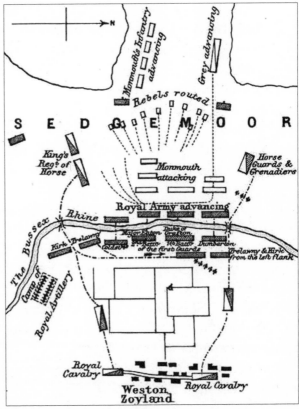

Above: The Battle of Tewkesbury, 1471.

Right: The Battle of Sedgemoor, 1685.

SELECT BIBLIOGRAPHY

Aethelweard's Chronicon

Annales Cambriae

Armes Prydein Fawr

Ashe, G., *The Quest for Arthur's Britain* (Paladin, 1968)

Barfield, O., *Saving the Appearances: A Study in Idolatry* (Barfield Press, 1988)

Baxter, R., *Reliquae Baxterianae* (1696)

Belloc, H., *Warfare in England* (1912)

Bhagavad Gita

Carlton, D., *Arthur: Warrior & King* (Amberley Publishing, 2018)

Cassius Dio, *Roman History*, ed. & trans. J. Jackson (Loeb Classical Library, 1925)

Charles-Edwards, T. M., *Wales and the Britons, 350–1064* (Oxford University Press, 2012)

Cowper, W., *Ode on Boadicea*

Drayton, M., *Polyolbion* (1612 & 1622)

Geoffrey of Monmouth, *Historia Regum Britanniae* (1136)

Gildas, *De Excidio et Conquestu Britanniae*

Graves, R., *The White Goddess: An Historical Grammar of Poetic Myth* (Faber & Faber, 1948)

Kightly, C., *Folk Heroes of Britain* (Thames & Hudson, 1982)

Malory, T., *Morte D'Arthur* (1485)

Moffatt, A., *The Sea Kingdoms* (HarperCollins, 2001)

Morris, J., *The Age of Arthur* (Macmillan, 1973)

Myers, J. N. L., *The English Settlements* (Clarendon Press, 1986)

Nennius, *Historia Brittonum*

Orwell, G., *The Lion & the Unicorn* (Secker & Warburg, 1941)

Reay, B. & MacGregor, J. F, *Radical Religion in the English Revolution* (Oxford University Press, 1984)

Reich, W., *The Mass Psychology of Fascism* (Farrar, Straus and Giroux, 1933)

Russell, J. B & Laycock, S., *UnRoman Britain: Exposing the Great Myth of Britannia* (The History Press, 2010)

Shakespeare, W., *Henry IV*

Shakespeare, W., *Henry VI*

Shaw, W., *History of the English Church During the Civil Wars & Under the Commonwealth* (Longmans, Green and Co., 1900)

Squire, J. C., 'Epigrams' (1916)

Tacitus, *Annals*, ed. J. Jackson (Loeb Classical Library, 1937)

Tacitus, *Agricola*, ed. D. R. Stuart (Macmillan, 1916)

The Anglo-Saxon Chronicle

The Book of Aneirin

The Battle of Maldon

The Black Book of Camarthen

The Mercian Register

Thompson, E. P., *The Making of the English Working Class* (Penguin, 1963)

Walter-Hodges, C., *The Namesake* (Bell, 1964)

Wall, M., *The Magical History of Britain* (Amberley Publishing, 2019)

Wood, M., *In Search of the Dark Ages* (BBC Books, 1981)

Yeates, S., J., *The Tribe of Witches: The Religion of the Dobunni & Hwicce* (Oxbox Books, 2008)

Zosimus, *Historia Nova*

ACKNOWLEDGEMENTS

Thanks are due to all the kind people who have assisted and encouraged me in the production of this book, especially Robert, Kevyn, Lyndon, David, Tim, John & Judy, Paul, Jane & the girls. I am grateful to the British Library for permission to use photographs. Individual photographers are credited alongside the captions. Every effort has been made to seek permission for copyright material. However, if I have inadvertently used copyright material without permission/acknowledgement I apologise and will make the necessary correction at the first opportunity.

INDEX